An extraordinary manuscript . . . Well done indeed! Aimee Murphy has managed to compile a powerful, in-depth and scholarly work with extensive research beyond anything I have ever read on the issues. Clearly, it is not an easy read (how could it be otherwise?) and while I am not a scholar, I care very deeply about the core tenets at issue and I have spent a good deal of my adult life publicly advocating and defending them. I wish the success of this remarkable work!

—**Martin Sheen**, Emmy- and Golden Globe-winning actor known for roles in *The West Wing*, *Apocalypse Now*, *The Departed*, *Grace & Frankie*, and *The Way*

This book is a must-read for all serious human rights advocates. In an in-depth, comprehensive examination of the life issues in modern society through the lens of the Consistent Life Ethic, a philosophy whereby all humans have the right to live a dignified life free of violence, Murphy calls out both major political parties in the US for their selective (dare I say "inconsistent"?) approaches to legalized violence, and connects all the dots with thoughtful evidence and research. Like-minded people who feel politically unhoused will find refuge in this passionate invitation to her organization, Rehumanize International, a movement dedicated to education, dialogue and action towards ending violence against humans while building a culture of life and peace. If you fancy yourself an honest defender of life, pick up this book. We have some serious work ahead of us.

—**Jeannie Gaffigan**, writer, producer, and *New York Times* bestselling author

A "Consistent Life Ethic" is a concept that many have never heard about or considered, and if for no other reason this new book is a vital contribution to the public discourse. My work is to stop executions ~~~ delight in the fact that opposition to capit

people diametrically opposed to each others' positions on other "life" issues. Aimee Murphy's book will help us all understand each other better, even if we are unwilling to adopt the "Consistent Life Ethic" on some of the life issues thoroughly examined herein.

—**Abraham J. Bonowitz**, co-founder and director, Death Penalty Action

Thorough and engaging, *Rehumanize: A Vision to Secure Human Rights for All* is fantastic. Aimee's passion and zest for life jumps through the pages and calls readers to action to make positive change in our broken world.

—**Catherine Glenn Foster**, president and CEO of Americans United for Life

Aimee Murphy asks the hard questions that test our commitment to protect human life and human dignity. Her primer is intelligent, instructive, and incisive about these overlapping challenges we face in today's society."

—**Gloria Purvis**, host of "The Gloria Purvis Podcast" with America Media and inaugural Pastoral Fellow with the Notre Dame Office of Life and Human Dignity at the McGrath Institute for Church Life

The time has come for a revolution of the heart, and in her book *Rehumanize: A Vision to Secure Human Rights for All*, Aimee Murphy shows the passion and provides the inspiration we all need for that revolution to begin within each and every one of us. Aimee has set about to build the foundation for a world that embraces the Consistent Life Ethic, and we are invited to join in, laying one brick at a time, taking one step at a time, toward a world where every human being is respected, valued, and protected

—**Tommy Tighe**, author of *Saint Dymphna's Playbook*

The consistent ethic of life should figure prominently in every discussion about the morality of laws and practices that permit the intentional destruction of human life. But toxic political partisanship and shallow public discourse regularly suffocate it. This book can help restore the consistent ethic to its rightful place. You don't have to agree with its every thought or proposal to grasp its enormous value or its timeliness.

—**Helen M. Alvaré**, the Robert A. Levy Chair in Law and Liberty at the Antonin Scalia Law School, George Mason University

The great tragedy of our time has been the seduction of so many in the pro-life movement into a false political agenda that pits the unborn against, rather than relates them to, all the other forms of human life God has made in his image and likeness. Aimee Murphy calls us back to the sanity of the Consistent Ethic of Life that the authentic gospel has always proclaimed. Thanks be to God for her work!

—**Mark P. Shea**, author of *The Church's Best-Kept Secret: A Primer on Catholic Social Teaching*

One of the best—if not the best—and most comprehensive writings on the Consistent Life Ethic to date. Aimee makes intellectual, yet easy-to-understand arguments. Thoroughly researched with fresh takes, both novices and veterans of the Consistent Life Ethic will benefit greatly from this book!

—**Christina (Christy) Yao Pelliccioni**, president of the Consistent Life Network

This book is a bold act of love. Aimee Murphy's genuine solidarity with every human being will inspire you to action.

—**Kelsey Hazzard**, founder and president of Secular Pro-Life

When you hear the words "pro-life," do you immediately think of a white male Republican legislator who is weirdly obsessed with sexual politics? Then you should meet Aimee Murphy, the badass, blue-haired, queer, Latina, disabled leader of the new pro-life generation. *Rehumanize: A Vision to Secure Human Rights for All* shows in plain and powerful prose the freedom and confidence that come from embracing life—life, plain and simple! Life for every living being, full stop, no exceptions, no backing down. Buy a copy for everyone you know.

—**Tim Wainwright**, co-founder
of Catholics for Social Action

Aimee Murphy brings passion and honesty to this review of violence in our culture and politics, and how we can resist it by upholding a consistent ethic of life and respecting the dignity of all human beings. Let's hope many hear and answer her call to counter violence with "connection, community, and rehumanization."

—**Kim Daniels**, co-director of the Georgetown
Initiative on Catholic Social Thought and Public Life

If, like me, you've found yourself diving deeper in recent years to issues of justice, human life and dignity, and the principles of nonviolence, Aimee's primer on the Consistent Life Ethic will no doubt be a convicting read. Transcending partisan politics *and* hyper-individualism, this book encourages us to examine our individual and collective consciences. Read it. Consider it. Wrestle with it. Discuss it. Let it strengthen your resolve to be your brother's and your sister's keeper

—**Kevin Heider**, singer/songwriter and
host of the "Song & Story" podcast

REHUMANIZE

Let's build a
culture of peace
and _LIFE_!

♡ Aimee Murphy

REHUMANIZE

A Vision to Secure
Human Rights for All

Aimee Murphy

New City Press
Hyde Park, New York

Published by New City Press
202 Comforter Blvd.,
Hyde Park, NY 12538
www.newcitypress.com

Rehumanize: A Vision to Secure Human Rights for All

Aimee Murphy

Cover design: Aimee Murphy
Layout and design: Miguel Tejerina

Library of Congress Control Number: 2022936601

ISBN: 978-1-56548-541-9 (Paperback)
ISBN: 978-1-56548-542-6 (E-book)

Printed in the United States of America

Contents

To Kairi, Elanor, Claudia, Josephine, and Helen,

My strong, brave, bold, loving girls:
May you benefit from the work we do today
To build the world beyond violence of tomorrow

A world where each and every human being is respected,
valued, and protected.

And if it has not yet come to be in your time
May you be the change—a catalyst—
For a revolution of encounter
Where all will respect and
Rehumanize.

~

beLOVEd,
Auntie Aimee

Series Preface

Does the book that you are about to read seem unusual? Perhaps even counterintuitive?

Good. The Magenta series wouldn't be doing its job if you felt otherwise.

On the color wheel, magenta lies directly between red and blue. Just so, books in this series do not lie at one limit or another of our hopelessly simplistic, two-dimensional, antagonistic, binary imagination. Often, in the broader culture any answer to a moral or political question gets labeled as liberal or conservative, red or blue. But the Magenta series refuses to play by these shortsighted rules. Magenta will address the complexity of the issues of our day by resisting a framework that unnecessarily pits one idea against another. Magenta refuses to be defined by anything other than a positive vision of the good.

The ideas in Magenta are crucial not only for our fragmented culture, but also for the Church. Our secular idolatry—our simplistic left/right, red/blue imagination—has oozed into the Church as well, disfiguring the Body of Christ with ugly disunity. Such idolatry, it must be said, has muffled the Gospel and crippled the Church, keeping it from being salt and light in a wounded world desperate for unity.

Magenta is not naïve. We realize full well that appealing to dialogue or common ground can be dismissed as a weak-sauce, milquetoast attempt to cloud our vision of the good or reduce it to a mere least common denominator. We know that much dialogic spade work is yet to be done, but that does not keep the vision of the Magenta Series (like the color it bears) from being *bold*. There is nothing half-hearted about it. All our authors have a brilliant, attractive vision of the good.

In the first book in the Magenta series, *Living the Feminist Dream*, Kate Bryan calls out what genuine feminism is—finding out who you are, who you were created to be, and every day living that out.

And in our second volume, *Keep at It, Riley!*, Noreen McInnes skillfully weaves a deeply personal testimony to the life and death of her parents, an intricate reflection upon the sacramental life of the Church and the depth and breadth of Catholic faith and spirituality.

We are so proud to be publishing Aimee Murphy's vision of a consistent life ethic. Long a champion of this way of thinking (and living), her particular vision has been very important for some time. But now, at this cultural moment, it is absolutely essential. Accessible and readable for many different people, this book will be especially resonant with young people who are committed to justice and nonviolence—but who are unsatisfied with the typical political and ideological paths offered to express their commitments. It is about as Magenta as a book can get.

Charles C. Camosy
Magenta Series Editor

Acknowledgements

First, God's grace and love is truly what carried me through the writing of each and every page. Thank you, Father, Son, and Spirit. I know that it is in Your Image I am made, and in knowing I am made for connection, community, and friendship, I am drawn closer to humanity.

Second, I must thank my home, my closest friend, my dear husband of ten years: Kyle Timothy. How he follows Thérèse's "Little Way" and lives his vows through a hundred different small acts of love and service every day has kept me alive, and has enabled me to get this passion project done. Thank you, my sweet babe: I couldn't have done it without you. I love you—with my all of me.

Third, I have to thank my team at Rehumanize International, who helped me to brainstorm, congeal, and focus the ideas within these pages. To Herb Geraghty and Grace Aquilina, who sat down with me for hours-long brainstorming sessions and gave invaluable input to many of the chapters; to Maria Oswalt, who helped iterate designs for the beautiful cover; to Sarah Slater, who reviewed all the legal shenanigans and gave me pep talks. And to our internal editors: John Whitehead and Kelly Matula, who did the hard work of fixing many of my grammar mistakes, typos, and clunky run-ons. All of you: Thank you for believing in me, in this project, and in the work that we are doing to build a culture of peace. Your help brought this book to life, and I'm greatly indebted to you for all that you've done.

Then I must thank my content reviewers: Mary Ann Augustine, Sarah Lohroff, Ismail Smith-Wade-El, and Zuri Davis—each of you brought your life experiences, your hearts, your minds, your whole selves to reviewing this project and helped me to make it the best it could be. I'm so grateful for your friendship and your openness to building a better world alongside me.

Next, I want to thank my family, both near and far, biological and chosen. There are too many of you to name, you know who you are and how dearly I love you. Thank you for all your prayers, kind words, and sweet care packages to me as I labored to bring this book into the world.

Of course, I must humbly extend my gratitude and appreciation to the team at New City Press who saw my proposal and took a chance on me. Matteo, Greg, Charlie, and Tom, all of you brought this home to your publishing house, and now that it's with you I couldn't imagine it anywhere else. Thank you for seeing my vision, and for making this book a beautiful reality.

Lastly, dear reader, I must thank you: for your commitment to human rights for all human beings, for reading this book, and for what you will do to change the world. . . Because, although I don't know *what* you will do to build a culture of peace and life, I *know that you must!* I *believe in you, and I'm here to walk with you. Onward!*

Chapter 1

A philosophy for all humanity

In picking up this book, you've proven that you care about making the world a better place. If we want to see authentic change in the world, each and every one of us needs to be invested in building a more humane future: the work that you are doing here matters. With *Rehumanize: A Vision to Secure Human Rights for All* I am hoping to lay the cornerstone of the solid foundation of a world beyond violence. I want to secure a future with human rights for all human beings that we will build together. This book is a basic introduction to a philosophy called the Consistent Life Ethic. In these pages you'll learn about our growing movement for human dignity for all and the issues of violence we work to end. I encourage you to use these pages for reference in all your future endeavors for human rights. As you read, and as you learn, I hope that you will be empowered through factual knowledge and equipped through ethical reasoning to work for a world where every human is respected, valued, and protected.

What is the Consistent Life Ethic?

The belief that all human beings, by virtue of their inherent human dignity, deserve to live free from violence.

Every act of violence against a fellow human—as an intentional use of force meant to harm or kill—is an attack on our shared inherent human dignity. Each human being, a member of a rational species, is unique: unrepeatable, inimitable, and irreplaceable. Each human being has a unique selfhood. You can't just swap out one person with another: any reasonable human would agree that switching out spouses or best friends for "a similar make and model" would disregard their dignity and diminish our own. We are more than the mere sum of our parts, or our traits. What makes us unique is not just our eye color or hair color or tone of voice or height or Myers-Briggs personality type. Human beings have an untouchable aspect of self, a *je ne sais quoi* to who we are that makes it impossible to substitute any one of us with another. If a human being is killed, someone irreplaceable and unique in all of time and space vanishes. This terrible reality is the reason why opposition to violence is foundational in ethics and philosophy. This truth of our human existence is the reason I embrace the Consistent Life Ethic (CLE).

In practice, the Consistent Life Ethic opposes every form of aggressive violence:

- Embryo destruction
- Abortion
- War
- Military torture
- Police brutality
- Torture in the justice system
- The death penalty
- Euthanasia and filicide
- Assisted suicide

- Abuse, enslavement, homicide, and every other form of aggressive violence against human beings.

This long list does not mean that the CLE does not value single-issue work: spending time and energy to end the death penalty, or to end abortion is good and necessary! The vital point is to maintain a Consistent Life Ethic in all that we do.

It is wrong, however, to claim the Consistent Life Ethic while undermining the work to end a particular form of violence. Sometimes conservative-leaning people back unjust wars that their political party supports; or liberal-leaning people support legal abortion because their political party does so. As Joseph Cardinal Bernardin, a key advocate in building the popular movement to support the Consistent Life Ethic, said,

> I know that some on the left, if I may use that label, have used the Consistent Ethic to give the impression that the abortion issue is not all that important anymore, that you should be against abortion in a general way but that there are more important issues, so don't hold anybody's feet to the fire just on abortion. That's a misuse of the Consistent Ethic, and I deplore it. . . I feel very, very strongly about the right to life of the unborn, the weakest and most vulnerable of human beings. I don't see how you can subscribe to the Consistent Ethic and then vote for someone who feels that abortion is a "basic right" of the individual. The consequence of that would be an absence of legal protection for the unborn.[1]

---

1. "Bernardin: Chicago's pastor on consistency and the '88 vote," interview in *National Catholic Register*, June 12, 1988, 7.

Though some political activists might devalue or exclude certain humans, adherents of an authentic Consistent Life Ethic never abandon any category of humans and thereby grow comfortable with violence.

How does this philosophy respond to the politically polarized "culture war"?

It's unfortunate that leaders at either end of the political spectrum use mental gymnastics to make exceptions to the rules of human rights and the right to life. Sometimes this gymnastic requires convincing yourself that the subjects of a proposed violence are less than human.

Those who identify with a Republican political agenda often support the death penalty because they think that the worst criminals "forfeit their humanity." However, no matter how grotesque their actions, murderers are still human beings, creatures inherently capable of reason as members of the human species despite having made poor choices in the past. This unchangeable humanity, not the actions of the human being, is what demands respect. Death row inmates may have done monstrous or beastly things, but they are human.

Those who identify with a Democrat, Green, or Socialist agenda, however, may maintain the same attitude perpetuated by Planned Parenthood counselors: the preborn human being is just a "blob of cells," or even a "parasite." Such dehumanizing terms camouflage the violence of abortion. But embryology clearly reveals that the product of a same-species conception is indeed a complete, whole, and differentiated member of the same species.[2] In short:

---

2.   See footnote 50 in chapter 2, "Embryo Destruction," for a substantial

dogs create dogs, cats create cats, and from the moment of fertilization human sperm and ova create a human beings. "Fetus" and "embryo" are demarcations for age, as are terms like infant, toddler, kindergartener, pre-teen, adolescent, adult, and aged. Through the mental gymnastics of exclusion we can convince ourselves that a proposed object of violence, although human, is not worthy of rights. Such justifications derive from an exclusionary ethics that regards some trait other than humanity as more valuable in the question of rights.

In the case of abortion, those who hold with policies favored by Democrats will raise the issue of bodily autonomy. They argue that a pregnant person's bodily autonomy has higher moral value than the right of the preborn child to continue living free from violence. In the case of war, those who hold with policies favored by Republicans consider the possibility of hitting an enemy target of military importance with greater value than the deaths of noncombatants. They argue that the right to "defense" has higher moral value than the lives of those who may be lost as "collateral damage" in acts of war.

In both these instances, someone's foundational human right to life is denied. But, of course, those who are killed, whose right to live free from violence is violated, can no longer exercise their rights to autonomy or just defense. The right to exist without harm is the first human right; all others depend on it. The exclusionary ethics of both hawkish Republicans and pro-choice Democrats result in discrimination based on characteristics like size, location, gender, religion, or race; but all human beings have human

---

list of citations from embryology textbooks.

rights. No exceptions. Indeed, they aren't "born rights" or "white rights" or "rich rights"—they are *human* rights.

Think about this: saying "I work for human rights" proclaims that each and every human being is valuable and worthy of protection. And those who make that claim but act contrariwise undermine their human rights work in any field, and cannot really claim to protect human rights at all. Those who ignore, condone, or commit violence violate the human rights and dignity of some humans. And human rights only for *some* aren't human rights at all.

Killing a human being irreversibly ends the life of a unique and unrepeatable self. When we kill, we don't kill a class of people. We snuff out individual lives. We bring to an end a singular human being who is worthy of a name and who has a past and would have a future. If we acknowledge that in any circumstance killing means ending an individual life, we can no longer reduce the action to a mere statistic. The quote commonly attributed to Josef Stalin is certainly true: "A single death is a tragedy; a million deaths is a statistic." Individual deaths can be teachable moments. We mourn the individual loss and the extinguishing of unique traits and one irreplaceable life. Many recognize the names George Floyd, Breonna Taylor, and Botham Jean; but when thousands die, their faces disappear, we lose the intimacy necessary to rehumanize the other.

Although the life of every singular human being is worthy of protection, many seek to protect only the "innocent," as if innocence is a human being's measure of worth. Certainly, no one is free from guilt—at some time, everyone probably has hit a sibling or a friend, or cheated on a test, or maybe even committed a grave wrong against a fellow human being. Yet many with a politically conservative stance use "innocence" to judge who deserves life. Surely not only the preborn children or infants yet to commit any wrong are the only ones worthy of life. And innocence, like age or ability, covers a wide spectrum. Drawing the line of "who is innocent enough to live" is an arbitrary metric. At what point do we say "Enough! It is enough that they are human!"

Innocence is a spectrum

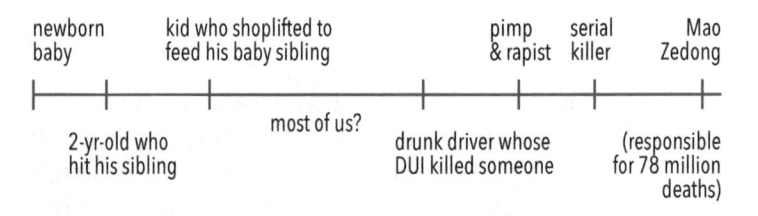

Any line we draw is arbitrary

Some consider "usefulness" to be the measure of a human being's worth, as if the ability to work were the end-all, be-all of humanity. Infants can't do much that is useful, yet their lives are protected. Aged or disabled persons often produce less than younger or nondisabled people, but their lives have value. Usefulness should not be the measure of worth, particularly because age or ability, like innocence, covers a wide spectrum. A line that specifies "who is useful enough to live" is arbitrary. At what point do we say "Enough! It is enough that they are human!"

Usefulness is a spectrum

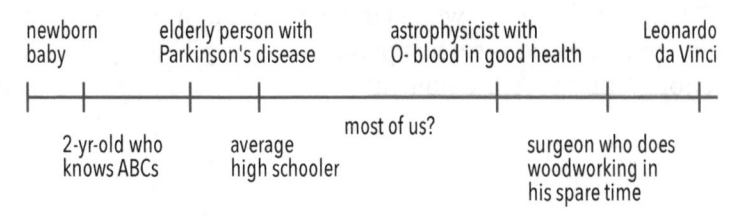

| newborn baby | elderly person with Parkinson's disease | astrophysicist with O- blood in good health | Leonardo da Vinci |

| 2-yr-old who knows ABCs | average high schooler | most of us? | surgeon who does woodworking in his spare time |

Any line we draw is arbitrary

As humans, our rational nature exists at every point of our lives: at conception and at the moment of death and everywhere in between. As long as we human beings exist, we have a rational nature. This nature, based on our capability as a species to be rational, is binary. It cannot be measured on a spectrum of usefulness or smarts. You either are a living member of a species with a rational nature, or you aren't. There's no "sort-of human."

And not even the worst action nor any amount of inaction can deprive us of this, our human nature. Our humanity is part of our essence: not a product of circumstance, age, ability, usefulness, or innocence. This value is unchangeable: it is not merely an opinion to be ignored by dictators or thrown out by lazy politicians—although they often try. Authentic justice derives from our shared human dignity, and human dignity requires respect in the culture, value in the community, and protection before the law.

It is a great social failure that our culture lacks an ethics of encounter. From either end of the philosophical and political spectrum we see double standards. For example, the title "pro-life" rings hollow if its cause is aligned with politicians who promote war, oppose immigration, and unwaveringly support the death penalty. That child in the womb has the potential to become a soldier on the battlefield, a refugee, or a prisoner on death row. That life must be valued at all stages. Likewise, the rhetoric of some politicians who make a show of opposing the death penalty can also ring hollow. Respect for the human life of a death row inmate is often aligned with the support for abortion, euthanasia, and torture. Even during the Obama administration, most liberals were stunningly silent in the face of wartime abuses committed under their watch. Such inconsistency stems from loving the nebulous "idea" of human rights more than loving and respecting the humans who hold those rights.

If we love and respect each and every human being, we must never directly kill any human being.[3] Each and every instance of human life, from conception to natural death must be respected. This principle stands at the center of the Consistent Life Ethic.

Regrettably, an "American first, human brother second" worldview and the related "America First" rhetoric that places political expediency ahead of true respect for all humanity has gained cultural prominence. But note what fourteen New England Catholic bishops wrote in response to the VietNam War:

> We must in conscience criticize the ethical validity of any doctrine, attitude or policy which seems to give

---

3. This maxim leaves room for the principle of double effect, and self-defense is provided for under these terms. For more information on this principle and what constitutes just defense, see the subsection of this chapter, "How do Consistent Life Ethic adherents respond to aggressive violence?" on page 27

American lives an intrinsic superiority over those of other people. Every human life, regardless of nationality, color or ideology is sacred, and its defense and protection must be of deep concern to us.[4]

Saying "only lives over here, in this country, at this age, in this socio-economic bracket matter" is discriminatory. There aren't "born rights" or "white rights" or "rich rights"—only human rights. And while these issues do differ, they are linked inasmuch as they compound disregard for the true, inherent value of human life. Honest human rights work doesn't leave some humans out: a culture of peace can be built only upon respect for the life and dignity of each and every human being.

Regrettably, the American two-party duopoly has generated the nightmare situation where, every two to four years, candidates offer voters no choice but to place one category of human beings above another based on political expediency and power. Republican candidates are likely to say they want to end or limit or reduce abortions; however, those same candidates are likely to condone or support the state-sanctioned violence of hawkish war policies, torture, capital punishment, harsh treatment of migrants and refugees, and support for police who often mistreat communities of color. Contrariwise, on the other side of the duopoly, Democratic candidates are more likely to support more humane policies on immigration, poverty, and criminal justice reform; yet

---

4. Catholic Bishops of the Boston Province, "Pastoral Letter on the Vietnam War," May 7, 1971, printed as "Bishops Urge 'Most Rapid Termination' Of Vietnam War" in the *Pilot*, Boston, MA, May 8, 1971, referenced by Robert F. Drinan in remarks to the U.S. House of Representatives, May 10, 1971, printed May 11, 1971, 14526-27, *govinfo.gov/content/pkg/GPO-CRECB-1971-pt11/pdf/GPO-CRECB-1971-pt11-3-3.pdf*.

they are more likely to condone or support the state-sanctioned violence of abortion on demand, embryonic stem cell research, or even the killing of vulnerable elderly and disabled populations through euthanasia or assisted suicide. As someone who embraces the Consistent Life Ethic, I refuse to vote for anyone who supports legal violence.

I cannot in good conscience vote for a candidate who supports abortion, or hawkish foreign policy, or torture, or euthanasia, or assisted suicide, or capital punishment, or police brutality, or human trafficking, or dismembering humans for political or social or scientific advancement—or any other form of aggressive violence. It is a low bar to demand that candidates oppose violence! It should be common sense that politicians oppose the intentional harming of any members of our human family. And yet we continue getting stuck in an ethical dilemma, having to choose "the lesser of two evils." Being asked over and over and over to support "the lesser of two evils" has resulted in our particular political moment, where evil keeps getting more and more entrenched.

Both sides of our modern political duopoly are bathed in violence. No mainstream political party consistently condemns violence against human beings. How do we escape a system of violence built to exclude outsiders and people of conscience? People of conscience need to stand up and demand better options. Instead of being forced to choose between one violent silo (whether Democrat or Republican) or another, we have to reject the false choices we've been led to believe we have to make and consistently uphold human rights for all human beings. We have to engage in creative nonviolent thinking to build a better, wholly life-affirming future.

Where does this philosophy come from?

Life philosophies based on consistent nonviolence and human equality have existed for millennia, but the modern Consistent Life Ethic movement can be traced back to the intersections of the anti-war and anti-abortion movements in the United States in the 1970s. The term "Consistent Life Ethic" may have begun with Joseph Cardinal Bernardin[5] or a US Catholic Bishops' staff member, Fr. J. Bryan Hehir.[6] This term is first mentioned in a July 1971 statement from Bishop Humberto Medeiros of Boston, coauthored by Fr. Hehir, "A Call to a Consistent Ethic of Life and the Law."[7]

This philosophy also was called "seamless garment," coined by Catholic pacifist Eileen Egan, also in 1971, in a pamphlet entitled "The Unborn Child and the Protection of Human Life."[8] The term reflects the "seamless garment" (John 19:23) that Jesus Christ wore at the time of his torture and that his executioners gambled for at his crucifixion because it would be worthless if divided. The garment is a metaphor for all human life not to be divided, because all acts of violence violate this holistic human dignity. Egan, who co-founded Pax Christi and was active with Catholic Relief Services in aiding war refugees, later said, "The protection of life is a seamless garment. You can't protect

5. D. Cosacchi and E. Martin, *The Berrigan Letters: Personal Correspondence between Daniel and Philip Berrigan* (Ossining, NY: Orbis Books, 2016), 13.

6. C.E. Curran, *Loyal Dissent: Memoir of a Catholic Theologian*. Moral Traditions series (Washington DC: Georgetown University Press, 2006), 103.

7. Thomas A. Nairn, ed., *The Consistent Ethic of Life: Assessing its Reception and Relevance* (Ossining, NY: Orbis Books, 2008), xii.

8. Mark Loyet, Catholic Diocese of Shreveport, "Fabric of the Seamless Garmet [sic]," *Catholic Connections*, January 2021, *issuu.com/catholicconnection/docs/january_2021_revised/s/11542546.*

some life and not others."[9] Her work and the Consistent Life Ethic movement that followed were influenced by her coworkers for peace and human dignity: Egan was a friend of Dorothy Day of the Catholic Worker movement and was also acquainted with Mother Teresa of Calcutta. Both women met Egan at a Catholic Worker House of Hospitality on the Lower East Side of New York City in 1960, again on a journey to Calcutta in 1970, and for one last time over tea at the Catholic Worker Maryhouse in New York in 1979.[10, 11]

The first organization explicitly dedicated to the CLE was the Consistent Life Network, which began as Pro-Lifers for Survival (PS) in 1979-1980.[12] Juli Loesch created the organization out of her horror that the larger anti-nuclear Mobilization for Survival network was promoting pro-abortion messaging in its information packet. Mobilization for Survival of Boston kicked the newly-created Pro-Lifers for Survival out of their network, so PS withdrew its application for membership and worked to create its own holistically life-affirming network of members. A similar political action group, JustLife, was founded in 1985 to sup-

9. Jean Driskell, "Catholic ethicist relates how respect for life is continuous teaching," *Georgia Bulletin*, February 23, 2017, *georgiabulletin. org/news/2017/02/catholic-ethicist-relates-respect-life-continuous-teaching*.

10. Eileen Egan. *Such a Vision of the Street: Mother Teresa—The Spirit and the Work* (Garden City, NY: Doubleday & Company, 1985), 125, 176, 283.

11. Nicholas Rademacher, "'To Relate the Eucharist to Real Living': Mother Teresa and Dorothy Day at the Forty-First International Eucharistic Congress, Philadelphia, Pennsylvania," *U.S. Catholic Historian* 27, no. 4 (2009): 59-72. *jstor.org/stable/40468602*.

12. Carol Crossed, "The Adventures of Prolifers for Survival—Scorned by Mobilization for Survival," *Consistent Life Network Blog*, December 1, 2015, *consistent-life.org/blog/index.php/2015/12/01/scorned-by-mobilization*.

port Consistent Life Ethic candidates for political office.[13] JustLife endorsed several candidates, but eventually faded. At the last meeting of Pro-Lifers for Survival in 1987,[14] the group of Consistent Life Ethic collaborators adopted Eileen Egan's term, calling itself the Seamless Garment Network.[15]

The term "Consistent Life Ethic" became popular in the 1980s. In the US this philosophy gained substantial momentum from Cardinal Bernardin of Chicago, who felt that Catholic Social Teaching demanded a holistic approach to issues of violence and human dignity. Beginning with his work as chair of the Ad Hoc Committee on War and Peace for the National Conference of Catholic Bishops, this work culminated with the publication of *The Challenge of Peace: God's Promise and Our Response*. The final section of this document connects reverence for human life and building peace in response to war.[16] In response to the letter, Fordham University invited Bernardin to present one of the first Gannon Lectures. Kenneth Briggs, a reporter for the *New York Times*, published a front-page article with the headline, "Bernardin Asks Catholics to Fight Both

13. Terry Mattingly, "Too conservative? Too liberal? No, it's JustLife," *City Edition*, October 31, 1992, *groups.csail.mit.edu/mac/users/rauch/nvp/consistent/justlife.html*.

14. Rachel M. MacNair and Stephen Zunes, eds., "Activists Reminisce: An Oral History of Prolifers for Survival," excerpted section from chapter 12 of *Consistently Opposing Killing: from Abortion to Assisted Suicide, the Death Penalty, and War* (Bloomington, IN.: Authors Choice Press/iUniverse, 2011), *consistent-life.org/blog/index.php/2017/05/30/oral-history-prolifers-survival*.

15. Carol Crossed, "Reminiscing on the Founding Meeting of the Consistent Life Network," *Consistent Life Network Blog*, June 8, 2016, *consistent-life.org/blog/index.php/2016/06/08/founding-meeting*.

16. National Conference of Catholic Bishops, *The Challenge of Peace: God's Promise and Our Response* (Washington D.C.: United States Catholic Conference, 1983).

Nuclear Arms and Abortion."[17] That piece kickstarted the movement for the Consistent Life Ethic.

The Consistent Ethic of Life: Assessing Its Reception and Relevance, a seminal analysis of this movement, notes that "Bernardin's consistent ethic is founded on the conviction that human life is sacred, a sacredness grounded in the belief that human beings are made in the imago Dei [image of God]." Bernardin and other major figures in this movement believed that "we have a personal as well as a social responsibility to protect and preserve human life at all stages of development and across the whole continuum of life." Ronald P. Hamel's analysis of the CLE agrees that "while distinct, these issues have a common foundation. Each has to do with the dignity of the human person and the sacredness of human life." One common criticism of the CLE is that this philosophy "flattens" distinct ethical issues into the same degree of importance, moral consideration, and urgency. However, as far back as Bernardin, leaders within the CLE movement have held that

> these threats to human life, both to the preservation of life itself (the right to life) and to the quality of life (promoting those rights that enhance life), are very distinct and require individual treatment... [and that] it is also important to recognize that not all issues have the same moral import (for example, abortion is qualitatively more morally grave than lack of health-care coverage). And, finally, while the [movement] must establish credibility across a wide range of life issues, individuals must establish priorities regarding their own public witness to life, while not denying the interdependence of the issues. The latter is critical. It would be inconsistent for

---

17.   Kenneth A. Briggs, "Bernardin Asks Catholics to Fight Both Nuclear Arms and Abortion," *The New York Times*, December 7, 1983, 1.

25

individuals to witness to life at one end of the spectrum of life issues while being insensitive or even hostile to life issues at the other end.[18]

Grassroots activists around the United States adopted this foundational understanding of the Consistent Life Ethic and in 2002 (after Bernardin's death), the Seamless Garment Network adopted the new name: "Consistent Life: a Network of Peace, Justice and Life."[19] The organization's current mission, vision, and purpose statements are direct:

> We are committed to the protection of life, which is threatened in today's world by war, abortion, poverty, racism, the death penalty and euthanasia. We believe that these issues are linked under a "consistent ethic of life." We challenge those working on all or some of these issues to maintain a cooperative spirit of peace, reconciliation, and respect in protecting the unprotected. We serve the anti-violence community by connecting issues, building bridges, and strengthening the case against each kind of socially approved killing by consistently opposing them all.[20]

Following the wave of anti-war, pro-life, and other human rights advocacy in the early 2010s, the Consistent Life Ethic has gained new partner organizations and voices.

The organization I founded, Rehumanize International (first named *Life Matters Journal* in 2011), is just one of the many groups founded by young activists with the CLE as our foundational philosophy. Young people crave the con-

---

18. Ronald P. Hamel, "The Consistent Ethic of Life: A Corrective Moral Vision for Healthcare," in *The Consistent Ethic of Life: Assessing its Reception and Relevance* (Ossining, NY: Orbis Books, 2008), 16-32.
19. Crossed, "Reminiscing."
20. Consistent Life Network "Vision & Mission," *consistentlifenetwork. org/mission.*

sistency, authenticity, and inclusion that the Consistent Life Ethic movement offers. We hope that you, too, will find your own niche within our movement, and find welcome, and belonging.

What does the Consistent Life Ethic look like in practice?

When we embrace the Consistent Life Ethic, we must stand for human rights for all human beings—and truly, authentically, love the human beings *behind* those human rights. We must live our lives with human dignity at the core of all our actions. We must not abandon some humans for political expediency. We must have empathy and compassion as we stand for the vulnerable and the marginalized. We must stand against dehumanization and actively seek to rehumanize victims of violence. We must stand against *all* violence against human beings, and work to create a world where every human is respected in the culture, valued throughout their life in society, and protected in the law from all forms of violence. To learn more about things you can do to get involved in CLE activism, see chapter 12.

How do Consistent Life Ethic adherents respond to aggressive violence?

If we place human life, human rights, and human dignity at the moral center of all action, then we must approach the questions of self-defense and community defense with utmost care. The Consistent Life Ethic sphere brings together folks from both just war theory and strict pacifist backgrounds to oppose all forms of aggressive violence. Both positions add something profoundly valuable to the conversation on violence, peacemaking, and building a way forward where every human is respected, valued, and protected. In turn, we must be brave enough to examine our own positions on defense, both personal and national, and see this philosophy's deeper implications on our action and policy.

Following a human-centered ethics, we should not ask "how can I use violent force against another human being?" but, "when a human (or group of humans) is under violent attack, what response respects the dignity of *all* involved?" Since all human beings have the same nature, the same intrinsic, immutable worth, aggressive violence is inherently incompatible with this dignity. Aggressive violence reduces humans' lives to mere means to an end.

Defensive action, however, falls into a different moral category. Harm committed during a rightly intended and rightly executed defensive action could be considered a double-effect. Now, what is double-effect?

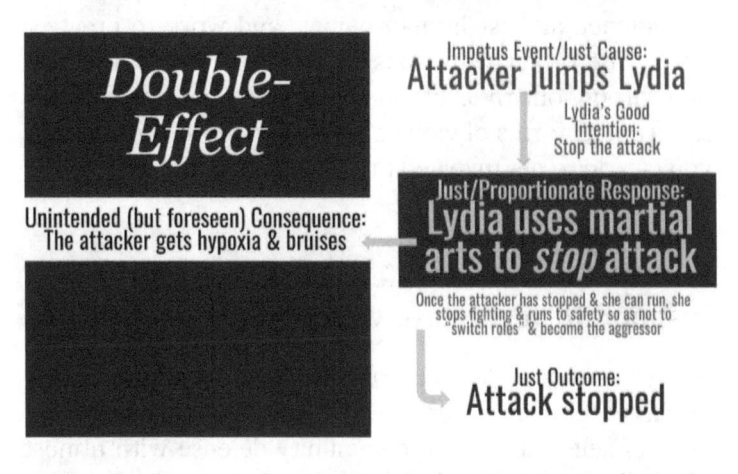

In the diagram above, the attacker jumping Lydia is the impetus event. By responding, Lydia's intention is to stop the attack. Her response itself is using her self-defense martial arts skills, including a limited choke hold to make the attacker pass out so she can get away. The response action itself is intended to stop the attack, not harm the attacker. The intention is good, the action is morally neutral, and the end result is that the attack was stopped. The side (or "double") effect of that intended response action might be that Lydia's martial arts response action may have left the attacker with some bruises, or a concussion, or slight hypoxia. Though these actions in the "double-effect" box are foreseeable, they are not intended harm.

The central point of double-effect is that an action meant to save a life, even one that causes foreseeable but unintended harm, may be permissible under the Consistent Life Ethic. This is so because each and every human being's life has equal worth; as such, we may never intentionally harm another, but we may protect our own life if it is imperiled. Just defense lies in balancing these two truths.

Holding all human life to be worthy of respect does not prohibit defensive action, but requires that any action be taken primarily for defense, for stopping an imminent threat to life. We should never intend to end the life of an attacker, but only to stop an ensuing attack. According to the CLE, every human being's life must be respected—*even* the lives of those who may be committing or who have already committed violence. What human beings do does not negate their inherent, immutable moral value.

In any violent attack, our first responsibility is to prevent, ward off, or defend against violent attack through the least violent means to effect a peaceful outcome. In some rare situations of personal defense, the least violent means to stop an attack may involve using violent defensive action, such as use of a gun. But the principle of double-effect applies in this situation—even if foreseen, the harm caused by such moral defensive action would be a side effect. Once the attacker has ceased aggressive action, however, it would be immoral for victims themselves to begin their own violent aggression, even if that aggression was geared towards preventing the original aggressor from ever attacking them again. In addition, the intentions and will of the defender determine the morality of such defensive action: if the direct will and intention is to kill (perhaps out of vengeance or zeal), then the action would violate respect for human dignity. In fact, such an action would demonstrate a selective preference between the human lives to be respected and those to be destroyed (in this case, the lives of those who have done bad things), which contradicts true respect for intrinsic human dignity.

There's a range of views on what people believe constitutes pacifism; ultimately, however, all pacifists refuse to respond to violence with violence. Many also disagree on the definition of "violence": Some would consider any use of a gun to be violent, but that learning a martial art like judo to stop an attack by turning the attacker's aggression against them is not violent. Nearly all pacifists I've encountered think that using guns or other lethal weapons violates the principle of last resort; they believe that even in interpersonal conflict, there is a nearly endless range of nonviolent responses to harm or threatened violence. Unfortunately, these skills in nonviolent de-escalation and conflict resolution are very rarely explored through trainings and educational opportunities, except in pacifist spaces.

Many who adhere to just war or just defense theory have a profound respect for those who choose not to defend themselves—who believe in literally turning the other cheek. It can be argued, though, that respecting every human being's life includes acknowledging a natural moral right to defend oneself and others from attack. No one, even pacifists, would decline to intervene if someone were trying to attack a two-year-old child. Within a peaceful paradigm, there indeed is a way to practice just defense. However, acknowledging a moral right to just defense does not mean that anything and everything done "in the name of defense" is morally permissible.

A common perception is that self-defense begins as a response to some sort of altercation. However, self-defense actually begins before an altercation even happens: It starts with awareness, and with thinking creatively about nonviolent solutions. It starts with building cultures of peace in society.[21] It starts with seeking to build community. It starts with a commitment to others' dignity. It also starts with preparing, as much as possible, least-force techniques of self-defense. Perhaps you could take a self-defense course, or a grappling-type martial arts course like Brazilian jiu-jitsu based on principles of peace and using the least force in self-defense. Ultimately, a truly just self-defense begins by evaluating what just defense requires and developing plans for peaceful resolution before difficult situations arise.

For human beings' lives to be truly respected across all time and space, our nations, militaries, and international institutions must hold with the same responsibility to respect and defend them in all cases.[22] The frequent dec-

---

21. Learn more about this in chapter 12, "Put These Ideas into Action".
22. A certain personalist line of thought in Germain Grisez's *Beyond the New Morality* demands that if every human life is infinitely valuable and worthy of protection, then treating even enemy combatants as "targets" to be killed is contrary to their inherent dignity. Intending to kill, even as a means to stop an attack, would be contrary to our shared inherent human dignity and not within the constructs of just defense.

larations that our current armed conflicts are "just wars" demonstrates practically zero understanding of what actually constitutes a just war. Here we ought to examine just war theory: How does a philosophy centered on human beings show us how to implement structures of just defense on a macro scale? And how is such a philosophy implemented on a micro, interpersonal scale? It may be especially difficult to propose just defense in our present age of gun-loving machismo, militarism and far-reaching violence enacted in the name of "liberty." To respect human lives in all circumstances, we must be willing to place ourselves in the uncomfortable position of standing against systems of power and violence.

To begin, a theory of just defense stipulates that all violent action must follow a just cause and therefore can only be defensive in nature, whether that action is defending our own lives, those of our fellow citizens, or potentially the lives of another nation or people. As an individual you can't start a fight because someone said something rude about your mom or stole something from you. You can't threaten someone who offends you; that is escalation. Initiating a fight does *not* qualify as self-defense. However, let's say someone near you is being attacked or you are being attacked. This is where your planned defensive response should kick in.

The very notion of "preemptive defense" is self-contradictory: It is immoral for me to break and enter into my neighbor's home and maim or kill that neighbor because I suspect that an attack might occur someday. Rather, a "defender" has to act in such a way as to respect the life and dignity of the person deemed to be the "aggressor." And because there is no absolute certainty until an action begins to take place, a "defending" nation cannot launch a preemptive strike in the name of defense.

Next, in order to respect the lives of every human being, be they individual attackers, militants, or civilians, violence or war must be used as a last resort. This aspect may be the most important element in the entire framework of just defense. Physical defense should be the last option. In situations of high conflict, the goal is de-escalation. In such circumstances, individuals and nations alike can benefit from apology, diplomatic conversation, and a non-threatening posture. Even when you're right, it is better to apologize than to get into an altercation that risks harm and violence and possible loss of life. If the other person or nation cannot be dissuaded from anger, then evading, leaving, or running is better than being put in a situation where self-defense might be necessary. Only when all other possibilities are exhausted may recourse to physical response be justified. Before war begins, during an attack, and in the aftermath, every diplomatic effort must be pursued so as to offer peace and demonstrate the utmost respect for life. "As a last resort" means that "pre-emptive defense" cannot be morally justified, because in taking such action, the "defending" nation has not sought all other means and options for peace. During an ensuing attack, however, it would be ideal to neutralize attackers' weapons to protect the peoples of the defending nation; with some current military technology this may be possible via non-violent means.

Two other aspects to be considered in determining the justness of a defense are the probability of success and proportionality of action. While it's hard to gauge the possible efficacy of personal self-defense, and though some defensive actions might have no guarantee of success (e.g., if you are a small person being attacked and kidnapped by a larger person), you still ought to defend yourself. If you want to remain alive and free, then giving everything you've got to fight back, even against a physically overpowering attacker, is vital. The standard of probable success is difficult to translate between the micro and macro, but it is vital in community and national defense. Probability of success may seem arbitrary and unfounded, but to best respect life, especially civilians' lives, a nation must consider whether defensive action might cause even greater loss of life, and only end in certain defeat.

Proportionality is crucial because that distinction prevents a defender from "switching roles" and becoming the attacker. If someone punches you in the face because of something you said about their favorite team, it would be disproportionate to shoot that person with a gun. The goal should always be to end the attack, not to kill the attacker. Proportionality on a national scale resembles this example. In waging war against an aggressor, a nation must take all action to avoid civilian casualties and "collateral damage"; any war's benefits must outweigh the likely negative effects. It is necessary that unjust killing and loss of life be prevented, and that a defender's motives remain rooted purely in defense of the nation and not in vengeful action.

This, of course, leads to motive: for a nation's self-defense to be just, like an individual's self-defense to be just, any violent action must be taken only as active defense. This means that we cannot seek out past aggressors out of a desire for vengeance, or zeal for one's own homeland; violent force can be employed only as a proportional last resort for current defense or protection. Defensive action is moral inasmuch as any death that results follows the principle of double-effect, and does not arise from an immoral desire to destroy a human being's life.

A last but not least requirement for just defense is the proper consent and authority of the defenders, also known as a requirement for "competent authority." Think about it this way: Every person has authority over themselves. Everyone has a right to defend themselves. Applying this rule can be highly situational, as when—for example—someone is being beaten or attacked in front of you. If the victim in question (e.g. an abuse victim) doesn't want you to use violence to stop the attack, then that individual's desire absolutely should be respected, and other means of intervention and de-escalation should be considered and used. In the case of national defense, for example, the United States Constitution requires that the president get consent from Congress to engage in war, and that Congress shall declare wars. This is to ensure that the people of the nation, who make up the military, support the decision to engage in a war.[23] The executive branch of government does not represent the whole of the nation, and does not even represent those everyday individuals in the military who would lay their lives on the line. To respect their lives, proper consent and authority must be exercised to give them agency in such a decision. This is much less a question in personal defense, because we act as agents for ourselves and make choices to defend our own persons and vulnerable others; but in the case of national conflict this question is of utmost importance so the lives of combatants who work to defend a nation are respected.

This is what constitutes a just defense of individual, community, and nation: proper consent and authority of the defending nation, proportionality and probability of success, motive and defensive nature of action, and use of violence and war as a last resort. All these aspects are present in personal defense, but are present in different

---

23. Because the military is composed of national citizens, they should be able to consent (or decline consent) to the use of force either in defending themselves or in defending others.

ways. Each is required for a national defense to be moral and just; this theory cannot be used to justify war *ex post facto*, but it is meant to guide and prevent unjust action. In truth, if all nations followed such a policy of ethics and just national defense, there would be no war at all.

All the principles listed above are tenets of just defense, adapted from just war theory. They are meant to be a strict guide for defensive action, not a permission slip to do anything in the name of "defense." Just war theory is often associated with Catholic thought (with St. Augustine in particular), but it arose in the pre-Christian era,[24,25] and its principles can be found across religious beliefs and humanist thought. I will review those principles again, so you can remember them.

War, when necessary, must be conducted according to these moral guidelines:

- Just cause
- Competent authority
- Proportionality
- Probability of success
- Last resort/Least force

Especially in the United States, but also all over the world, citizens and peoples everywhere have the responsibility to hold accountable those nations who engage in military conflict, to demand that they act according to principles of just defense. It makes one wonder whether it is possible to justly serve in any modern techno-

---

24. Rory Cox, "Expanding the History of the Just War: The Ethics of War in Ancient Egypt," *International Studies Quarterly* 61, no. 2 (2017): 371.

25. Gregory Raymond, *The Greco-Roman Roots of the Western Just War Tradition* (Oxfordshire, England: Routledge, 2010).

logical military, considering that the history of military action in the twentieth and twenty-first centuries has been steeped in unjust, often cruel, and systemically dehumanizing violence.

We must consider the technology placed in the hands of soldiers and these weapons' relation to the nature of war: How can we instill the defensive and human-centered nature of justice that must be upheld in any war instead of the "patriotic" priorities such as zealous love of country or the vengeful aims directed at the vague concept of "terror"? And how can we possibly engage in wars in which we seek not to kill, but only to defend ourselves? So many modern weapons have been invented only for the purpose of killing in the most effective manner possible, from machine guns to grenades, bombs to chemical warfare. If soldiers are trained with these weapons, trained to kill most effectively, instead of learning best practices of defense, we do not train defenders, but killers. And in training how to kill, we teach killing as a means of defense, instead of defense first, with the possibility of death as a side effect. With modern weapons, a truly just war seems impossible. Holding our militaries and our governments accountable is of the utmost importance if we wish to see peace and true proper respect for human life and dignity.

As neighbors to our fellow human beings, we have a responsibility to hold others accountable for their actions and to stop abuses of human dignity through the abuse of the term "just war." We would not tolerate for one instant a neighbor coming into our home in the name of "defense" and hurting us because he thinks we might, someday, be planning to attack him. Likewise, police actions such as firing bullets at, kicking, or otherwise abusing nonviolent actors (such as US protestors exercising their First Amendment rights to free speech and assembly) should not be tolerated. And finally, actions like capital punishment are unnecessary in the developed world for the safety and defense of the public, and as such, can only be seen as used for vengeance. We should hold both our neighbors and our local authorities accountable for unjust action in the name of defense.

I hope that this analysis of defense through the Consistent Life Ethic framework, helps to illuminate the issues of personal and national defense in light of the dignity of the human person. We must uphold every human being's life. We must seek not to justify our actions, but first and foremost to act justly. In coming to see these problems from a perspective of respect for all life, we can hold both neighbor and nation accountable for their actions contrary to life and engender such an attitude in our culture so that together, we may work to seek peace.

Who can support the Consistent Life Ethic?

This human-centered ethic is universally under-standable and agreeable. Though the terminology "Consistent Life Ethic" originated in Catholic circles, many CLE advocates have come to this philosophy because of their roots in one or more other ideologies. People from all different backgrounds, races, faiths, and politics embrace it because at its core it is centered on human dignity. Here, I want to explore just some of the backgrounds that led modern advocates to embrace the Consistent Life Ethic philosophy.

Humanism

In a nutshell, this philosophy (said to have begun in the fourteenth and fifteenth centuries) places humans at the center of ethical action and seeks to promote human flourishing through uplifting the individual (who often lives in the context of human community).[26] Though not all humanists support the Consistent Life Ethic, advocates like atheist humanist Nat Hentoff have supported a consistent ethic of life based on the idea of the "indivisibility of life," therefore advocating against war, the death penalty, euthanasia, and abortion.[27]

Feminism

Among the many and diverse feminisms, there is a rich history of pro-life leaders. Women's rights organizers of the suffragist era might not have called themselves "feminists," or "pro-life," but in a conversation following the tragic decision of *Roe v. Wade*, the feminist author of the Equal Rights Amendment (ERA) Alice Paul intimated to Feminists for Life founder Pat Goltz that nearly all first-wave feminists had been anti-abortion.[28]

The definition of feminism as based in the shared, equal humanity of men and women includes three core principles that clearly lie within a consistent and intersectional feminism: equality, non-discrimination, and nonviolence. Equality for all human beings means that all

26. "Humanism," in *obo* in Renaissance and Reformation, *oxfordbibliographies.com/view/document/obo-9780195399301/obo-9780195399301-0002.xml.*
27. Nat Hentoff, "The Indivisible Fight for Life," presented at an AUL Forum, 19 October 1986, Chicago, *groups.csail.mit.edu/mac/users/rauch/nvp/consistent/indivisible.html* .
28. "First Wave Feminists," Feminists for Life, *feministsforlife.org/gallery/firstwavefeminists.*

of us share equally in our inherent human dignity, regardless of gender identity, race, religion, politics, age, size, sexual orientation, ability, or any other circumstance. Non-discrimination follows directly from the principle of equality because any act of discrimination (be it sexism, racism, ageism, ableism, etc.) contradicts equal human dignity. Non-discrimination lived in the real world means that all human beings have the same right to live a life free from violence, based on their inherent equal human dignity.

Many activists have found their way to the Consistent Life Ethic through the exploration of feminism, including organizations such as Feminists for Life, Feminists Choosing Life of New York, and others. I also credit my own embrace of the CLE with a foundational understanding of human equality through the lens of feminism, and when sharing how all struggles for human dignity are interconnected, often refer to pro-life feminist, disability self-advocate, and CLE activist Fannie Lou Hamer: "Nobody's Free Until Everybody's Free."[29]

Non-Aggression Principle

Murray Rothbard laid out the authoritative definition of the Non-Aggression Principle in his 1974 essay "War, Peace, and the State":

> No one may threaten or commit violence ("aggress") against another man's person or property. Violence may be employed only against the man who commits

---

29. Fannie Lou Hamer, "Nobody's Free Until Everybody's Free," Speech Delivered at the Founding of the National Women's Political Caucus, Washington, D.C., July 10, 1971. Included in *The Speeches of Fannie Lou Hamer: To Tell It Like It Is*, eds. Maegan Parker Brooks and Davis W. Houck (Jackson, MS: University Press of Mississippi, 2013).

such violence; that is, only defensively against the aggressive violence of another. In short, no violence may be employed against a non-aggressor.[30]

This philosophy is the guiding principle behind most modern libertarian philosophy, and those who recognize the humanity of the preborn child have often formed libertarian pro-life coalitions. These have included the late Doris Gordon and her grassroots organization, Libertarians for Life.[31] Outsider politicians like Ron Paul have been said to embrace a Consistent Life Ethic and are partly credited with inspiring a resurgence of CLE advocates during election seasons between 2000 and today.[32]

Personalism

Personalism, a fairly recent philosophy, crystallized in Europe during the first half of the twentieth century in response to the radical and dehumanizing modern movements of individualism and (individualism's opposite) collectivism. Spurred by the oppression of violent ideologies like Nazism in Germany and Marxist-Leninist Communism in Russia, the dignity of the incommunicable[33] individual

---

30. Murray Newton Rothbard, "War, Peace, and the State," in *Egalitarianism as a Revolt Against Nature, and Other Essays*, 2nd ed. (Auburn, AL: Ludwig Von Mises Institute, 2000), 115–32.
31. "Libertarians for Life," l4l.org.
32. Nicholas Neal, "No Aggression, No Homicide: Being Libertarian & Consistent Life," *Life Matters Journal* 1, no. 2 (December 2011): 26-27.
33. Here, I'm using the word "incommunicable" in the manner of Personalist philosopher John F. Crosby, as in his seminal book *The Selfhood of the Human Person*, published by The Catholic University of America Press in 1996, and from his article "The Incommunicability of Human Persons," *The Thomist: A Speculative Quarterly Review* 57, no. 3 (1993): 403-442. doi:10.1353/tho.1993.0020. His use of the word seems to encompass the idea that each human individual's selfhood cannot be contained within words or captured with nameable traits,

was held up as key to human flourishing; simultaneously, however, the Personalist movement abhorred the toxic apathy of individualism. Personalism's moral locus is the human person: a being with rational nature who exists in the context of community.

The first stirrings of this movement, which included popular Catholic thinkers like John Henry Cardinal Newman and Karol Wojtyla (later Pope John Paul II), can be traced to proto-Personalist Immanuel Kant, whose moral imperative rests on the central idea that all humans must be treated based on their inherent dignity:

> The human being (and in general every rational being) exists as an end in himself, not merely as a means to be used by this or that will at its discretion; instead he must in all actions, whether directed to himself or also to other rational beings, always be regarded at the same time as an end.[34]

The Personalist movement that followed Kant's first intimations of human dignity as the center of moral action was heavily French in origin. This movement can be traced back to Jacques Maritain and his Thomistic Personalism, Gabriel Marcel and his Existentialist Personalism, the catalogs of *Esprit* published by the Communitarian Personalist Emmanuel Mounier, and the later Metaphysical Personalism of Maurice Nédoncelle. They saw Personalism as:

> an option in favor of the person that took from individualism its defense of the rights of the subject and

---

that something in us as members of the human species is ineffable and makes it such that each of us is unique, unrepeatable, and irreplaceable because of this unnameable selfhood.

34. Immanuel Kant, *The Groundwork of the Metaphysics of Morals*, trans. Mary Gregor (Cambridge, UK: Cambridge University Press, 1997), §4:428.

from collectivisms their ethical tension towards the construction of a common project. . . the primacy of the person before society balanced by the correlative obligation to serve the same society through a commitment that could demand serious sacrifices.[35]

Many Consistent Life Ethic advocates today have found their philosophy holistically articulated within Personalist writings.

Religions and the Consistent Life Ethic

Many religions have a version of a Golden Rule ("Do unto others as you would have them do unto you.") or a Silver Rule ("Do not do unto others what you would not like done to you."), or rules of non-aggression or non-violence, which can easily be interpreted into a consistent ethic of life. Some of those are featured here:

Buddhism, Jainism, Hinduism

Within these three religions based in India, there is a central thread of *ahimsa*, which in Sanskrit means "non-injury." Ahimsa, as a central belief of these religions is "the ethical principle of not causing harm to other living things." As such, ahimsa translates into vegetarianism in the daily life of Buddhist, Jainist, and Hindu believers, and "Mohandas K. Gandhi extended ahimsa into the political sphere as satyagraha, or nonviolent resistance to a specific evil."[36] Many adherents of the Consistent Life Ethic have come from Buddhist and Hindu backgrounds. Many

---

35. Juan Manuel Burgos, An *Introduction to Personalism*, trans. R.T. Allen (Washington, D.C.: The Catholic University of America Press, 2018), 16.
36. "Ahimsa," *Encyclopedia Britannica*, February 19, 2015, *britannica. com/topic/ahimsa.*

may even adopt the CLE because of the principle of non-violence towards all, without necessarily using the term "Consistent Life Ethic," because that phrase was popularized only recently in the United States, at first by Catholic activists.

Confucianism

Within *The Analects* of Confucius, there is a dialogue concerning a central teaching that may serve as a foundational guide for a good life:

> Zigong asked: "Is there a single word that can serve as a guide to conduct throughout one's life?"
>
> Confucius said: "Perhaps the word 'shu,' 'reciprocity': 'Do not do to others what you would not want others to do to you.'"[37]

This principle is, again, a version of the Silver Rule, which generally proposes an ethic of nonviolence and support for human dignity.

Judaism

In the Babylonian Talmud, the teachings of a Silver Rule are presented as the center and root of all Jewish teachings: "A prospective convert asked Hillel to teach him the entire Torah while standing on one foot. Hillel replied, 'What is hateful to yourself, do not do to your fellow man. That is the whole of Torah and the remainder is but commentary. Go and study it.'"[38]

---

37. Confucius, *The Analects of Confucius*, trans. R. Eno, 2015, §15.24, *chinatxt.sitehost.iu.edu/Analects_of_Confucius_(Eno-2015).pdf*.
38. Babylonian Talmud, Shabbat 31a.

Islam

There are strong traditions of Muslim pacifism and non-violence that hearken to the story of Muhammad's nonviolent struggle against oppression in Mecca before his *hijra* to Medina.[39,40] Respect for human life is woven throughout the pages of the Qur'an. For example, Surah (chapter) 5, Ayat (verse) 32 reads: "The Almighty says: And if any one saved a life, it would be as if he saved the life of all of humanity." Additionally, several parts of the Qur'an point to principles of non-aggression and to peace: "Fight in the cause of Allah those who fight you, But do not transgress limits; For Allah loveth not transgressors."[41] And "fight them on, until there is no more tumult or oppression, and there prevail justice and faith in Allah."[42] This points to a principle of just self-defense with clear limits based on the idea of the inherent dignity of even those against whom a Muslim might be fighting.

Christianity

The stories contained within the New Testament include the Golden Rule. Jesus of Nazareth tells his followers, "In everything, do to others what you would have them do to you, for this sums up the Law and the Prophets,"[43] and "Love your neighbor as yourself."[44] In a bold passage from the Gospel of Matthew Jesus challenges many Christians:

---

39. Glenn D. Paige, Chaiwat Satha-Anand (Qader Muheideen), and Sarah Gilliatt, eds., *Islam And Nonviolence* (Honolulu, HI: Center for Global Nonviolence, 2001).
40. Elise Boulding, *Cultures of Peace: The Hidden Side of History* (Syracuse, NY: Syracuse University Press, 2000), 57.
41. Surah 2, Ayat 190
42. Surah 2, Ayat 193
43. Holy Bible, New International Version, Matthew 7:12
44. Holy Bible, New International Version, Matthew 22:39

You have heard that it was said, "Eye for eye, and tooth for tooth." But I tell you, do not resist an evil person. If anyone slaps you on the right cheek, turn to them the other cheek also. . . [and] you have heard that it was said, "Love your neighbor and hate your enemy." But I tell you, love your enemies and pray for those who persecute you.[45]

Many believers interpret these passages to support a Consistent Life Ethic, non-aggression, and even Christian pacifism.

Seeing that such diverse people have embraced the Consistent Life Ethic, we discovered a basic foundation for reaching out to anyone from any background to have good, productive conversations about this consistent philosophy of human dignity and nonviolence. Because we share a core, foundational principle—our inherent human dignity—we know that the Consistent Life Ethic applies to every human. Because these principles have universal applicability, we understand that we must respect and care for every human with whom we interact. This leads us to practice radical inclusivity: when we embrace the Consistent Life Ethic, we understand that our movement to end violence against human beings requires the most urgent action, and everyone must take part. In our movement, every human truly stands for the rights of every human.

The Consistent Life Ethic and the scope of this book

At Rehumanize International, the team I work with focuses primarily on issues of violence that, even in this

---

45. Holy Bible, New International Version, Matthew 5:38-44

day and age, remain legal. Though we do unequivocally oppose human trafficking and domestic violence and homicide, these practices are widely illegal all over the globe, and have neither the near-universal cultural acceptance nor the legal standing that, for example, abortion or war share in nearly every nation. Violence that is legal presents an especially egregious violation of human dignity, in that the victims are often so totally dehumanized that their deaths go by unmarked, their dignity buried under political posturing and rhetoric in an attempt to "justify" the violence itself. Sometimes that rhetoric is ableism, sometimes ageism or racism or sexism or other ideas about our value being determined by our circumstances. And sometimes, like in the case of abortion, the "justifications" like ageism and ableism overlap and combine to dehumanize the vulnerable.[46] So, we spend our limited time and energy working to end legal acts of violence (i.e. those that are included by name in the table of contents). I do want to make clear that in focusing on these particular issues of violence, we should never intend to undermine the work others are doing to end acts

---

46. Likewise, we want to acknowledge my choices in separating these various issues of violence in the table of contents. For example, "Violence in Response to Disability" could easily include sections on police brutality, embryo destruction, the death penalty, and abortion. Ableism is rampant in our society and impacts every corner of our work. But I opted to put abortion and embryo destruction as primarily related to violence within the context of reproduction, and police brutality and the death penalty within the section on violence in response to crime, more for the sake of organizing similar broader themes. But it's worth noting that the Consistent Life Ethic movement tends to understand well the intersectionality of human lives, and how, for example, the death penalty, in addition to being primarily a response to crime, is often ableist. I encourage you to look for these connections as you read this book and then move forward in your own work for human dignity and human rights.

of violence within our given social context that persist, even though they are already illegal.

Additionally, there are issues such as poverty, access to healthcare, or systemic discrimination that many in the Consistent Life Ethic movement consider ancillary because they are not *direct* acts of violence. Nonetheless, as a matter of course I care passionately about addressing these issues, ending all forms of dehumanization, and upholding human dignity. Even if we ended all aggressive violence, we would need to work to protect and bolster the dignity of our fellow humans. Because people from almost every socio-political background embrace the CLE, well-intentioned people may well come to different and varied solutions to these problems. I encourage every person who reads this book to think and act creatively—alongside the oppressed—to resolve these problems; ultimately, as long as you have the inherent dignity of each and every human being at the center of your work, a day will surely come when not only violence but also poverty and all forms of discrimination become things of the past. The chapters that follow will walk you through the facts about various issues of legal violence by 1) explaining the methods used within that act of violence, 2) assessing the ethical implications that follow from applying the Consistent Life Ethic to the facts of that violence, 3) exploring the history of cultural acceptance and public policy around that act of violence, to equip you with knowledge of some precedent in the law for any work you might do related to that act of violence, 4) public policy suggestions for ending that act of violence.

In many of the illustrative examples and much of the historical analysis, I will draw connections to the wider worldwide society, but I will focus largely on my own nation and culture—the United States—both because it is where I have the most experience and because of its current status as global hegemon. I hope it is clear that I want to end violence all over the world, not simply in my own nation; but as with most things, the bulk of my knowledge and activism being closest to home is a sound principle. Additionally, in presenting the methods used to harm and kill humans, I obviously do not mean to say that the method of the action determines its wrongness. The moral problem lies in the intentional harm and killing, not how it is done. I merely present the methods to better equip you to dialogue about the issues.

Next, each of these chapters will include common questions related to that act of violence and answers from a Consistent Life Ethic perspective, to demonstrate how to discourse about these issues. Then, each chapter will include some discussion questions particularly geared towards kickstarting stimulating discourse in your own book club or reading group of peers, friends, or colleagues. Lastly, there are suggestions for further reading that I hope will launch your continued learning on CLE topics, and motivate you to act.[47]

Again, thank you for picking up this book and for making a conscious effort to learn, grow, and (as several modern authors have paraphrased Gandhi) "be the change you wish to see in the world." I hope you find this whole text to be engaging, challenging, and encouraging!

Discussion Questions

1. Before you opened this book, how familiar were you with the concept of the Consistent Life Ethic? Where

---

47. The titles suggested in this and future chapters for further reading may not be written from a Consistent Life Ethic perspective, and I do not necessarily endorse all of the positions these sources take. I present them with a hope that the earnest but critical reader will learn something valuable from them.

had you heard of it? How did that context impact what you originally thought of it?

2. When have you seen people get excluded from justice movements or organizations over unrelated issues (like religion, sexual orientation, or socioeconomic background)? How did that make you feel?

3. At the beginning of this reading, which of the topics within our conception of the Consistent Life Ethic do you take particular issue with? Which do you feel profoundly undereducated about?

4. What practical actions do you hope or plan to take to develop nonviolent conflict resolution skills? How will you endeavor to live by these principles and work to make defensive violence a last resort in your life?

Further Reading Suggestions

1. Rachel MacNair and Stephen Zunes, *Consistently Opposing Killing: from Abortion to Assisted Suicide, the Death Penalty, and War* (Westport, CT: Praeger Press, 2008).

2. Thomas A. Nairn, *The Consistent Ethic of Life: Assessing Its Reception and Relevance* (Ossining, NY: Orbis Books, 2008).

3. Mary Krane Derr, Rachel MacNair, and Linda Naranjo-Huebl, editors, *ProLife Feminism: Yesterday and Today* (Bloomington, IN: Xlibris, 2006).

4. Juan Manuel Burgos, *An Introduction to Personalism* (Washington, D.C.: The Catholic University of America Press, 2018).

5. Glenn D. Paige, Chaiwat Satha-Anand (Qader Muheideen), and Sarah Gilliatt, editors, *Islam and Nonviolence* (Manoa, HI: Matsunaga Institute for Peace, 1993).

6. Rob Arner, *Consistently Pro-Life: The Ethics of Bloodshed in Ancient Christianity* (Eugene, OR: Pickwick Publications, 2010).

7. Mark Andreas, *Sweet Fruit from the Bitter Tree: 61 Stories of Creative & Compassionate Ways out of Conflict* (Boulder, CO: Real People Press, 2011).

8. Rachel M. MacNair, *Perpetration-Induced Traumatic Stress: The Psychological Consequences of Killing* (Westport, CT: Praeger Press, 2002).

9. Eli S. McCarthy, editor, *A Just Peace Ethic Primer: Building Sustainable Peace and Breaking Cycles of Violence* (Washington, D.C.: Georgetown University Press, 2020).

Ending Violence
in Reproduction

We have treated the loss of our fetuses as a theoretical loss, a sad-but-necessary loss, as of civilians in wartime. We have not yet realized that the offspring lost are not the enemy's, nor our neighbor's, but our own. And it is not a loss of inert, amorphous tissue, but of a growing being unique in history.

–Frederica Mathewes-Green

Chapter 2

Embryo destruction

Though the new technologies of in-vitro fertilization and embryonic stem cell research seem to promise groundbreaking solutions to medical problems, we must never use violence to achieve scientific progress.

What is Embryo Destruction?

At the moment a human ovum (egg) is fertilized by a human sperm (or also by a new technology called somatic cell nuclear transfer)[48] a new, differentiated, unique, whole,[49] and living member of the human species begins to exist.[50] In

---

48. Masahito Tachibana et al., "Human Embryonic Stem Cells Derived by Somatic Cell Nuclear Transfer," Cell 153, no. 6 (May 2013): 1228-38, doi.org/10.1016/j.cell.2013.05.006.

49. When I say "whole" in this context, I mean "a unity," a 'total organism," which is different from "a fully mature being." By way of comparison, a toddler, too, is whole, a total organism, despite the fact that toddlers are developmentally immature. We would say that the human toddler is a whole toddler, a whole human; toddlers are complete for the stage that they are in; and if you add time and nutrition, they will develop into the same being, but at a later developmental stage/age.

50. Here, there could be a nearly endless list of citations from various biology textbooks, ranging from middle school level to medical

the modern era, if not implanted into the womb, many pre-natal humans created in-vitro (outside of the human body, literally "in the glass"), are treated as property: discarded like trash or used as if they were merely "medical waste."

In-Vitro Fertilization: Embryo Commoditization and Destruction

In-vitro fertilization (IVF), a common method of assisted reproductive technology (ART), is often used to overcome various conditions of infertility, or to offload the work of pregnancy to surrogates. In this process, typically several eggs are inseminated to create a new tiny human being.[51] The treatment of these preborn children is often dehumanizing. They may be named in legal contracts as "products" of conception that could be transferred to any "owner."[52] They may be killed—and all killing is a kind of violence—by being "discarded."

---

school level. We will include a cross-section of several: First, "Human development begins at fertilization when a sperm fuses with an oocyte to form a single cell, the zygote. This highly-specialized, totipotent cell marks the beginning of each of us as a unique individual." (Moore, Persaud, Torchia. *The Developing Human: Clinically Oriented Embryology*, 10th edition [Philadelphia, PA: Elsevier, 2016], 11). Other textbooks with relevant quotations include: T.W. Sadler, *Langman's Medical Embryology*, 11th edition (Philadelphia, PA: Lippincott & Wilkins, 2010), 13; Ronan O'Rahilly and Fabiola Müller, *Human Embryology and Teratology*, 3rd edition (New York: Wiley-Liss, 2011), 8; William J. Larsen, *Essentials of Human Embryology*, (New York: Churchill Livingstone, 1998), 1-14; Keith L. Moore, *Before We Were Born: Essentials of Embryology*, 7th edition (Philadelphia, PA: Saunders, 2008), 2; Campbell, Williamson, and Heyden, *Biology: Exploring Life* (Needham, MA: Pearson, 2004), 192-97.

51. Mayo Clinic, "In-vitro fertilization (IVF)," *mayoclinic.org/tests-procedures/in-vitro-fertilization/about/pac-20384716*.

52. Walther Bennett Mayo Honeycutt, "Frozen Embryos: The Law at a Crossroads," *wbmhlaw.com/2020/02/25/frozen-embryos-the-law-at-a-crossroads/*

In countless cases these tiny humans are commod-itized, as in the shocking history of Kim Kardashian and Kanye West, who specifically chose male embryos because they "wanted an heir."[53] In addition to choosing for genetic sex, the commoditization phenomenon is glaringly obvi-ous in the possibility of "designer babies": babies chosen for their particular eye color, hair color, height, etc.

This consumerist mindset is compounded by the sheer number of embryos that are created, sometimes twenty or more in one IVF egg-harvesting cycle.[54] Many more embryonic humans are created than would likely ever be implanted and parented. People often are happy with parenting one or two children, and yet have left some-times more than a dozen embryos in cryogenic freezers. There, the embryos are unable to live and grow, but also are unable to die. More than four hundred thousand embryonic-stage children are indefinitely frozen in the US.[55] Even when these embryonic humans are allowed

---

53. Tyler Johnson, "Kim Kardashian Only Received Male Embryos Dur-ing IVF; Kanye Wanted 'an Heir,' Source Claims," *The Hollywood Gos-sip*, June 24, 2015, thehollywoodgossip.com/2015/06/kim-kardashi-an-only-received-male-embryos-during-ivf-kanye-wante/.

54. This section from a news story on a recent study from the UK was very eye-opening for us: "More than 1.625 million eggs in the UK were retrieved from 147,274 women between this timeframe. In all, 172,341 fresh oocyte retrieval cycles took place. Overall, a total of 931,265 embryos resulted from the 1.625 million eggs retrieved—a fertilisation rate of 57 per cent. Of the embryos created, 22 per cent, or 209,080, were transferred into the uterus, while a slightly higher proportion (24 per cent, or 219,563) were frozen. . . . Most of the embryos that weren't transferred (54 per cent) were likely discarded after patients paid for several years of maintaining them in storage." Jonathan Chadwick, "IVF clinics are retrieving 'far too many' eggs from women, with over 50 collected in some procedures, experts warn," *Daily Mail*, June 29, 2021, *dailymail.co.uk/sciencetech/article-9736663/Clinics-retrieving-eggs-IVF-patients-study-suggests.html*.

55. Lesley Stahl, "A Surplus of Embryos," CBS *News*, February 10, 2006, *cbsnews.com/news/a-surplus-of-embryos/*. Given that this report is

to be adopted (after the original parents decide they do not want to have any more children and abandon their embryonic children to a registry for donation), they are often treated not as inherently valuable human beings with their own rights and self-ownership, but as medical material, as property. In fact, the transfer of embryos falls under contract law, not adoption law.[56]

Embryonic Stem-Cell Research:
Embryo Commoditization and Destruction

The first derivation of embryonic stem cells was from mouse embryos in 1981. After lengthy study of the biology of mouse embryonic stem cells, a method to derive stem cells from human embryos and grow the cells in the laboratory was developed in 1998. This practice brought with it myriad ethical issues.[57]

To distinguish embryonic stem-cell research from other research, we must first learn some definitions. A stem cell is any type of cell which, when it divides, cre-

---

over fifteen years old, it's entirely probable that there are more than the four hundred thousand embryos listed here currently in cryogenic freezers around the nation. Another piece referenced above, "Frozen Embryos: The Law at a Crossroads," from Walter Bennett Mayo Honeycutt, estimates about eight hundred thousand embryos were being kept in freezers in 2020.

56. The National Registry for Adoption page, "Embryo Adoption: Legal Contract: Making It Legal," quotes from the Embryo Adoption Awareness Center: "Just to be very clear and transparent on all levels, in the U.S. embryo adoption is not considered a legal form of adoption because embryos are considered property, not people. Therefore, the process is governed by property contract law, not by adoption law. We are applying the best practices of adoption to the whole process, but adoption law does not apply." *nrfa.org/embryo-adoption-legal-contract-making-it-legal/*.

57. J A Thomson, et al. "Embryonic stem cell lines derived from human blastocysts." *Science* 282, no. 5391 (1998): 1145-47.

ates two daughter cells, "one of which is destined to become something new and one of which replaces the original stem cell."[58] There are two different kinds of stem cells: human embryonic stem (HES) cells and adult stem (AS) cells—that come from different sources. HES cells are derived from human embryos that are destroyed to harvest the stem cells. AS cells, on the other hand, are derived from developed and differentiated tissues that do not require the destruction of the individual; they may be found in the brain, placenta, bone marrow, muscles, liver, and elsewhere.[59]

Stem cells have differing levels of plasticity (meaning, the ability to change, or in this case, to become different types of cells):

- Totipotency: The quality of being able to develop into a complete human organism.[60] Only embryos have totipotent stem cells.

- Pluripotency: The quality of being able to form any of the many kinds of adult tissues in a body. Both HES cells and adult induced pluripotent stem (iPS) cells fit this categorization.

- Multipotency: The quality of being able to form a limited but substantial number of adult tissues. Many types of adult stem cells have this capacity.

58. Maureen Condic, "The Basics about Stem Cells," *First Things* 119 (January 2002): 30–31.
59. Christopher Thomas Scott, *Stem Cell Now: From the Experiment that Shook the World to the New Politics of Life* (New York: Pi Press, 2006), 65–69.
60. This stage refers to the very early embryonic stage in which cells, if removed from the embryo, can develop as a complete human organism. This can produce identical twins.

- Unipotency: The quality of being able to create only one type of tissue.[61,62]

The profound plasticity of pluripotent stem cells has resulted in an expectation of near-endless possibilities for cures for diseases. However, because pluripotent cells are far less controllable than multipotent cells and can become any adult tissue, they are also much more likely to overdevelop and become teratomas, a type of tumor.[63]

Human Embryonic Stem cells are derived from two slightly different but ethically similar sources:

- From discarded embryos that are remaining after IVF fertility treatments;[64] or,

- Through the creation of embryos via Somatic Cell Nuclear Transfer (SCNT).[65]

The derivation of the usable HES cells begins with the growth of the human embryo to the blastocyst stage, at which time there is an inner cell mass (ICM) surrounded by an outer layer of cells (trophectoderm).[66] Functionally, the process of ESCR means tearing apart that embryonic

---

61. Christina Healy, "Therapies that Respect Life: The Different Types of Stem Cell Research," *Life Matters Journal* 5, no. 3 (November 2016): 1-2.
62. Thomas B. Okarma, "The Technology and Its Medical Applications," in *The Human Embryonic Stem Cell Debate*, eds. Suzanne Holland, Karen Lebacqz, and Laurie Zoloth, (Cambridge, MA: The MIT Press, 2001), 15-26.
63. Monya Baker, "Why HES Cells Make Teratomas," *Nature News*, March 5, 2009, *nature.com/stemcells/2009/0903/090305/full/stem-cells.2009.36.html.*
64. J.A. Thomson, et al, "Embryonic Stem Cell Lines Derived from Human Blastocysts," *Science* 282, no. 5391 (November 1998): 81145-81147. DOI: 10.1126/science.282.5391.1145
65. Tachibana et al, "Human Embryonic Stem Cells Derived," 1228-38.
66. James A. Thomson, "Human Embryonic Stem Cells," in *The Human Embryonic Stem Cell Debate*, eds. Suzanne Holland, Karen Lebacqz, and Laurie Zoloth (Cambridge, MA: The MIT Press, 2001): 15-26.

human's body for the purpose of "scientific research": the ICM is removed from the embryo to allow for experimentation on the HES cells, thereby killing them.[67] At this point, there is no known method of HES research that does not require the killing of the embryonic child as part of the process.[68]

A Brief Ethical Analysis of Embryo Destruction

All human beings have the same intrinsic nature and dignity, no matter how they were conceived. The circumstances of how sperm and egg got in place and joined together has zero impact on the nature and dignity of the embryonic child as a human. The killing of embryonic children is reprehensible and contrary to the Consistent Life Ethic. Treating young humans as property to be discarded or "used" should never be considered an option, whether within the IVF industry or in scientific research using embryonic stem cells in an effort to find cures for ailments. Even though the proposed ends of achieving a successful pregnancy or curing debilitating diseases are both positive outcomes, humans should never be used merely as the means to an end. To do so would violate the inherent dignity of the victims discarded or destroyed in the process.

---

67. Thomson, J.A., et al. "Embryonic Stem Cell Lines Derived from Human Blastocysts."
68. Tandis Vazin and William J Freed, "Human embryonic stem cells: derivation, culture, and differentiation: a review," *Restorative Neurology and Neuroscience* 28, no. 4 (2010): 589-603.

History of Policy and Culture around Embryo Destruction

Though research on human embryos is explicitly prohibited in five countries (Austria, Lithuania, Poland, Slovakia, Tunisia) and restricted or unknown in a handful more (Germany, Italy, Peru, Colombia, Ecuador, Costa Rica, El Salvador), it is allowed and often funded by the governments of dozens of nations worldwide, typically up to fourteen days after fertilization.[69]

In the United States, HES research has been hotly contested since 1975, when the Department of Health, Education, and Welfare (now the Department of Health and Human Services) adopted the rules and regulations for human embryonic research set by the National Commission for the Protection of Human Subjects of Biomedical and Behavioral Research.[70] Subsequent presidential administrations have allowed or disallowed the creation of embryos for scientific research, the divide usually falling along Democratic or Republican party lines.[71] Since 1996, the Dickey-Wicker Amendment has been attached to the appropriations bills for the Departments of Health and Human Services, Labor, and Education each year, prohibiting the use of federal funds for creating, destroying, or knowingly injuring human embryos.[72] Nonetheless, at this time, the NIH still does HES and fetal tissue research.

69. "World Stem Cell Policies," The Hinxton Group, *hinxtongroup.org/wp.html.*

70. U.S. Congress. H.R.7724, "National Research Act (1974)," *congress.gov/bill/93rd-congress/house-bill/7724/titles.*

71. "A Brief History Of U.S. Stem Cell Policy," Research America, *researchamerica.org/advocacy-action/issues-researchamerica-advocates/stem-cell-research/brief-history-us-stem-cell.*

72. Megan Kearl, "Dickey-Wicker Amendment, 1996," *The Embryo Project Encyclopedia,* Arizona State University, August 2010, *embryo.*

Ironically, HES cells have failed to meet scientific expectations, while AS cells have far exceeded them. Adult stem-cell research has been highly successful at developing therapies and treatments for more than seventy conditions, including leukemia, MS, and sickle cell anemia. Embryonic stem cell research, however, has yet to have an effective treatment or cure attributed to it, due in large part to immune rejection and tumors.[73] Not only is AS cell research more fruitful and effective, but most importantly, it does not kill any humans, embryonic or otherwise. Despite the lack of productive HES therapies in the twenty years of development, there is still a push from many scientists and celebrities to pursue HES research, and in many nations around the world it remains legal and government funded.

A Brief Potential Nonviolent Policy Solution to the Problem of Embryo Destruction

Solving the problems of embryo destruction will not be easy; in dozens of nations around the world, whole industries are devoted to the status quo practices of IVF and ESCR. A firm first step toward ending embryo destruction would be to limit the number of embryos that are allowed to be created in any given assisted reproductive technology procedure. For example, Germany has a policy where a maximum of three embryos may be created in vitro, and all of them must be implanted, thereby eliminating the possi-

---

asu.edu/pages/dickey-wicker-amendment-1996#:~:text=The%20
Dickey%2DWicker%20Amendment%20is,or%20knowingly%20injur-
ing%20human%20embryos.

73. D. Prentice, "Adult Stem Cells," Appendix K in *Monitoring Stem Cell Research: A Report of the President's Council on Bioethics.* Washington, DC: Government Printing Office. 2004, 309-346.

bility of hundreds of thousands of tiny humans being stuck in freezers or being abandoned and treated as detritus by the medical establishment.[74]

We must speak out against this industry, which leaves thousands of embryonic children frozen, at risk of being torn apart for their body parts to promote "scientific advancement." The intrinsic human worth of every child, at whatever age, deserves to be respected. We must unequivocally end embryonic stem cell research, make it illegal, and give the hundreds of thousands of embryonic children currently captive in cryopreservation the care and families that they deserve through gestation and embryo adoption.[75]

74. Volha Parfenchyk and Alexander Flos, "Human dignity in a comparative perspective: embryo protection regimes in Italy and Germany," *Law, Innovation and Technology* 9, no. 1 (2017): 45-77.

75. Some Catholic moral theologians (like Nicholas Tonti-Filippini) think that "there is no moral way out" of the conundrum of thousands of embryos stuck in freezers, and that the "solution" is to "let the embryos expire" by intentionally thawing them without giving them care. I would argue that this "quick fix" is actually a genocide of these tiny humans by forced starvation: dependent humans (like these embryos) deserve access to nutrition and shelter provided by their caregivers/guardians, and intentionally "thawing" them without placing them in a uterine environment (or potentially in the future, an artificial womb) to give them access to nutrition would be a form of violence. For more on the Catholic debate on embryo adoption, see the following piece and the associated links: Rebecca Taylor, "What is the Pro-Life Catholic View of Human Embryo Adoption?", *LifeNews*, June 29, 2011, *lifenews.com/2011/06/29/what-is-the-pro-life-catholic-view-of-human-embryo-adoption/*.

Addressing Common Arguments in Support of Embryo Destruction

Personhood

"It's not a person."

Such a statement echoes a position like that of utilitarian philosopher Peter Singer, who maintains that even one-year-old toddlers, or intellectually disabled adults are not persons because they are not capable of higher-order thought, which is his standard of personhood. By his standard, animals like adult pigs, dolphins, and chimpanzees would be persons, but not human infants. Herb Geraghty, Executive Director of Rehumanize International explains that we must protest this standard:

> This very concept of personhood is an illegitimate social and legal construct that throughout history has been used almost exclusively to discriminate against whole classes of human beings. The Consistent Life Ethic calls us to stand for human rights, not person-rights, because the definition of who can or can't be a person is ultimately a political and ideological debate that ignores basic scientific facts. If there could ever be a category of "human non-persons" then personhood is either a useless signifier at best or dangerous and deadly at worst. If we are going to claim to be supporters of "human rights," we must apply them to all humans.[76]

---

76. Herb Geraghty, "Human Rights for Every Human Being," talk presented at Rehumanize Conference 2021, online, September 4, 2021.

"Thousands of embryos die by miscarriage every day and we don't grieve those losses as a society."

Natural deaths do not justify intentional violence. Many of the embryonic children lost early in pregnancy are mourned by their families,[77] and those who aren't may not be grieved either because their parents didn't yet know of their existence, or because there is a common taboo around mourning such young life, often tied up with cliché phrases like: "well, you can just try again," or "at least you know you can get pregnant." The death of individual human beings who we didn't know existed wouldn't mean that they didn't exist or that their life didn't matter.

"If a fertility clinic were on fire and you had the chance to save a newborn or a petri dish with twelve embryos in it, you'd almost certainly save the infant."

The emotionally-fraught triage decisions we might make during a high-stress emergency don't neces-sarily speak to the moral worth of the humans we could save in these circumstances. For example: if instead it were a burning school and my own niece was one of ten children stuck inside, no one would blame me for emotionally choosing to save my niece; likewise, this choice says nothing about the moral value of the other nine children who I could not save. Additionally, there are other factors that go into a decision like this, including whether the humans in question have a likelihood of surviving. A newborn is much more likely to survive this scenario than

---

77. Elizabeth Leis-Newman, "Miscarriage and loss," *American Psycho-logical Association Monitor on Psychology*, 43, no. 6 (June 2012): 56, *apa.org/monitor/2012/06/miscarriage*.

embryos in a petri dish, who would likely not survive the thaw that would come even if I did save them from perishing in the fire; this reality doesn't touch their innate human dignity. Additionally, similar to the trolley problem often cited in these moral equations, discussants often assume the disposability of certain humans. Instead of accepting that some humans are discardable in our moral calculus, I think it's worth the work to conceive of creative solutions that can try to save all lives in danger.

Science Denial

"It's not (a) human."

As mentioned under the section "What is Embryo Destruction?" earlier in this chapter, science points to the fact that sperm-egg fusion at fertilization creates a new, living, distinct, unique, and unrepeatable human organism. Such an organism is of a wholly different kind than body parts like gametes (sperm and egg) and has internally-directed growth and selfhood. Essentially, since conception, you have always been you. Since conception, I have always been me; the only things that have been added are nutrition, time, and education.

"Different religions believe that life begins at different times (first breath, quickening, conception), so the law should respect those beliefs."

Though we live in a religiously plural society and we honor a freedom of religion, no religion can be allowed to violate the foundational human right to live free from violence. Without this right, no other rights can truly be said to exist, because all hinge on the first right to live. If a religion holds a belief that is not in accord with the scientific consensus, then although its members may be free to hold that belief, it should not dictate law. Our laws should be dictated by science and principles of human dignity.

Scientific Advancement

"Not allowing ESCR is killing patients who need this research."

This argument is based on a utilitarian idea of personhood that values some humans over others, thereby creating a grotesque hierarchy or caste system of human dignity and rights. The stance that refusing to kill embryos does violence against others comes from a grave misconception concerning the nature of aggressive violence. Protecting the dignity of a vulnerable group and refusing to use or harm its members for our own ends is the antithesis of violence.

"The potential for lifesaving cures from embryonic stem cell research outweighs the moral issues with experimenting on embryos."

When research on embryonic stem cells began, journalists gushed over the possibilities for curing disease and ethical objections were swept to the side as obstacles in the way of medical progress. Especially in light of years of evidence to the contrary, it is time to stop destroying human lives for the sake of experimentation. We may not intentionally harm humans even if scientific research on their bodies could potentially create medical cures. We may not do evil that good may come of it.

Hardship of Infertility

"Infertility is awful; we should be helping infertile couples have children."

> This topic is deeply personal to me, a young woman struggling with infertility for more than nine years. I've always desired to be a mother to many children. Nonetheless, the hardship of infertility doesn't justify using these embryonic children as commodities in the IVF process. There are many alternative forms of natural and pre-conception reproductive technologies that assist the couple in conceiving a child and maintaining a pregnancy. Additionally, if you disagree with me that IVF inherently commoditizes the child, there are even nonviolent options within the realm of assisted reproductive technology (ART), the foremost of which is simply not creating excess embryos beyond what the people involved would reasonably implant and parent.

"Having a baby is a good thing."

> If families facing infertility decide to pursue artificial reproductive technologies (specifically in-vitro fertilization), there remains a massive moral quandary: in this process, children are created as a commodity, as something "deserved" by parents, not as good in their own right but existing for the good of the parents. They are created to fulfill a desire in the parents, not loved for themselves.[78] The phenomenon of treating embryos

---

78. On a related note: some folks have asked me: isn't it also possible that naturally conceived children also can become a status symbol, an object, a means to an end? The answer is a resounding yes. Whether it's wealthy suburbanites who have themselves sterilized after having their two children (a boy and a girl, of course) or the fundamentalist couple who have a large brood to be an outward sign of their virtue and faithfulness, treating children as commodities can

as goods is perhaps most glaringly obvious when parents select embryos based on their (sometimes eugenic) desires. These ideas of choosing a color and size are more apt for buying a car than loving a new human being into the world. The embryonic children are created in a process that treats them as property, as mere medical material. Of course, any children conceived this way still share the same inherent human dignity as any of us, because our dignity isn't reliant on how we were conceived or how our parents treat us. And any children conceived through the commoditizing practice of IVF, by their nature, deserve to be cared for: to be loved, cherished, and provided for in the context of a family.

Discussion Questions

1. How does it make you feel to realize the scientific evidence that human lives begin at the moment of fertilization? What part of you might still struggle with that knowledge?

2. Why do you think members of the scientific community so easily dehumanize embryonic humans? How do concepts such as ageism, sizeism, ableism, or our prejudices about "how humans should look" impact this dehumanization?

3. What other stories are you aware of concerning humans being dehumanized and used in medical research, treated as if their selfhood didn't matter? How do those stories impact how you see the preborn child (victim) killed in ESCR?

---

be found in all social circles.

Further Reading Suggestions

1. Samuel B. and Maureen L. Condic, *Human Embryos, Human Beings: A Scientific and Philosophical Approach* (Washington, D.C.: The Catholic University of America Press, 2018).

2. O. Carter Snead, *What It Means to Be Human: The Case for the Body in Public Bioethics* (Cambridge, MA: Harvard University Press, 2020).

3. Robert P. George and Christopher Tollefson, *Embryo: A Defense of Human Life* (New York: Doubleday, 2008).

Chapter 3

Abortion

Pregnancy presents some of the most physically demanding circumstances that a human can undergo. Abortion may be a heated issue when parents and their preborn children are painted as "at odds" with each other, but when we start with the facts and the Consistent Life Ethic, we find a clear way to nonviolence and solidarity.

What is Abortion?

Science tells us that the product of same-species reproduction is a unique, differentiated, whole, living member of the same species. The biology is clear: in reproduction with two human parents, at the moment sperm meets egg at fertilization, a new human being comes into existence.[79] Embryology textbooks recognize the scientific truth that once fertilization has occurred, an individual life has begun

---

79. The question of "personhood" is often brought up in conversations about abortion to justify the act of abortion because the prenatal child is often treated as "non-person." This question will be addressed in greater depth later in this chapter, under the section, "Addressing Common Arguments in Support of Abortion page 86.

and that life's development is self-directed,[80] despite great dependency upon the parents.[81]

Abortion, the termination of a pregnancy, includes the death of the embryo or fetus. For this book, we will only be discussing the case of elective or induced abortion (as opposed to "spontaneous abortion," also known as miscarriage). Such abortions are currently carried out using five different methods.[82]

---

80. When I say "self-directed" here, I mean that the growth of embryos is caused by the embryos themselves, just as growth of an infant or toddler or adolescent would be self-directed by their genome. That is, the organization and reproduction of cells to form, grow, and maintain organs, bones, and other tissues is caused within the organism itself, from its DNA. Like all organisms, the human embryo and fetus needs external nutrition to grow, but that does not mean that the parent providing the nutrition is directing that growth. For more on this process, See *Human Embryos, Human Beings* by Samuel B. and Maureen L. Condic.

81. Here, there could be a nearly endless list of citations from various biology textbooks, ranging from middle school level to medical school level. We will include a cross-section of several: First, "Human development begins at fertilization when a sperm fuses with an oocyte to form a single cell, the zygote. This highly-specialized, totipotent cell marks the beginning of each of us as a unique individual." (Moore, Persaud, Torchia, *The Developing Human: Clinically Oriented Embryology*, 10th edition [Philadelphia, PA: Elsevier, 2016], 11). Other textbooks with relevant quotations include: T.W. Sadler, *Langman's Medical Embryology*, 11th edition (Philadelphia, PA: Lippincott & Wilkins, 2010), 13; Ronan O'Rahilly and Fabiola Müller, *Human Embryology and Teratology*, 3rd edition (New York: Wiley-Liss, 2011), 8; William J. Larsen, *Essentials of Human Embryology* (New York: Churchill Livingstone, 1998), 1-14; Keith L. Moore, *Before We Were Born: Essentials of Embryology*, 7th edition (Philadelphia, PA: Saunders, 2008), 2; Campbell, Williamson, and Heyden, *Biology: Exploring Life* (Needham, MA: Pearson, 2004), 192-97.

82. Illustration and description of abortion procedures by former abortionist and medical professional Dr. Anthony Levatino may be found at *AbortionProcedures.com*. Further often-euphemized descriptions of abortion procedures can be found at the Induced Abortion Q&A produced by the American College of Obstetricians and Gynecologists at *acog.org/Patients/FAQs/Induced-Abortion*.

- RU-486 or Mifeprex (The Abortion Pill)

  These pills deplete the hormones needed to maintain the uterine lining and placenta, the source of nutrition and shelter for the tiny preborn child. They are used in conjunction with Cytotec (misoprostol), which causes strong contractions and the expulsion and fatal starvation of the child.

- Vacuum Aspiration

  Used only in the first trimester, in this procedure the physician inserts a hollow suction tube into the dilated cervix. Using a vacuum with twenty-seven times the power of a typical household vacuum, the tiny human is torn into pieces and the body parts are pulled through a hose into a bottle.

- D&C (Dilation and Curettage)

  This procedure, used typically after fourteen weeks, is similar to the vacuum aspiration abortion, but after the child is suctioned out of the uterus, a small loop-shaped steel knife (called a curette) is used to cut up the placenta and umbilical cord. The uterus is then suctioned out to ensure none of the child's tiny body parts have been left behind.

- D&E (Dilation and Evacuation)

  Used generally in second-trimester abortions, the cervix is first dilated substantially. The doctor inserts narrow forceps-like pliers into the uterus to grasp an arm or leg, and, with a twisting motion, tears the limb from the child's body. The spine is snapped and the skull crushed. After the procedure, body parts are counted to ensure nothing of the child has been left in the uterus.

- Induction/Prostaglandin Abortion

For this procedure, the physician will inject digoxin or potassium chloride into the child's heart to cause a heart attack and kill the preborn human being. Labor is induced to deliver an already dead child. Sometimes, the babies are delivered alive and left to die by starvation or neglect.[83,84]

Ultimately, all versions of elective abortion, when "successful," result in the intentional death of the preborn human being. Abortion providers all over the world have admitted on the record that abortion is killing—it causes harm and it ends the life of a living human child.[85] Indeed,

---

83. According to a CDC report, of all live-birth infant deaths in a twelve-year period (2003-2014), 24.3 percent could definitively be classified as involving an induced termination (elective abortion). See "Mortality Records with Mention of International Classification of Diseases-10 code P96.4 (Termination of Pregnancy): United States, 2003-2014," Centers for Disease Control, reviewed April 2016, *cdc.gov/nchs/health_policy/mortality-records-mentioning-termination-of-pregnancy.htm.*

84. At least one former nurse has testified in front of the US Senate Judiciary Committee on the Born Alive Abortion Survivors Protection Act, telling her story of seeing a baby left to die without medical care or food after a failed induction termination abortion. See Jill Stanek Testimony, Born Alive Abortion Survivors Protection Act Hearing, US Senate Judiciary Committee, February 11, 2020, *judiciary.senate.gov/imo/media/doc/Stanek%20Testimony.pdf.*

85. For more on this crucial topic, read Sarah Terzo's extensive research on this subject at *clinicquotes.com.*

the term "failed abortion" generally applies only when the child *isn't* killed by the procedure.[86,87,88,89]

A Brief Ethical Analysis of Abortion

The facts presented to this point demonstrate that the human zygote/embryo/fetus is a living, unique, whole, differentiated member of the human species. Abortion intentionally kills that human being through starvation, dismemberment, or poisoning, and as such is an act of aggressive violence. When we abide by the Consistent Life Ethic, we acknowledge that we must speak out against acts of violence such as abortion and work to end them, no matter how politically inconvenient it might seem. The preborn child is just as much a human being as you or any other are a member of the species *homo sapiens*, despite differences in age, development, location, ability, or otherwise. What gives us our inherent value and rights is our

86. Adam Eley and Jo Adnitt, "The failed abortion survivor whose mum thought she was dead," BBC *News*, June 5, 2018, *bbc.com/news/health-44357373*.

87. Anna North, "Republicans are bringing back a bill to protect 'abortion survivors,'" Vox *News*, February 11, 2020, *vox.com/policy-and-politics/2019/2/25/18239964/born-alive-abortion-survivors-protection-2020-sasse*.

88. Daniel Roshan and Boris Petrikovsky, "Pregnancy Outcomes After Failed Abortion," *Obstetrics & Gynecology* 107, no. 4 (April 2006): 97S.

89. It must be noted here that the term "failed termination" or "failed abortion" for instances when the child isn't killed indicates that the ultimate goal of abortion is not bodily autonomy and an end to the condition of pregnancy (nor even freedom from the responsibilities of parenting, because many survivors born alive during abortion procedures are indeed placed with adoptive families), but rather that the goal of abortion is a dead child. This dark reality is something with which pro-choice people must wrestle, and pro-life people must remember in all discourse around this tragic topic.

humanity—and all preborn humans share in that equally, too. So we must work to bring an end to abortion and, in solidarity, accompany parents experiencing unexpected or difficult pregnancies.

History of Policy and Culture around Abortion

One common argument goes: "Abortion has always happened, therefore it should be safe and legal." In addition to the fact that this argument is not a good reason to accept acts of violence generally, it also doesn't speak to the legal history of abortion, the historical recognition of the rights of the preborn child, and the larger cultural shift towards recognition of the rights of all human beings.

Though the US Supreme Court argued that "restrictive criminal abortion laws. . . [were] of relatively recent vintage," historical evidence demonstrates that many ancient cultures respected the life of the preborn child.[90] References in the Babylonian Code of Hammurabi, the Assyrian Tiglath-Pileser's laws, the legal code of the Hittites, the hymns of ancient Egypt, the Vedas and Vinayas of the Buddhists, and the Indian Code of Manu all exhibit respect for the preborn child, and many of them specifically prohibit abortion.[91,92] Additionally, one of the most famous enduring documents of the pre-modern era is the

---

90. *Roe v. Wade*, Majority Opinion by Blackmun of US Supreme Court, 1973, 129.
91. Eugene Quay, *Justifiable Abortion: Medical and Legal Foundations* (Washington DC: Family Life Bureau for National Catholic Welfare Conference, 1961), 400-405.
92. Harold O.J. Brown, "What the Supreme Court Didn't Know," *Human Life Review* 1, no. 2 (1975): 7-8.

Hippocratic Oath, which specifically states that physicians will not "give to a woman a pessary to produce abortion."[93] English Common Law precedents leading up to American colonial law were rather unclear on the legal status of the preborn child; however, a 1716 ordinance by the Common Council of New York City that required the licensing of midwives explicitly prohibited abortion.[94,95] Although Common Law didn't seem to indicate that abortion was always wrong (often due to the outdated distinguishing line of "quickening"), the life of the preborn child clearly was the primary factor in determining whether acts of abortion should be legal.[96] Unfortunately, according to the limited science of the time, it was not thought that the preborn child was alive until the sensation of movement could be felt outside the womb ("quickening").[97] After the ovum was discovered in 1827, the science of embryology began to demonstrate more clearly how the conception of all mammals (including human beings) truly functions.[98] Before the beginning of the Civil War thirty-one US states

93. Arturo Castiglioni and E. B. Krumbhaar, A History of Medicine (A.A. Knopf: New York, 1958), 227.

94. Dennis J. Horan and Thomas J. Marzen, "Abortion and Midwifery: A Footnote in Legal History," in New Perspectives on Human Abortion, eds. Thomas Hilgers, Dennis Horan, and David Mall (Frederick, MD: University Publications of America, 1981), 199-200.

95. Cyril Means, The Law of New York Concerning Abortion and the Status of the Foetus, 1664-1968: A Case of Cessation of Constitutionality (New York: New York Law School, 1968), 411, 419.

96. Stephen M. Krason and William B. Hollberg, "The Law and History of Abortion: The Supreme Court Refuted," in Abortion, Medicine, and the Law, eds. J. Douglas Butler and David F. Walbert (New York: Facts on File Publications, 1986), 206-7.

97. Robert M. Byrn, "An American Tragedy: The Supreme Court on Abortion," Fordham Law Review 41, no. 4, 816.

98. Joseph Needham, A History of Embryology, 2nd revised edition (Cambridge: Cambridge University Press, 1959).

had adopted legislation punishing abortion.[99] Additionally, tort law in the United States began to recognize that the preborn child was not a part of the mother's body in *Bonbrest v. Kotz* (1946). Prior to *Roe*, laws in sixteen states allowed for parents to bring wrongful death suits after the death of their preborn child, and in a wrongful birth suit brought in 1967 the New Jersey Supreme Court decided with clarity that the "[rights of children] to live is greater than and precludes [the parents'] right not to endure emotional and financial injury."[100,101]

In the early twentieth century, several nations outside the United States adopted laws permitting abortion. The Soviet Union, under Lenin's leadership, released a decree in 1920 that allowed abortion for any reason, with no limits other than that any abortion must be performed by a trained physician.[102] Mexico and Poland signed laws in the 1930s that supported legal access to abortion after rape.[103,104] And in 1935, to promote "racial hygiene," Nazi Germany began promoting eugenic abortion for women who had hereditary disorders.[105] In the late 1930s and early 1940s, a handful of

---

99. Quay, *Justifiable Abortion*, 447-520.
100. William J. Maledon, "The Law and the Unborn Child: The Legal and Logical Inconsistencies," *Notre Dame Lawyer* 46, no. 2 (1971): 359.
101. *Gleitman v. Cosgrove*, New Jersey Supreme Court, 1967.
102. People's Commissariat of Health, On The Protection of Women's Health, "Decree on Abortion," Issued November 18, 1920. *soviethistory.msu.edu/1917-2/the-new-woman/the-new-woman-texts/on-the-protection-of-womens-health/*
103. Alexandre Peyrille, "Mexico City to Legalize Abortion Despite Protests," *Banderas News*, April 2007, *banderasnews.com/0704/nr-despiteprotests.htm*.
104. Julia Hussein, Jane Cottingham, Wanda Nowicka and Eszter Kismodi, "Abortion in Poland: Politics, Progression and Regression," *Reproductive Health Matters* 26 no. 52 (2018): 11-14, *tandfonline.com/doi/full/10.1080/09688080.2018.1467361*.
105. Robert E. Proctor, *Racial Hygiene: Medicine Under the Nazis* (Cam-

other nations legalized abortion, typically in limited circumstances. And in 1948, in a tragic turn of events that shows how issues within the CLE truly are linked, Japan enacted their Eugenic Protection Act, which allowed abortion. The Act was adopted partly in response to the impacts of World War II and the ensuing post-war occupation.[106] And from the 1950s through the late 1960s, several other nations and many US states gradually legalized abortion.

In 1973, the Supreme Court of the United States (SCOTUS) handed down a 7-2 decision that legalized abortion in all fifty US states based on a trimester model that attempted to "balance" maternal autonomy and the "potentiality of human life."[107] Despite the embryological evidence to the contrary, in his majority opinion Justice Harry Blackmun argued that because "those trained [in] medicine, philosophy, and theology are unable to arrive at any consensus" on when the life of a human being begins, the Court was "not in a position to speculate at the answer."[108]

Since 1973, dozens of anti-abortion laws have been written and passed on a state level, seeking to limit abortion under the *Roe* framework. In 1992, the Supreme Court heard *Planned Parenthood v. Casey*, contesting one such pro-life law. The ruling affirmed the core of the ruling in the precedent of *Roe*, but overturned the trimester-based "compelling interest" standards, holding instead that abortion may be prohibited only after viability and restricted only if the

---

bridge, MA: Harvard University Press, 1989), 366.

106. John Whitehead, "The Wages of War: How Abortion Came to Japan," *Consistent Life Blog*, July 24, 2018, *consistent-life.org/blog/index.php/2018/07/24/abortion-japan/*,

107. Roe v. Wade

108. Jesse Choper et al. *Leading Cases in Constitutional Law: A Compact Casebook for a Short Course*, 2016 edition (St. Paul, MN: West Academic Publishing, 2016).

legal restrictions do not present an "undue burden" upon the woman.[109,110] This standard has been upheld in Supreme Court cases contending over the piecemeal state-based anti-abortion legislation since, including in *Whole Woman's Health v. Hellerstedt*, and *June Medical Services, LLC v. Russo.* At the time of this writing, the Supreme Court is deliberating *Dobbs v. Jackson Women's Health Organization*, the subject of a 2020 Mississippi law that acknowledges fetal rights and bans abortion after fifteen weeks.[111] Some in the formidable legal movement to end abortion in the United States speculate that the *Dobbs* case may result in *Roe* being overturned, and the US example is one that other nations' pro-life movements often look to emulate.

Nevertheless, according to the Guttmacher Institute, the research arm of Planned Parenthood, in 2017 862,320 legal elective abortions were performed.[112] The primary

---

109. *Planned Parenthood of Southeastern PA v. Robert P. Casey*, Supreme Court of the U.S., 1992.

110. It must be mentioned here that this standard of "viability" is inconsistent because it is constantly changing with the advent of new medical technologies. According to the text of *Planned Parenthood v. Casey*, when *Roe* was decided in 1973 viability was understood to be at twenty-eight weeks gestation, and when Casey was decided in 1992, viability was closer to twenty-four weeks. Yet, at the time of this writing, so much has advanced in NICU technology that the earliest known preemie to survive and thrive was born at just twenty weeks. (To learn more about this resilient little one, read Susan-Elizabeth Littlefield's piece for CBS Minnesota, "Baby Richard Thrives as He Breaks Guinness World Record," June 23, 2021, *minnesota.cbslocal.com/2021/06/23/baby-richard-thrives-as-he-breaks-guinness-world-record/*).

111. Amy Howe, "Court to weigh in on Mississippi abortion ban intended to challenge *Roe v. Wade*," SCOTUSblog, May 17, 2021, *scotusblog.com/2021/05/court-to-weigh-in-on-mississippi-abortion-ban-intended-to-challenge-roe-v-wade/*.

112. The Guttmacher Institute, "Induced Abortion in the United States," September 2019, *guttmacher.org/fact-sheet/induced-abortion-united-states*.

abortion provider in the US, the corporate healthcare conglomerate Planned Parenthood, performs 35 to 40 percent of all abortions nationwide. In its corporate report for fiscal year 2019-2020, Planned Parenthood listed 354,871.[113] A May 2021 Pew survey found that "59% [of U.S. adults] say abortion should be legal in all or most cases, while 39% say it should be illegal in all or most cases."[114] Our culture accepts using the violence of abortion to solve the problems associated with an unplanned or difficult pregnancy. In most cases, however, the actual problems in such "crisis pregnancies" won't be addressed by killing the preborn child. According to the Guttmacher Institute's most recent study, the reasons most frequently cited [for having an abortion] were that "having a child would interfere with [her] education, work or ability to care for dependents (74%); that she could not afford a baby now (73%); and that she did not want to be a single mother or was having relationship problems (48%)."[115] The larger problem behind such justification for abortion is that our culture is not oriented towards the natural and completely normal processes of pregnancy or raising children. Our culture considers the cisgender wombless male body as normative; because of this, menstruation is seen as "disgusting" and taboo, preg-

113. Planned Parenthood Federation of America, "2019-2020 Annual Report," 2021, *plannedparenthood.org/uploads/filer_public/67/30/67305ea1-8da2-4cee-9191-19228c1d6f70/210219-annual-report-2019-2020-web-final.pdf*.

114. Hannah Hartig, "About six-in-ten Americans say abortion should be legal in all or most cases," Pew Research Center, May 6, 2021, *pewresearch.org/fact-tank/2021/05/06/about-six-in-ten-americans-say-abortion-should-be-legal-in-all-or-most-cases*.

115. Lawrence B. Finer et al, "Reasons U.S. Women Have Abortions: Quantitative and Qualitative Perspectives," *Perspectives on Sexual and Reproductive Health*, September 2005, *guttmacher.org/journals/psrh/2005/reasons-us-women-have-abortions-quantitative-and-qualitative-perspectives*.

nancy is treated like a disease, and birth and child-rearing are a "burden."[116] These patriarchal structures present the violence of abortion as a "solution," but the actual solution will come only by reorienting society around the reality that humanity is continued only through pregnancy, birth, and child-rearing, and by reorienting institutions to support these aspects of the human experience not only because they are typical, but because they are good.

Although in this section I focus on the United States, the nation I call "home," the laws and norms of other nations are worth mentioning here, especially regarding sex-selection abortion and forced abortion. The misogynistic cultural expectations in India and China, for example, consider males to be "more desirable" than girl children.[117] As a result, in these countries many females have been aborted, especially in China, which maintained its "One-Child Policy" until 2015. Forced abortions of second children were pushed on countless women there, even those who deeply desired their babies.[118] Disturbingly, the culture has so deeply dehumanized preborn children that such violence was often overlooked, even by women's rights activists in the US and elsewhere.

---

116. Erika Bachiochi, "Embodied Equality: Debunking Equal Protection Arguments for Abortion Rights," *Harvard Journal of Law & Public Policy* 34, no. 3 (Summer 2011), *papers.ssrn.com/sol3/papers.cfm?abstract_id=1873485.*

117. Robin Maria DeLugan, "Exposing Gendercide in India and China," *Current Anthropology* 54, no. 5 (University of Chicago Press, 2013): 649–650.

118. Fresh Air radio show, "How China's One-Child Policy Led to Forced Abortions, 30 Million Bachelors," NPR, February 1, 2016, *npr.org/2016/02/01/465124337/how-chinas-one-child-policy-led-to-forced-abortions-30-million-bachelors.*

A Brief Potential Nonviolent Policy Solution to the Problem of Abortion

At minimum, the law should protect the right of every human being to live free from violence. Because elective abortion kills an innocent human being, it must first be clearly stated that the act should *never* be legal. This remains difficult to accomplish in the nation where I live because abolishing abortion would require either a constitutional amendment, or that the Supreme Court overturn the precedent of *Roe* and *Casey*; in the meantime, many state-level legislatiors and organizations are working within the "undue burden" framework to try to protect the preborn.

All of this said, incarcerating post-abortive people and providers will not build a culture of life; instead of expanding the retributive model of incarceration to include abortion, it should be seen as the often-coerced, communal trauma that it is and gear our justice system towards healing and restoration, particularly for the women who have had abortions.[119] Additionally, solutions must be promoted that protect and support unborn human beings as well as their parents, such as paid family leave, an end to pregnancy discrimination in all areas of schooling and employment, and access to affordable childcare and healthcare. After all, to eliminate abortion, the perceived need for it must also be eliminated. Pro-life work must include dismantling the systems of oppression that

---

119. If you'd like to see more about one foundational idea that centers the human dignity of both the preborn child and those who have had abortions in a post-Roe justice framework, I encourage you to read my collaborative white paper on this subject, "Restore the Heart: Healing the Communal Trauma of Abortion through a Restorative Justice System," published in 2020. You can access it here: *rehumanizeintl.org/justice-after-roe*.

drive the demand for abortion such as poverty, racism, and misogyny.[120] Whether these ancillary actions are done within the law, or on a cultural level by changing hearts and minds, charitable giving, or other grassroots mutual aid and activism, we must be working to create a world where abortion is *both* illegal and unthinkable.

Addressing Common Arguments in Support of Abortion

Many arguments to support abortion are also used to support embryo destruction. Chapter 2, "Embryo Destruction," presents the arguments related to the personhood of the preborn and science denial.

Bodily Autonomy

"It's my body, it's my choice."

> Fundamentally, every act of violence starts with a choice. At least two bodies are involved in every pregnancy: that of the pregnant person and that of the preborn child, both of whom have a right to their own body and to live free from violence. The state does not violate bodily autonomy by preventing one human from doing violence (or contracting another person to do violence) to another human, particularly those who are smaller, vulnerable, and defenseless, such as prenatal humans.

---

120. To learn more about ways you can work to uproot these forms of dehumanization (and others), see chapter 11, "Resisting the Inculturation of Violence," on page 243.

"It should be a legal form of violence like self-defense."

First, a fetus is not an aggressor: babies aren't capable of being aggressive; they do not have that capacity. If the extremely rare situation arises where continuing a pregnancy (due to a medical condition such as severe infection/sepsis) could lead to death, there are non-violent ways within medical practice to manage that situation while respecting the dignity of both humans involved. For example, a preterm delivery of the child could be done, wherein both the mother and child receive medical care to attempt to save both lives. Most maternal mortality in the US is caused by health conditions such as hypertension, pulmonary issues, infection, and hemorrhage,[121] most of which can be safely managed by a competent and attentive medical team without the need for abortion to save the mother's life. Even back in 1967, before *Roe v. Wade*, Alan Guttmacher, the former head of Planned Parenthood, said: "Today it is possible for almost any patient to be brought through pregnancy alive, unless she suffers from a fatal disease such as cancer or leukemia, and if so, abortion would be unlikely to prolong, much less save [her] life."[122] This is especially true when we consider that abortions performed in the later stages of pregnancy take two to four days on average, due to the need to soften the cervix,[123,124] whereas a preterm live

121. "Pregnancy Mortality Surveillance System," CDC, 2017, *cdc.gov/reproductivehealth/maternal-mortality/pregnancy-mortality-surveillance-system.htm*.

122. Alan Guttmacher, "Abortion Yesterday, Today, and Tomorrow," in *The Case for Legalized Abortion Now* (Berkeley, CA: Diablo Books, 1967), 3.

123. "Surgical Abortion (Second Trimester)," UCLA Health, *uclahealth.org/obgyn/surgical-abortion-second-trimester*

124. "Third-Trimester Abortion," Boulder Abortion Clinic, P.C., *drhern.*

delivery would take only a few hours for a c-section[125] and up to a couple of days for induction;[126] an abortion for a complication would take substantially longer.

Pregnant Persons' Wellbeing

Socioeconomic reasons: "They already have kids"; "they're in poverty"; "they're in school"; "they can't afford a baby right now"; "they're facing career/academic discrimination"; etc.

I acknowledge that on many levels our society has an appalling lack of care for families, but violence does not solve any of these difficult socioeconomic situations. Instead of accepting the legal starvation, dismemberment, or poisoning of preborn humans, we should be fighting for economic justice for families and to end the patriarchal structures that favor the cisgender wombless male body in most social and economic contexts. Additionally, though programs don't always provide for all housing, healthcare, and food needs, there are some resources in the social safety net to help pregnant people and their families through these hard situations. For example, there are government programs that pregnancy resource centers and other nonprofit organizations often point their clients to in times of need.[127] We should focus on expanding social welfare programs

com/third-trimester-abortion/.

125. "Emergency C-Section: Why They're Needed and What to Expect," *Healthline*, last updated July 31, 2020, *healthline.com/health/pregnancy/emergency-c-section#takeaway*

126. "When Waiting for Baby Isn't Safe: Inducing Labor," Premier Health, October 25, 2016, *premierhealth.com/your-health/articles/women-wisdom-wellness-/when-waiting-for-baby-isn-t-safe-inducing-labor*

127. One website with a comprehensive list of pregnancy resource centers is: *americanpregnancy.org/resources/provider-search/*.

to meet the needs of families in all circumstances, not on expanding access to violence through abortion.

"She shouldn't have to carry 'the rapist's baby.'"

Our first response to this argument must be heartfelt compassion for the survivors of sexual violence. Their healing and wellbeing are vital. This is a really heavy topic, and one that is really close to my heart, personally.

When I was sixteen, I was date raped by an ex-boyfriend. Months went by, and I still hadn't had a period: I thought that I was pregnant with his child. I was emotionally wracked, thinking of nothing but abortion. When he threatened to kill me if I didn't have an abortion, I suddenly realized how abusive he'd been—he was telling me, "You're an inconvenience to me and to my future, therefore I'm going to kill you." I realized that I didn't want to be like him; I couldn't use violence to get what I wanted in life. In that moment, I knew that if I were pregnant, the child within me would be deserving of the same rights that I had: the foremost of which was to live free from violence.

Rape is a terrible crime, a horrific act of violence: But adding the violence and trauma of abortion on top of it will not heal the wound that sexual violence leaves. Instead, it passes the violence and oppression on to a defenseless child, yet another victim of the rape who did not choose to be in this situation. As a survivor, I know that abortion would solve nothing, and would have compounded the trauma by adding perpetration-induced traumatic stress to the mix. Instead, I know that what I needed was competent, trauma-informed mental healthcare, and access to support from my friends and family. A huge part of that is just believing survivors and walking with them as they seek healing, whether they choose to report the rape or not.

"He'll kill me if I don't have an abortion."

Similar to above, our first response should be compassion: What she is telling you is that she is a victim—at this very moment—of domestic violence. Whether it is her boyfriend, spouse, or parents, this threat should be received as real and dangerous.[128] The first thing you should ask is, "Are you safe?" Remind her that she can report such threats to the authorities and seek shelter from her abuser and get out of that abusive situation. Consider helping her reach out to a local domestic violence shelter or resource center, along with a pregnancy resource center to affirm her right to keep her child and get her financial and housing help, if she needs it. As with the answer above as well, remind her that the violence of abortion will not solve the abusive situation that she is in: Killing her child will not remove her from the abusive situation; it will only heap more trauma on a defenseless victim.

Mental health concerns: "They are suicidal or have PTSD"; "they have gender/pregnancy dysphoria"; etc.

People with mental health concerns deserve to get the mental health treatment that they need during these difficult situations.

---

128. Pregnant people are especially at high risk of domestic violence; it is common for partners and family members to threaten to kick them out on the street or to harm them physically, including death. Around 20 percent of pregnant women are harmed by domestic violence, and in the United States homicide is the leading cause of death for pregnant people. See "Domestic Violence and Pregnancy Fact Sheet," National Coalition Against Domestic Violence, 2004, *vawnet.org/sites/default/files/assets/files/2016-09/DVPregnancy.pdf*.

Killing a child will not solve mental illness. For people in circumstances like these, we should seek all proactive nonviolent care options.

Physical health concerns: "She has gestational diabetes"; "they have mirror syndrome"; "she's worried about dying" (maternal mortality is particularly high in communities of color). As stated above, medical practice has many nonviolent options for managing most of these situations while still respecting the dignity of both humans involved. In the case of high maternal mortality in communities of color, we need to provide culturally competent healthcare to pregnant people, particularly those in Black and Indigenous communities who have been historically marginalized by medical practices that favor white bodies.[129]

"This is an ectopic pregnancy."

Ectopic pregnancy is an exceptional but not uncommon instance in which the embryo implants outside of the uterus, typically following a case of endometriosis where the endometrial-type tissue grows outside the typical uterine location, often in a fallopian tube which cannot enlarge to accommodate the growing prenatal child.[130] In an ectopic pregnancy, the embryo's continued growth poses a potential danger of fallopian

129. "Racial and Ethnic Disparities Continue in Pregnancy-Related Deaths," CDC, September 5, 2019, cdc.gov/media/releases/2019/p0905-racial-ethnic-disparities-pregnancy-deaths.html.
130. American Society for Reproductive Medicine. *Ectopic Pregnancy: A Guide for Patients*, Revised 2014. reproductivefacts.org/globalassets/rf/news-and-publications/bookletsfact-sheets/english-fact-sheets-and-info-booklets/booklet_ectopic_pregnancy.pdf.

tube rupture and ensuing hemorrhage and/or sepsis for the pregnant person. If the fallopian tube ruptures, the embryo will die in the process, and the pregnant person is likewise at an elevated risk of death from the infection of these diseased tissues.

At this time, the most common treatments for ectopic pregnancies include "therapeutic abortions" that aim to remove the embryo through targeted medication or surgery in order to save the pregnant person's life and potentially preserve future fertility.[131] Continuing the ectopic pregnancy does pose a likely threat to the life of the pregnant person and continuing the pregnancy could easily result in the death of both parent and child. I believe this might perhaps be the only case in which such removals could be morally licit as a form of self-defense against imminent death because the child's presence is precisely the reason the pregnant person could die, and intentionally removing the embryonic human could be an example of double-effect (explored further in the subsection of chapter 1, "How do Consistent Life Ethic adherents respond to aggressive violence?"). The American Association of Pro-Life Obstetricians and Gynecologists' statement on the matter briefly explores this ethical nuance:

> The intent for the pro-life physician is not to kill the unborn child, but to preserve the life of the mother in a situation where the life of the child cannot be saved by current medical technology. . . the American Association of Pro-Life Obstetricians recognizes the unavoidable loss of human life that occurs in an ectopic pregnancy, but does not con-

---

131. "Ectopic Pregnancy: Diagnosis & treatment," Mayo Clinic, updated March 12, 2022, *mayoclinic.org/diseases-conditions/ectopic-pregnancy/diagnosis-treatment/drc-20372093*

sider treatment of ectopic pregnancy by standard surgical or medical procedures to be the moral equivalent of elective abortion, or to be the wrongful taking of human life.[132]

As with the distinction within the CLE movement between strict pacifism and just defense adherents, some pro-lifers believe that even these "therapeutic abortion" procedures violate their conscience against violence because the act could be construed as direct, intended violence. In their assessment, using a *very* strict model of double-effect, the best potential response to ectopic pregnancy properly diagnosed prior to tube rupture would be a surgical removal of the diseased endometrial tissue, perhaps including the embryo, whose death would be foreseen but not the intended purpose of the surgery. Furthermore, they would propose that surgeons helping pregnant people in this situation (particularly those who badly wanted their child) should be exploring the medical possibility of removing the embryo from the diseased tissue in the fallopian tubes and then attempting to re-implant the embryo in the proper place within the uterus,[133] but that option hasn't been well-explored and therefore is not common practice at this time.[134]

---

132. "What is AAPLOG's Position on Treatment of Ectopic Pregnancy?" American Association of Pro-Life Obstetricians and Gynecologists, July 2010, *aaplog.org/what-is-aaplogs-position-on-treatment-of-ectopic-pregnancy/*

133. L. B. Shettles, "Tubal embryo successfully transferred in utero," *American Journal of Obstetrics and Gynecology*, 163: 6 Pt 1 (1990) 2026–2027. *ajog.org/article/0002-9378(90)90794-8/pdf*.

134. Patricia Santiago-Munoz, "The truth about ectopic pregnancy care," The University of Texas Southwest Medical Center blog, October 22, 2019, *utswmed.org/medblog/truth-about-ectopic-pregnancy-care/*.

Preborn Humans' Circumstances

"The baby has been diagnosed with a (fatal) fetal abnormality/disability."

> Though this situation can be difficult for the family, violence against a vulnerable disabled child is not an acceptable response. Instead, families in this situation should be provided with ample resources on how to care for a child with the condition in question, and on disability justice, palliative care (if necessary), and communities of support.

"The kid will end up unloved in foster care/poverty."

> First, a person's life is no less valuable and worthy of respect and care just because that person grew up in foster care or in poverty: remember that those who've experienced this situation realize that you're actually saying that they'd be better off dead! Second, the primary goal of foster care is family reunification, and it is a social good that we have systems in place to protect a child's welfare while allowing birth parents to make an effort to improve and amend their lives (when necessary). Though the foster system admittedly needs much work and reform, it is nothing short of discriminatory to suggest the violence of abortion remain legal because of the possibility of children ending up in that system.

Societal Impact

"There's an ongoing climate crisis and overpopulation is contributing to it."

Contrary to popular belief, overpopulation is a myth often used by global elites to justify population control efforts among the poor and "undesirable." In fact, as stated by anti-racist activist Sangeetha Thanapal,

> the truth about population growth and its impact on the environment is obscured. The places with high levels of population growth account for just 10 percent of lifestyle consumption emissions while the richest in the world make up half of the total emissions ... Positing population as an environmental problem is an eco-fascist tactic that considers poor people, black and brown people etc., as the problem.... Pointing the finger at the poorest among us and demanding that they stop having babies is eugenicist rhetoric. Instead of looking at how capitalism uses resources at an unsustainable rate, environment groups that use the overpopulation argument seek to reduce the human population.[135]

Thanapal also quotes activist and author Naomi Klein, who points out that the regions with "the highest levels of population growth, (are) the poorest parts of the world with the lowest carbon footprints."[136] The ongoing climate crisis is more a question of consumption and distribution of resources than the sheer number of humans on the planet. Indigenous, Black, and other activists of color (including climate activists) have loudly rejected the racist theory of overpopula-

---

135. Sangeetha Thanapal, "Environmental movements need to critique capitalism, not overpopulation," *Eureka Street*, November 3, 2020, *eurekastreet.com.au/article/environmental-movements-need-to-critique-capitalism—not-overpopulation*.

136. Adryan Corcione, "Eco-fascism: What It Is, Why It's Wrong, and How to Fight It," *Teen Vogue*, April 30, 2020, *teenvogue.com/story/what-is-ecofascism-explainer*.

tion and its associated efforts to kill off children or coercively sterilize their parents.[137]

"If abortion is banned, crime rates will go up because many of the children conceived will become criminals."

This argument, popularized by the book *Freakonomics*, essentially states that the children who are being aborted are those who would be unwanted and therefore would be more likely to become criminals.[138] Whether this is true or not, it is not a moral justification for the violence of abortion. A child's wantedness does not impact that child's inherent dignity or rights; instead, the solution to unwantedness is to build up a culture that sees and protects the value of each and every child, and promotes love and appreciation of all children, regardless of how wanted they might have been at the time of their conception.

"Paying for WIC/maternal welfare for these poor children will require an increase in taxes."

Eliminating groups of humans who are "tax burdens" does not solve socio-economic injustice and poverty. Killing all foster kids or all disabled people who receive welfare benefits is not just or good. Consider that instead

---

137. There are numerous examples of this sort of statement that can be found from many activists on Twitter. See *twitter.com/* (and insert each of the following after the slash) BRATZULA/*status/1407377823447330818*, jessicawins/*status/1412774077069070339*, MankaMenga/*status/1303284203107291136*, HarryBackwood/*status/1463901223292215301*, Survival/*status/1329369984095621122*, algebrandis/*status/1378601528320212993*.

138. Steven D. Levitt and Stephen J. Dubner, *Freakonomics: A Rogue Economist Explores the Hidden Side of Everything* (New York: William Morrow Publishing, 2005), Ch. 4.

of funding violence like massive US military spending, we could be using our taxes to support the needs of the poor and vulnerable in a way that helps them access basic needs such as food, water, and housing.

"Illegal abortions will happen anyway, and thousands of women will die."

We understand that our current culture often drives women to feel that they need abortion; this is deplorable and the injustice of it must be addressed. Our first response to those who are seeking abortion should be compassion. It's worth mentioning, though, that the number of women who died by illegal abortions in the pre-Roe era was highly exaggerated by the leaders of the abortion movement. In his 1979 book *Aborting America*, Dr. Bernard Nathanson, the former head of NARAL wrote,

> How many deaths were we talking about when abortion was illegal? In NARAL, we generally emphasized the frame of the individual case, not the mass statistics, but when we spoke of the latter it was always 5,000 to 10,000 deaths a year. I confess that I knew that the figures were totally false and I suppose that others did too if they stopped to think of it. But in the "morality" of our [pro-abortion] revolution, it was a useful figure, widely accepted, so why go out of our way to correct it with honest statistics? The overriding concern was to get the laws eliminated, and anything within reason that had to be done was permissible.[139]

---

139. Bernard Nathanson, *Aborting America* (New York: Doubleday, 1979), 193.

Additionally, it must be noted that we do not think that violence against humans should be made to seem sterile by being moved into a legal, clinical setting. When I think of this argument, I remember that rape, though illegal, is still shockingly common. And as a rape survivor, I cannot imagine someone suggesting that because rape is still common, that it should be made "safe and legal and accessible." Likewise, abortion being legalized and moved into a clinical setting does not reduce the violence against the preborn victim, but only serves to assuage the conscience of those participating in the violence itself.

"Abortion clinics do some good things, so don't protest them or attempt to shut them down."

Imagine a center that provided low-cost childcare, but the staff also killed at least one of the toddlers in their care every day. Would we contract with them for our after-school daycare program? No! In fact, if we knew such an organization existed, we would work to shut it down. We should not allow an organization that kills human beings to exist—much less an organization that includes killing as part of its profit model. Places like Planned Parenthood perform abortions; and since we know that every "successful" abortion kills a human being, we should not allow them to remain open so long as they perform abortions. When we promote (or even permit) an organization that advocates for and takes part in the killing of preborn children, we too are complicit in the attitude that will sacrifice children for convenience, we too are complicit in the blood money given to an organization that kills our pre-born human siblings, we too are complicit in death. A life-affirming response, instead, would be to create and fund accessible, free, or low-cost women's health and sexual wellness clinics that wouldn't refer for or participate in abortions.

Discussion Questions

1. Before reading this chapter what notions did you have about abortion, the preborn, and the people who have abortions? Has any of that shifted in learning more?

2. Why do you think abortion has become such a ubiquitous "solution" to problems such as poverty, relationship issues, and discrimination?

3. What in our cultural discourse on abortion have you found to be harmful? What would have been impactful and helpful for you in changing hearts and minds on this often-heated subject?

Further Reading Suggestions

1. Clarke D. Forsythe, *Abuse of Discretion: The Inside Story of Roe v. Wade* (New York: Encounter Books, 2013).

2. Dr. Bernard Nathanson, *The Hand of God: A Journey from Death to Life by the Abortion Doctor Who Changed His Mind* (Washington, DC: Salem Books, 2013 reprint).

3. Sue Ellen Browder, Subverted: *How I Helped the Sexual Revolution Hijack the Women's Movement* (San Francisco: Ignatius Press, 2019).

4. Trent Horn, *Persuasive Pro Life: How to Talk about Our Culture's Toughest Issue* (El Cajon, CA: Catholic Answers Press, 2014).

Ending Violence
in War

Every gun that is made, every warship launched, every rocket fired signifies, in the final sense, a theft from those who hunger and are not fed, those who are cold and are not clothed. . .This is not a way of life at all, in any true sense. Under the cloud of threatening war, it is humanity hanging from a cross of iron.

~Dwight D. Eisenhower

Chapter 4

Warmaking

During conflict between two nations, or attacks on human rights outside their own borders, states have often responded with the intense violence of war. But the Consistent Life Ethic calls us to reflect deeply on questions surrounding combat: Where does protecting the vulnerable end and becoming an aggressor begin? And is it even possible at all for modern warfare to be conducted ethically?

What is War?

War is violent conflict at the highest level between nations, states, and communities who have taken up arms against fellow humans. Wars are waged today using some of the most advanced military technology ever seen. Automatic assault weapons, advanced robots, fighter jets, attack drones, and highly specialized bombs are just some of the high-tech tools of violence to which militaries around the world have access with the advancement of the global military arms trade.

Nowhere is the danger from military technology clearer (or more worrying) than with nuclear weapons. Global inventory of nuclear weapons, both deployed and undeployed, currently adds up to 13,410 warheads, with about 1,800 "on high alert, ready for use on short notice,"[140] 91 percent of which are held by Russia and the United States.[141]

Nuclear weapons established a new way of understanding war between nations, and therefore a new way of understanding the relationships between nations. Some see the nuclear threat as the foundation of peace (or, at least, a lack of conflict). Security, then, rests on deterrence, and deterrence becomes the foundation of how we relate to others. If each country is building up a store of weapons that cause indiscriminate damage, then their ways of relating to each other will always be mediated by this threat. Nuclear weapons set the relationship between peoples as one of threat and coercion. True peace can never be achieved, because the tense order exists only because of the threat of devastating violence.

Increased military technology, particularly on the scale of nuclear weapons, is often seen as a provocation to other countries, who may feel that they need to increase their own defense technology simply to protect themselves. More and more money, time, and talent are invested into the military-industrial complex, making it harder and harder for anyone to back down. The monetary costs of this are staggering—but the human costs are more staggering still.

"We don't do body counts,"[142] US General Tommy Franks told reporters—it was a line that would quickly become

---

140. Hans M. Kristensen and Matt Korda, "Status of World Nuclear Forces," Federation of American Scientists, *fas.org/issues/nuclear-weapons/status-world-nuclear-forces/*.

141. Kristensen and Korda, "Status of World Nuclear Forces."

142. John M. Broder, "A Nation at War: The Casualties; US Military Has No Count of Iraqi Dead In Fighting," *New York Times*, April 2, 2003, ny-

infamous. Cold and casual, General Franks's remark called attention to an aspect of war sometimes overlooked in discussions about defense: war makes it easy to see human lives as expendable, necessary losses or human capital in a global negotiation. War draws our eyes away from individual human beings toward the "bigger picture"; mass death is easier to think of in the abstract. Even when we are not the ones doing the killing, war makes it easier for us to dehumanize.

The "human costs" of war are numerous, and many extend long after the war is fought. The US and other international forces "regularly pay out cash when their troops 'inadvertently' cause the injury or death of civilians, or inflict damage to property."[143] While these payments are certainly a necessary step in redressing wrongs, they also often end up revealing the dehumanizing nature of the military's treatment of civilians. Even when the claims are accepted, they are often still objectifying, as in the case of one claims receipt that listed "death of wife" under the heading "supplies and services"; under quantity, the numeral 1; and then listed the "unit price" of the woman as $2,500.[144]

Dehumanization and total violence are part and parcel of modern warfare, but the history of warmaking wasn't always quite this brutal. The technological changes of the past 125 years revolutionized war and in turn, in some way, shape, or form have touched nearly everyone alive today.

---

times.com/2003/04/02/world/nation-war-casualties-us-military-has-no-count-iraqi-dead-fighting.html.

143. Emily Gilbert, "The Gift of War: Cash, Counterinsurgency, and 'Collateral Damage,'" *Security Dialogue* 46, no. 5 (October 1, 2015): 403–21. https://www.jstor.org/stable/26292326.

144. Gilbert, see Figure 2. Death of wife, in "The Gift of War : Cash, Counterinsurgency, and 'Collateral Damage.'"

A Brief Ethical Analysis of War

Some say war and conflict are unavoidable; some say they are natural to human psychology. What gets abstracted in such statements is that war and conflict at root are, in the words of philosopher Thomas Nagel, "relations between persons."[145] Whatever else you think war and conflict may be, it is important to remember that when we think about and make decisions regarding war, war disrupts or destroys personal relationships. The question should not be "How much violence can we get away with?", but rather, "Is violence ever an appropriate way to relate to others, and if so, in what circumstances?" What other ways of relating can be tried before resorting to violence?

By its nature, war makes it hard to think of people *as* human. It's easier to think of them euphemistically, as targets or "collateral damage," and the waging as being done by an impartial bureaucracy rather than individual people who call the shots. Euphemisms make war seem necessary and scientific, but they distract us from the humanity of all involved and our responsibilities to each other. We need to consider what consideration must be given to how we relate to each other, to other nations, that honor the human dignity of all involved.[146] War happens between humans and to humans; it is not an abstract theory or inevitable force.

---

145. Thomas Nagel, "War and Massacre," *Philosophy & Public Affairs* 1 no. 2 (1972): 123–44. *jstor.org/stable/2264967*.

146. It should be noted that some (myself included) think that applying popular modern ethical theorist Germain Grisez's Personalism as laid out in *Beyond the New Morality* necessitates that no one may intentionally take the life of another human being, up to and including two soldiers facing each other. If one soldier were to shoot at another from an opposing army, the shot would still have to meet the requirement of double-effect, not intending to harm or to kill but only to stop an ongoing attack. To learn more about double-effect

In her essay "Accidents Don't Just Happen: The Liberal Politics of High-Tech Humanitarian War," Patricia Owens points out that the recent trend of construing civilian deaths as "accidents" shows how a refusal to acknowledge the relational responsibility inherent in making choices regarding war and allows us to normalize small massacres.[147] Attempting to alleviate responsibility and make violence ourselves appear more humane in our violence, Owens writes, is a failure to take responsibility for our actions:

> The effect of this refusal to admit responsibility is analogous to Hannah Arendt's understanding of bureaucracy, what she calls "rule by Nobody." In its extreme form, individuals are "de-humanized," becoming mere functionaries and cogs in "an intricate system of bureaus." However, although nobody is held responsible, this "'nobody'" still rules. It is not "no-rule rule"; "it may indeed, under certain circumstances, even turn out to be one of its cruellest . . . versions," for it is "impossible to localize responsibility and to identify an enemy." Indeed, in a world of seemingly autonomous machines fighting "digital-age" war, blaming humans, holding anyone responsible, seems even less plausible.[148]

Dehumanization goes both ways: not only are the victims dehumanized, but those who should be held responsible are seen as "functionaries and cogs." Those who call the shots, who decide who lives and who dies, remain

---

and just defense, read "How do Consistent Life Ethic adherents respond to aggressive violence?" page 27.

147. Patricia Owens, "Accidents Don't Just Happen: The Liberal Politics of High-Technology 'Humanitarian' War." *Millennium* 32, no. 3 (2003): 595–616. DOI:10.1177/03058298030320031101.

148. Owens, "Accidents," 608.

invisible. Wars seem too large and too complicated for people to have responsibility in them, and immoral actions are explained away as necessary.

One frequently cited moral system in decisions regarding war is just war theory. As I mentioned in the chapter 1 subsection "How do Consistent Life Ethic adherents respond to aggressive violence?", this theory holds that a war can be considered just if it meets certain criteria: it has a just cause, right intention, and a probability of success; it is waged by a proper authority; it is a last resort; and its intention is proportional to the harms the war will cause. Just war theory is a valuable framework, and is certainly helpful in many cases. Unfortunately, though, it does not necessarily make choices simple. As with any ethical framework, how to apply it is often ambiguous, and, unfortunately, its ambiguity can be used to justify abhorrent action. Just war theory should be used to plan future actions based on what is just according to the human dignity of all, not as a bludgeon to silence good-faith protestors against war and aggressive violence.

Deciding whether and how a war could be justly waged is the bare minimum. We need to make sure our decision-making is informed by the humanity of everyone involved, and just war theory's principles can't be set aside once they've been used to accommodate the desire for war. Just war theory's applicability to modern warfare is especially important in discerning whether to use nuclear weapons; unfortunately, this is often where just war theory is often left behind.

Nuclear arms can never be weapons of a just war. Though some proponents of maintaining nuclear arsenals might argue that nuclear weapons are useful as a deterrent to war, nuclear weapons deter war only by the possibility of mutually assured destruction. They function as deterrents only if used against civilian city centers. Because intentionally killing hundreds of thousands of innocent human beings is inherently unjust, retaining nuclear weapons (whether deployed or non-deployed) is contrary to human dignity and a culture of peace.

Nuclear weapons must not be stockpiled, let alone used, just because another nation possesses them. The injustice of other nations should not be used to dislodge another nation's moral compass and provoke it to evil. Belief in a human-centered ethics and practice requires an end to all nuclear arms and a ban on the development of weapons of mass destruction. Instead, the world's vast military technology should be ordered towards anti-ballistic missile defense systems to prevent a nuclear weapon from ever touching down. As long as the United States and other nuclear-armed nations maintain their arsenals, they are guilty of planning and preparing for indiscriminate and disproportionate uses of force—in effect, for committing war crimes.

Ultimately, though, all foreign policy should be ordered towards diplomacy, peace, and human dignity. Indeed, if all nations were acting justly, ordering their actions towards the dignity of each and every human being—both within and outside their borders—there would never be a reason for war, and there certainly would never be an unjust war.

History of Policy and Culture around War

Sadly, war has been a long-standing human tradition. Archaeological discoveries have revealed the existence of bows in Mesopotamia as early as 10,000 BCE, and pictographs of war found in Kush date back to 3500 BCE.[149] The

---

149. "War in Ancient Times," *World History Encyclopedia*, *worldhistory. org/war/*.

first written documentation of war comes from 2700 BCE between Elam and Sumer.[150]

Ancient military tactics involved organized lines of armed infantry "shock troops" meant to try to break the line of defense.[151] With the advent of cavalry, chariots, and even ships, the tactics added small improvements like the phalanx formation, but over many millennia changed relatively little. These tactics were implemented during Roman military conquests of much of the European continent, of Byzantium (and later Constantinople); during the Mongolian conquest of much of Asia; by European nations' conquest of Africa and India; and countless other skirmishes and territorial battles worldwide between tribes, clans, and dynasties. Only when gunpowder became available were tactics forced to shift in response to the more lethal weaponry developed in China and other Eastern nations.[152] By the thirteenth century, proper guns were found in several Eastern countries, and in the fourteenth and fifteenth centuries, guns and gunpowder were making their way west, changing the field of war forever and precipitating the wholesale colonization of the Americas and the subjugation of Indigenous peoples. As the United States rushed to empire in the late nineteenth century, war began to change even more with the invention of new, grisly technologies.

With the First World War, begun in 1914, warmaking followed a trajectory toward "more effective" mass violence as deaths topped five million in just the first year.[153] Total

---

150. "War in Ancient Times."
151. "War in Ancient Times."
152. "Gunpowder." *Encyclopedia Britannica, britannica.com/technology/ gunpowder.*
153. "How Modern Weapons Changed Combat in The First World War," Imperial War Museums, *iwm.org.uk/history/how-modern-weapons- changed-combat-in-the-first-world-war.*

war became the standard: every aspect of entire nations was directed towards fighting this war, such that selective service drafts were implemented for the first time in many nations, and whole centers of industry were retooled towards creating weapons and other mechanisms of war.[154] New technology like quick-fire artillery, poison gas, and flamethrowers brought immense death and destruction and pushed militaries to trench warfare;[155] but the advent of airplanes meant that a whole new dimension could be exploited to attack military headquarters and civilian city centers.[156]

During World War II, the most evident case of total war in human history, most large nations on the planet devoted all their energies and resources toward defeating their enemies. Combat resembled that of the First World War in many ways, although with substantially increased sophistication and power in many technologies. The most massive shift, however, came with the development of nuclear weapons. Albert Einstein insisted that whoever had this power would win the war, and feared that the Nazis would achieve this hugely destructive milestone first.[157] J. Robert Oppenheimer and his Manhattan Project raced to harness the power of the atom first, and on August 6, 1945, the US Army Air Force *Enola Gay* dropped an atomic weapon

---

154. "Total War," *Encyclopedia Britannica,* britannica.com/topic/total-war.

155. "How Modern Weapons Changed Combat in The First World War," and "How Gas Became a Terror Weapon In The First World War," Imperial War Museums, *iwm.org.uk/history/how-gas-became-a-terror-weapon-in-the-first-world-war.*

156. "Firsts of the First World War," Imperial War Museums, *iwm.org.uk/history/firsts-of-the-first-world-war.*

157. Trevor Lipscombe, "Einstein Feared a Nazi Atom Bomb—But Immigrants Made Sure the U.S. Got There First," *Time,* August 2, 2019, *time.com/5641891/einstein-szilard-letter/.*

named "Little Boy" on the Aioi Bridge in Hiroshima, obliterating the Japanese city.[158]

War had changed, permanently. In *The Absolute Weapon: Atomic Power and World Order* (1946), Bernard Brodie and other war theorists comment on the significance of nuclear weapons, "Thus far the chief purpose of our military establishment has been to win wars. From now on its chief purpose must be to avert them."[159]

Warmaking adapted to this modern era, trying to avert all-out nuclear war by relying on strategic alliances formed through treaty organizations and resorting to fewer declarations of war by states in the cold war that followed. On August 9, 1945, less than a week after the conclusion of the Potsdam Conference that attempted to establish a lasting peace in Europe, and just one day after Russia's entrance into the war against Japan, the US military dropped the "Fat Man" plutonium nuclear weapon on Nagasaki.[160] Victory came for the US in the Pacific Theater shortly thereafter, but the cost was unutterable: all told, both atomic bombs had instantly killed over 120,000 Japanese people, most of them civilians.[161] Just a year and a half later, the largest nuclear powers (the Soviet Union and the United States) slid into the Cold War, a hostility that held the whole world in terrified tension.[162]

---

158. "The Most Fearsome Sight: The Atomic Bombing of Hiroshima," The World War II Museum, August 6, 2020, *nationalww2museum.org/ war/articles/atomic-bomb-hiroshima*.

159. Frederick S. Dunn et al, *The Absolute Weapon: Atomic Power and World Order*, ed. Bernard Brodie, Yale University Institute of International Studies (New York: Harcourt Brace & Company, 1946).

160. Sarah Pruitt, "Hiroshima, Then Nagasaki: Why the US Deployed the Second A-Bomb," History.com, July 21, 2020, history.com/news/ hiroshima-nagasaki-second-atomic-bomb-japan-surrender-wwii.

161. "The Most Fearsome Sight," The World War II Museum.

162. Erin Blakemore, "What was the Cold War—and are we headed to another one?" *National Geographic*, March 23, 2022, nationalgeograph-

The Truman Doctrine of intervention wherever communism threatened to gain power began a series of proxy wars between the US and the USSR, the first of them in Greece and Turkey. To help ease the fears of their non-nuclear allies around the world, the United States signed on to NATO—the North Atlantic Treaty Organization—with Canada, Belgium, Denmark, France, Iceland, Italy, Luxembourg, the Netherlands, Norway, Portugal, and the UK. All signing parties declared that "an armed attack against one or more. . . [is] an attack against them all," indicating that the nuclear powers would come to the defense of smaller, non-nuclear powers.[163]

In effect, the combination of the Truman Doctrine, the new existence of NATO, alongside the reality of a Cold War and trying to avert nuclear mutually assured destruction, propelled the US and its allies into the space race along with a series of "small" proxy "conflicts" against Soviet principles and communist alignment, none of them properly declared wars. Over the decades, the Soviet Union's empire expanded, as did that of the US and of NATO. Children and families in both nations practiced bomb drills, prepared bomb shelters, and learned to dehumanize and distrust those from the "enemy" empire. Countless other nations were dragged into the proxy wars between the two nuclear superpowers, until the USSR eventually disbanded in 1991. Dreadfully, in light of the Russian invasion of Ukraine in February of 2022, the whole world is anxious at the possibility of yet another Cold War—and with it, the threat of nuclear devastation.

Despite the effort to avoid nuclear warfare, many nations still drafted soldiers to fight their conflicts.[164]

ic.com/culture/article/cold-war.
163. The North Atlantic Treaty, Washington D.C., April 4, 1949.
164. Even today, there are young men being conscripted to fight (some

However, one statistic about drafted infantry troubled military leaders: During the battles of WWII, it was found that "on average, no more than 15 percent of the men had actually fired at the enemy.... The best showing that could be made by the most spirited and aggressive companies was that one man in four had made use of his fire power."[165] As US Lt. Colonel Dave Grossman responded in assessing this statistic, these low firing rates proved "the simple and demonstrable fact that there is within most men an intense resistance to killing their fellow men. A resistance so strong that, in many circumstances, soldiers will die before they can overcome it."[166] So in the shift after World War II, the training for infantry evolved to promote a dehumanized, violent mindset.

To increase the firing rate for soldiers, the Army took great steps to condition soldiers to be comfortable with killing. World War II infantry training had involved shooting practice on the standard, round bullseye targets, but in the years that followed WWII, the US Army replaced the bullseye circles with human-shaped targets.[167] They taught

---

against their conscientious objection) in the Russian army. See Mary Ilyushina, "As Russia drafts young men, some fear ending up on Ukraine's front line," *Washington Post*, April 1, 2022, washingtonpost. com/world/2022/04/01/russia-military-army-conscripts-draft/. Though Ukraine isn't forcing men to fight at the time of this writing, they are requiring men between the ages of 18 to 60 to remain in the country instead of fleeing as refugees with their families. See Lorenzo Tondo, "Ukraine urged to take 'humane' approach as men try to flee war," *The Guardian*, March 9, 2022, theguardian.com/global-development/2022/mar/09/ukraine-urged-to-take-humane-approach-as-men-try-to-flee-war.

165. S.L.A. Marshall, *Men Against Fire: The Problem of Battle Command* (Norman, OK: University of Oklahoma Press, 2000), 54.

166. Lt. Colonel Dave Grossman, *On Killing: The Psychological Cost of Learning to Kill in War and Society* (Boston MA: Little Brown, 1995), 4.

167. Catherine Ryan and Gary Weimberg, *Soldiers of Conscience* (Berkeley, CA: Luna Productions, 2007).

the soldiers "reflexive fire training," which conditioned these troops to bypass their human moral reasoning by firing quickly. As stated in Rob Arner's *Consistently Pro-Life: The Ethics of Bloodshed in Ancient Christianity*,

> The Army gradually increased the [weapons'] fire rates in the following wars, so that it grew from World War II's 25 percent, to 55 percent in the Korean conflict, to upwards of 80 percent in Vietnam. In modern conflicts, such as in Iraq, the fire rate is well over 90 percent as the training soldiers receive works hard to condition the suppression of the innate instinct against killing.[168]

This dehumanizing training and subsequent increased fire rate points to distressing evidence that militaries fail to consider the impact of Perpetration-Induced Traumatic Stress (PITS) and overall mental health on their soldiers.[169] Indeed, the threat to life isn't over when the deployment is—in the US, seventeen veterans (largely from low-income communities) commit suicide every day,[170] and the suicide rate rises as high as twenty-two a day if you count active duty members, National Guardsmen, and reservists.[171,172]

168. Rob Arner, *Consistently Pro-Life: The Ethics of Bloodshed in Ancient Christianity* (Eugene, OR: Pickwick Publications, 2010), 42.

169. On the subject of Perpetration-Induced Traumatic Stress, I highly recommend Rachel M. MacNair's work, including her book *Perpetration-Induced Traumatic Stress: The Psychological Consequences of Killing*.

170. "2019 National Veteran Suicide Prevention Annual Report," Office of Mental Health and Suicide Prevention, US Department of Veterans Affairs, mentalhealth.va.gov/docs/data-sheets/2019/2019_National_Veteran_Suicide_Prevention_Annual_Report_508.pdf.

171. Leo Shane III, "New veteran suicide numbers raise concerns among experts hoping for positive news," *Military Times*, October 9, 2019, militarytimes.com/news/pentagon-congress/2019/10/09/new-veteran-suicide-numbers-raise-concerns-among-experts-hoping-for-positive-news/.

172. Although they disproportionately struggle with suicidal ideation and PTSD, veterans often face months-long waits for appropriate care.

It is impossible to calculate all whose lives have been affected by war, as in the cases of pandemics aggravated by war, loss of access to drinking water or food, and inability to access healthcare. Perhaps the struggle to determine any clear figure to document the cost—human and otherwise—shows that the effects of war are too extensive to be grasped or controlled; therefore, war should be invoked with the utmost caution.

A Brief Potential Nonviolent Policy Solution to the Problem of War and International Conflict

Too often war is seen in the abstract, as an unstoppable force or inevitable disaster. The Consistent Life Ethic makes us take a step back and ask the hard questions. If we look at war relationally, we are forced to think of ourselves as responsible for our actions and to see our actions as having serious consequences. Working for peace in a violent world is difficult, and the solutions will take a lot of work. But it is necessary work if we want to make sure all our actions reflect the dignity of every person.

War is rarely our only choice—and when it is our "only choice," usually we've ignored every opportunity to achieve

---

Given that the US military targets low-income communities for recruitment, and many economically marginalized youth see in the military a way out of poverty because of the guaranteed income and healthcare, the neglect to proactively protect soldiers' mental health functionally treats the poor infantry as discardable collateral—which should lead us to ask whether everyone is given a real choice in making this sacrifice. See Nick Martin, "The Military Views Poor Kids as Fodder for Its Forever Wars," *The New Republic*, January 7, 2020, newrepublic.com/article/156131/military-views-poor-kids-fodder-forever-wars.

peace along the way.[173] Instead of focusing our attention and funding on militarization, we must mediate conflicts without violence as much as possible.

A first step towards limiting the opportunities for unjust war would be to stop funding the military industrial complex. The financial incentive for military contractors to build infrastructure for war conflicts with efforts for diplomacy and peacebuilding. The movement for peace is a vastly underfunded, grassroots effort; while weapons manufacturers make billions by pushing government leaders to see war as "the answer." The billions spent each year on military expenditures could be diverted toward crucial domestic needs such as healthcare, housing, and education.

Another major step to build a strong foundation of peace and end the stalemate of deterrence would be to abolish nuclear weapons. Though the United Nations Treaty on the Prohibition of Nuclear Weapons went into effect on January 22, 2021, none of the nuclear powers have ratified or adopted it.[174] The anxieties of the nuclear powers regarding abolition and the imbalance of power are addressed in a white paper, "Toward the Abolition of Strategic Nuclear Weapons" (2016), in which I and several coauthors create an outline for gradually reducing the number of nuclear weapons to zero.[175]

---

173. Matthew Evangelista, "Coping with 9/11: Alternatives to the War Paradigm," Watson Institute, June 16, 2011, *watson.brown.edu/costsofwar/files/cow/imce/papers/2011/Coping%20with%20911.pdf*.

174. United Nations, "Treaty on the Prohibition of Nuclear Weapons," July 7, 2017 adoption, January 22, 2021 in force, *un.org/disarmament/wmd/nuclear/tpnw/*.

175. Jason Jones, John Whitehead, and Aimee Murphy, "Toward the Abolition of Strategic Nuclear Weapons: A Just War Analysis of Total War," *Life Matters Journal* and *I Am Whole Life*, August 6, 2016, *rehumanizeintl.org/nukes*.

Civilians don't have direct power over the military, but there are still actions that we can take to end war. We can protest, and vote for government leaders who accept the tenets of just war theory. A first step would be enforcing the "proper authority" requirement—in the US we can do so by demanding that all wars be approved by Congress, and voting out those who don't hold our Executive Branch accountable for the billions spent and lives lost to our continuing unjust wars.[176] There are endless ways to promote peace, and Rehumanize International (the organization I founded) is a member group of World Beyond War, which has education resources and a substantial list of ideas we can take to end war and build peace.[177]

Addressing Common Arguments in Support of War and National Defense

National Defense

"They're going to attack us; if we attack them first we can prevent the attack."

> We know from experience that the government/ media give information on foreign military powers to the public that is often either wrong or built on lies.[178] It is impossible to tell the future. Furthermore, our

---

176. To learn more about all of the requirements of just war theory, see the section "How do Consistent Life Ethic adherents respond to aggressive violence?" in chapter 1, on page 27.

177. You can find this list at *worldbeyondwar.org/abolish/* .

178. Uri Friedman, "The Ten Biggest American Intelligence Failures," *Foreign Policy*, January 3, 2012, *foreignpolicy.com/2012/01/03/the-ten-biggest-american-intelligence-failures/*.

own "pre-emptive strikes" give those nations a "just cause" to engage us in further war. Finally, even if one subscribes to just war theory, pre-emptive strikes are never a tool of a just war. For more information on this, see "How do Consistent Life Ethic adherents respond to aggressive violence?" in chapter 1.

"We must slow/stop the spread of terrorism because they all hate us and our freedom."

It is common sense that bombing civilians has not made and will not make them less likely to support acts of vengeance against other nations. Many modern acts of terrorism are retribution against a long history of colonial military violence; as long as we continue to bomb and shoot civilians, we will see a perpetual cycle of war and blowback.[179] The best way to stop the spread of terrorism is to bring our troops home and promote nonviolent peacebuilding efforts that uphold the human dignity of all.

"Our freedoms are being threatened."

Though I particularly sympathize with those who've lost loved ones in terrorist attacks like those on the World Trade Center and the Pentagon on September 11, 2001, terrorism is addressed not by inflicitng government-sponsored terrorism on the civilians of other nations, but by promoting human dignity and peace.

---

179. Charlotte Morris, "To What Extent Has U.S. Foreign Policy Contributed to an Increase in Religious Inspired Terrorism since 1945?" *Journal of Global Faultlines* 6, no. 2 (2019): 186–203. DOI: 10.13169/jglobfaul.6.2.0186.

Additionally, the freedoms of the average American have been more deeply curtailed and impacted by the US Patriot Act[180] and the extralegal killings of civilians (like Anwar and Abdulrahman al-Alwaki[181]) than they might have been by the threat of overseas terrorists.

National Interests

"We must support American interests around the world."

Typically, "American interests" do not refer to the individual or even the collective interests of the average American citizen, but rather to the business interests of a select elite group. The human cost of war (foreign civilians, combatants, and American military members) outweighs the potential profit of a select group of shareholders. The authentic interests of Americans are best served by the universal promotion of human rights and dignity, not by war.

A Global Police

"The world needs a 'global police.'"

No single nation has the right to act as a police force for the entire world. When military force is used in places (like Libya or Afghanistan) to "impose democracy" or "end terrorism," they almost always have

---

180. Freedom House, "Today's American: How Free? - The civil liberties implications of counterterrorism policies," May 2, 2008, *refworld. org/docid/491013161d.html.*
181. Steve Nelson, "Drone Memo Justifying Assassination of U.S. Citizen Released," *U.S. News & World Report,* June 23, 2014, *usnews.com/ news/articles/2014/06/23/drone-memo-assassination-us-citizen- anwar-al-awlaki-released.*

been left worse off and unquestionably more war-torn.[182] Additionally, it's worth noting that the US is allied with several countries who engage consistently in violations of human dignity,[183] so its foreign policy "picks and chooses" about which humans to care about and which we allow to be violated.

"But wars ended the injustices in the Holocaust, chattel slavery in the US, etc."

Defense of vulnerable people is a moral good and atrocities like genocide and slavery absolutely should be ended; however, the way that we engage these moral evils and attempt to end them should also be ethical and just because we must value each and *every* human being as the unrepeatable, inherently valuable self that they are. In our efforts to protect and uphold the dignity of vulnerable people who have been victims of violence, we must make sure that the dignity of those "on the other side" in such conflicts is still respected. For more about a theory of just defense, please see "How do Consistent Life Ethic adherents respond to aggressive violence?" on page 27.

---

182. For one opinion on this, see the following quote from Ben Rhodes, who served as a top foreign policy adviser to President Obama: "Look at the countries in which the war on terror has been waged: Afghanistan. Iraq. Yemen. Somalia. Libya. Every one of those countries is worse off today in some fashion. The evidentiary basis for the idea that American military intervention leads inexorably to improved material circumstances is simply not there." From: Ezra Klein, "Let's Not Pretend That the Way We Withdrew from Afghanistan Was the Problem," *The New York Times*, August 26, 2021, nytimes.com/2021/08/26/opinion/afghanistan-us-withdrawal.html

183. Jeffrey Fields, "Why repressive Saudi Arabia remains a U.S. ally," *The Conversation*, March 3, 2021, theconversation.com/why-repressive-saudi-arabia-remains-a-us-ally-156281.

"If we leave the nations in which we've intervened, there will be a vacuum of power and more violence."

Oftentimes, outside militaries are one of the biggest contributors to violence in these nations. We can still engage in diplomatic and humanitarian efforts in countries and regions where human dignity is attacked, but we should reject war as the "solution" to problems of violence and dehumanization.

Preventing (Further) War

"Nuclear weapons and mutually assured destruction (MAD) will prevent further war"

This is addressed somewhat in the section above on "A Brief Ethical Analysis of War." The threat of mutually assured destruction and the wholesale decimation of humanity and life on Earth is inherently unjust and contrary to human dignity. Provoking "good behavior" by holding a gun to someone's head (or to their family members) is violent coercion and is not a solid foundation for a culture of peace; likewise, threatening all of humanity with extinction through the use of nuclear weapons is not the path we should take.

"Support our troops"

"Our military (and organizations such as NATO) do good work: aid, humanitarian projects, etc."

Similar to my answer in chapter 3 to the question about the good that abortion providers do, an organization that promotes and perpetuates violence, no matter how much good it may do, must never be supported.

I am not opposed to the existence of a military per se, but conducting a just war using current military technology is questionable. Instead, military energies must be diverted from the killing machine we are conditioned to accept to a more authentically defensive and nonviolent approach to conflict. Additionally, treaties and organizations to enforce or enact those treaties are necessary, but not when they are used to justify and support violence, such as war. The act of fighting wars must be separated from humanitarian aid, so that in conscience citizens can fund humanitarian and nonviolent organizations, and defund those that are violent and warlike.

"Support our troops!" Or "Bashing war hurts our soldiers' morale."

Each member of our military—like all members of our human family—has inestimable dignity and worth. I think that this is best honored by valuing their lives as precious and worthy of protection, instead of wasting those lives in unjust conflicts around the world. We should bring our troops home, provide them alternatives to the career they currently have in service to a violent employer, and end unjust war.

Discussion Questions

1. How is peace more than the mere absence of violence?
2. Considering all the requirements for a war to qualify as "just," how can World War II be classified as a just war? What about World War I? What about the US military engagement in the Middle East? More recently,

what about US and NATO involvement in the conflict between Russia and Ukraine?

3. What do you think it means to be a "peacemaker"?

Further Reading Suggestions

1. S.L.A. Marshall, *Men Against Fire: The Problem of Battle Command* (Norman, OK: University of Oklahoma Press, 2000).

2. Kent Shifferd, Patrick Hiller, and Phill Gittins, A *Global Security System: An Alternative to War* (Charlottesville, VA: World Beyond War, 2018).

3. Kathleen Belew, *Bring the War Home: The White Power Movement and Paramilitary America* (Cambridge, MA: Harvard University Press, 2019 reprint).

4. Glen H. Stassen, editor, *Just Peacemaking: The New Paradigm for the Ethics of Peace and War* (Bohemia, NY: Pilgrim Press, 2008).

Chapter 5

Military torture

In a misplaced effort to gain vital tactical information during wartime, or to disgrace and shame the enemy, many militaries and governments violate human rights by using their power to dehumanize prisoners of war by inflicting severe pain, suffering, and trauma.

What is Torture?

Torture is the use of violence for a tactical purpose, such as gaining strategic information, forcing a confession, or meting out punishment, typically committed by a person of authority, such as a public official (including military personnel). Though torture in war is prohibited in international law by several statutes, several nations in every region of the world still engage in it.[184,185]

---

184. Amnesty International, "Torture," *amnesty.org/en/what-we-do/torture/*.

185. Domestic justice and prison systems commit torture that will be covered later, in chapter 7. They've been separated because, frankly, there's too much material and nuance necessary to cover the discussion of torture in just one chapter.

Historical torture included grotesque tools such as the rack, Cat-o-Ninetails, the Judas Cradle, or the Brazen Bull,[186] so modern methods might seem less gruesome because they appear "sterilized" in comparison. Torture was employed heavily by both the Axis and Allied powers during World War II, including forced labor camps, physical degradation, medical torture, and brutalization of prisoners, particularly the Jewish people systematically dehumanized and exterminated under Nazi rule. It's worth mentioning, as well, that the Japanese also engaged in widespread torture of POWs,[187] and neither the US nor the UK can claim to have fought "a clean war," because they too engaged in torture (and, as Peter Schrijvers documents, mass rape).[188,189]

In the past two decades of the War on Terror waged by the United States and allied nations since 2001, torture methods have often been called "enhanced interrogation" techniques to sanitize the intentional cruelty.[190] Perhaps the most famous form of "enhanced interrogation" used at the military base at Guantánamo Bay, Cuba, was water-

---

186. Steven Casale, "9 Medieval Torture Devices and Methods That Date Back to the Ancient World," *The Archive*, October 23, 2015, *explorethearchive.com/9-torture-methods-of-the-ancient-world*.

187. Clare Makepeace and Meg Parkes, "VJ Day: Surviving the horrors of Japan's WW2 camps," BBC News *Magazine*, August 15, 2015, *bbc.com/news/magazine-33931660*.

188. Ian Cobain, "How Britain tortured Nazi PoWs: The horrifying interrogation methods that belie our proud boast that we fought a clean war," *The Daily Mail*, 26 October 2012, *dailymail.co.uk/news/article-2223831/How-Britain-tortured-Nazi-PoWs-The-horrifying-interrogation-methods-belie-proud-boast-fought-clean-war.html*.

189. Peter Schrijvers, *The GI War Against Japan: American Soldiers in Asia and the Pacific During World War II* (New York: NYU Press, 2005), 212.

190. Mark Tran, "Q&A: Torture and 'enhanced interrogation,'" *The Guardian*, April 18, 2008, *theguardian.com/world/2008/apr/18/usa.terrorism*.

boarding. The name may sound benign, but what the prisoner endures is horrific:

> [Waterboarding] calls for the prisoner to be strapped down on his back, usually with his feet elevated. Typically the prisoner's face is covered with a towel (to collect moisture) or cellophane (to increase breathing difficulty) and water is poured over his face. The result is simulated drowning. Sometimes the technique results in death by heart attack or stroke. Other times it causes long-lasting psychological damage to the prisoner.[191]

More recently, *The New York Times* exposed some of the torture methods used on prisoners at Guantánamo and other CIA black sites as illustrated by Abu Zubaydah, a former prisoner there who was the first to endure waterboarding torture:

> One [of Abu Zubaydah's drawings] shows the prisoner nude and strapped to a crude gurney, his entire body clenched as he is waterboarded by an unseen interrogator. Another shows him with his wrists cuffed to bars so high above his head he is forced on to his tiptoes, with a long wound stitched on his left leg and a howl emerging from his open mouth. Yet another depicts a captor smacking his head against a wall.[192]

Mohammed El-Gharani, one of many teenagers who were arrested in Iraq, Saudi Arabia, and Afghanistan after

---

191. James L. Dickerson, *Inside America's Concentration Camps: Two Centuries of Internment and Torture* (Chicago: Lawrence Hill Books, 2010), 247.

192. Carol Rosenberg, "What the C.I.A.'s Torture Program Looked Like to the Tortured," *The New York Times*, December 4, 2019, *nytimes. com/2019/12/04/us/politics/cia-torture-drawings.html.*

the 9/11/2001 terrorist attacks,[193] recounts the beatings, compulsory nudity, sexual threats, electroshock torture, sensory deprivation, and sleep deprivation he was forced to endure as a mere teenager.[194]

Perhaps the worst instances of torture in the War on Terror, though, were waged by US Military Police at Abu Ghraib prison in Iraq. The Taguba Report exposed the cruelty inflicted by military personnel against detainees, including:

> (1) "Punching, slapping, and kicking detainees [and] jumping on their naked feet"; (2) "Videotaping and photographing naked male and female detainees"; (3) "Forcibly arranging detainees in various sexually explicit positions for photographing"; (4) "Forcing detainees to remove their clothing and keeping them naked for several days at a time"; (5) Forcing naked male detainees to wear women's underwear"; (6) "Forcing groups of male detainees to masturbate while being photographed and videotaped"; (7) "Arranging naked male detainees in a pile and then jumping on them"; (8) "Positioning a naked detainee on a . . . box, with a sandbag on his head, and attaching wires to his fingers, toes, and penis to simulate electric torture"; (9) "Writing 'I am a Rapest' (sic) on the leg of a detainee alleged to have forcibly raped a 15-year-old fellow detainee, and then photographing him naked"; (10) "Placing a dog chain or strap around a naked

---

193. "Guantánamo's Children: The Wikileaked Testimonies," UC Davis Center for the Study of Human Rights in the Americas, January 10, 2008, Last Revised: March 22, 2013, *humanrights.ucdavis.edu/reports/Guantánamos-children-the-wikileaked-testimonies/Guantánamos-children-the-wikileaked-testimonies.*

194. Jérôme Tubiana and Alexandre Franc, *Guantánamo Kid: The True Story of Mohammed El-Gharani* (London: SelfMadeHero, 2019).

detainee's neck and having a female Soldier pose for a picture"; (11) "A male MP (military police) guard having sex with a female detainee"; (12) "Using military working dogs (without muzzles) to intimidate and frighten detainees, and in at least one case biting and severely injuring a detainee"; and (13) "Taking photographs of dead Iraqi detainees."[195]

Another method of torture used for the US military's interrogation program in the War on Terror included solitary confinement, sometimes within "a mattress-sized cell from which [the detainee] was allowed to leave only two or three times a week, usually in the dead of night so that he [would] not see sunlight."[196] Though modern torture is often sanitized using language like "enhanced interrogation," its intent matches the brutal medieval torture of old: to dehumanize, demean, and psychologically break detainees through many different forms of pain and suffering.

A Brief Ethical Analysis of Military Torture

Human beings have intrinsic value and no crime, serious as it may be, can remove it. To deserve human rights, you don't have to be innocent—it's enough that you're human. Torture doesn't recognize the humanity of interrogated persons: it reduces them to objects to be manipulated, or obstacles to achieving some end. Many detained individuals are innocent of any terrorist acts when arrested and therefore any harm inflicted upon them would be inherently aggressive.

---

195. "U.S. Abuse of Iraqi Detainees at Abu Ghraib Prison," *The American Journal of International Law* 98, no. 3 (July 2004): 591–96. doi. org/10.2307/3181656.
196. Dickerson, *Inside America's Concentration Camps*, 249.

However, even if *guilty* terrorists were the only ones tortured, torture would still be an act of aggressive violence against people who could otherwise be safely incarcerated in order to prevent them from harming society. Additionally, torture is not a defensive action necessary to keep people safe. Ultimately, torture is an act of aggressive violence against a detained person or prisoner, and as such is prohibited according to the Consistent Life Ethic.

Beyond being morally wrong, it's worth noting that torture has also been shown to be ineffective and impractical. Even declassified CIA interrogation manuals, which were used to train torturers, don't portray torture as a particularly successful interrogation technique: To quote the 1983 Human Resources Exploitation Training Manual: "Intense pain is quite likely to produce false confessions, fabricated to avoid additional punishment."[197,198]

As neurologist Lawrence Hinkle explains, "Any circumstance that impairs the function of the brain potentially affects the ability to give information as well as the ability to withhold it."[199] Dr. Darius Rejali, a modern expert on torture, states that the terror and extreme stress of

---

197. U.S. Central Intelligence Agency, "1983 Human Resources Exploitation Training Manual," 1983, K-11, accessed via third-party site, *documents.theblackvault.com/documents/cia/HumanResourceExploitationManual-CIA.pdf*.

198. Interestingly, the 1983 Human Resources Exploitation Training Manual explicitly prohibits several acts of torture (under "Coercive Techniques" in section K) because they are contrary to policy, US law, or international statutes. Though training likely shifted between 1983 and the early 2000's, several of these prohibited (or highly discouraged), torturous actions were used against detainees at Abu Ghraib in the early 2000s.

199. Lawrence Hinkle, Jr., "The physiological state of the interrogation subject as it affects brain function," in *The Manipulation Of Human Behavior*, eds. Albert D. Biderman and Herbert Zimmer. (New York: John Wiley & Sons, 1961), 19.

torture often makes people "more dogmatic and tenacious," thus more committed to not talking, or it causes them to dissociate to withstand enormous amounts of pain.[200] Furthermore, traumatic pain and exhaustion can cause even cooperative individuals to have trouble recalling information; in their exhausted and pain-addled state, they may give false information they believe is correct, or the "heightened suggestibility," caused by the pain, might cause them to start believing whatever they think the torturer believes.[201]

Some people will talk to get the torture to stop, some will purposely lie, others will give misleading information because they are unable to think straight, and a few others will give correct information.[202] Combine this situation with the fact that torturers may not be very good at judging the veracity of a confession, and it is obvious that this leads to a serious glut of information that intelligence seekers will need to verify. In other words, torture gives intelligence seekers more data to work with, but it also requires the extra work of verifying and sifting through those high amounts of data, much of which is purposely misleading and false.[203] So not only is torture ethically wrong, but all we gain from it is dubious information at enormous institutional and moral costs.

200. Jean Maria Arrigo, "A Utilitarian Argument Against Torture Interrogation of Terrorists," *Science and Engineering Ethics* 10, no. 3 (2004): 7.

201. Darius Rejali, *Torture and Democracy* (Princeton, NJ: Princeton University Press, 2009), 466.

202. U.S. Central Intelligence Agency, "1983 Human Resources Exploitation Training Manual."

203. Rejali, *Torture and Democracy*, 161, 175.

History of Policy and Culture around Military Torture

Historically, torture (like many other forms of violence) was thought to be acceptable, and human dignity was seen as subordinate to other sociocultural goods. The pre-Christian Roman Empire commonly used floggings and crucifixions as forms of torture and state-sponsored retributive justice. Regrettably, the Christian cultures that followed the Roman Empire's adoption of Christianity also promulgated widespread use of torture to interrogate prisoners or to attempt to get them to recant heresies or do penance for misdeeds. This use of torture included the abuses of the Inquisition, the Salem witch trials, and myriad other instances of state-sponsored cruelty throughout Western European nations and their later colonies.[204]

Colonial powers around the world have repeatedly tortured Indigenous people. The fledgling US employed one of the earliest uses of death marches and concentration camps for "enemy nations": the Trail of Tears and the reservation system that treated the native people as enemies and prisoners.[205,206]

We often associate World War II with Nazi concentration camps full of Jewish and Roma people; but the United States and Canada employed concentration camps on a

---

204. Brian A. Pavlac, *Witch Hunts in the Western World: Persecution and Punishment from the Inquisition Through the Salem Trials* (Westport, CT: Greenwood Press, 2009).

205. Dickerson, *Inside America's Concentration Camps*, 13-38.

206. Concentration camps are meant to hold a high concentration of "undesirable" people, particularly those seen as potential or real enemies; these Indian reservations were the first example of this in the US.

massive (if less violent) scale, too.[207,208] "[W]ithin minutes after the attack on Pearl Harbor, the territorial governor of Hawaii suspended the writ of *habeas corpus*" and power was handed over to General Walter Short, who then declared martial law.[209] Because Hawaii was still a territory, "the government could suspend the right of *habeas corpus* . . . because [it] was. . . not a state."[210]

Only months later, on February 19, 1942, the US issued Executive Order 9066 and just five days later Canada followed suit with Order-in-Council PC 1486.[211,212] During the years of internment that followed, thousands of innocent Japanese-Americans were given a number, and forced to "unburden" themselves of all homes and businesses and move to dehumanizing concentration camps where they were constantly patrolled, deprived of proper food, and threatened with violence from the looming guard towers.[213] The guards sometimes forced the Japanese-American prisoners to stand in their underwear and sandals at machine-gunpoint in freezing temperatures.[214]

---

207. I often ponder whether the US use of internment camps during WWII is the reason why our military intelligence didn't register the many internment camps around Germany and Poland full of Jews and other "undesirables" as worth looking into. To this day, this thought haunts me.

208. "Internment of Japanese Canadians," *The Canadian Encyclopedia*, last updated February 28, 2022, thecanadianencyclopedia.ca/en/article/internment-of-japanese-canadians.

209. Dickerson, *Inside America's Concentration Camps*, 47.

210. Dickerson, *Inside America's Concentration Camps*, 56.

211. Executive Order 9066, February 19, 1942; General Records of the United States Government; Record Group 11; National Archives, *ourdocuments.gov/doc.php?flash=false&doc=74*.

212. Order-in-Council 1486, February 24, 1942, Government of Canada Archives, recherche-collection-search.bac-lac.gc.ca/eng/home/record?app=fonandcol&IdNumber=1447094.

213. Dickerson, *Inside America's Concentration Camps*, 66-72.

214. Dickerson, *Inside America's Concentration Camps*, 142-143.

The Nazi concentration camps took the abuse of prisoners a massive, horrific step further:[215] The victims of Nazi concentration camps (who were often Jewish or Roma) were subject to physical degradation, forced starvation, beatings, exposure to the elements, forced labor, flogging, and hanging torture.[216] Some prisoners, particularly the disabled, were taken to centers where they were subject to grotesque and dehumanizing medical experimentation and then killed (if the experimentation didn't kill them first).[217] On top of all of this horror was the systematic extermination of those deemed "undesirable" (like the Roma, Jewish, and gay people) at death camps, where tens of thousands of innocent people were gassed or shot for the "crime" of existing.

In the wake of the atrocities inflicted during World War II around the world, torture was finally outlawed internationally in 1948 by the Universal Declaration of Human Rights, which states in Article 5 that "no one shall be subjected to torture or to cruel, inhumane or degrading treatment or punishment."[218] This prohibition was expanded further by the Geneva Conventions III and IV in 1949, which address the Treatment of Prisoners of War and

---

215. However, Nazis were heavily influenced in their torturous practices by the genocidal treatment of Black, Indigenous, and other people of color within the United States. See Ira Katznelson, "What America Taught the Nazis," *The Atlantic*, November 2017, theatlantic.com/magazine/archive/2017/11/what-america-taught-the-nazis/540630/.

216. Auschwitz-Birkenau Memorial and Museum, "Other Punishments," auschwitz.org/en/history/punishments-and-executions/other-punishments.

217. "The Doctors Trial: The Medical Case of the Subsequent Nuremberg Proceedings," United States Holocaust Memorial Museum, archived from the original on 20 April 2008, retrieved 23 March 2008, web.archive.org/web/20080420105201/http://www.ushmm.org/research/doctors/indiptx.htm.

218. United Nations, "Universal Declaration of Human Rights," 1948, un.org/sites/un2.un.org/files/udhr.pdf.

relative to the Protection of Civilian Persons in Times of War, respectively.[219],[220] The UN Convention Against Torture and Other Cruel, Inhuman or Degrading Treatment or Punishment entered into force in 1987.[221]

Though both torture and extended internment of innocents violate international law, governments have often continued to engage in torture. Sometimes, torture is chalked up to the ignorance of the Geneva Conventions and international human rights standards on the part of military personnel.[222] However, sometimes governments (including the United States) search for ways to justify flouting international laws against torture.[223] For example, a confidential report compiled for Secretary of Defense Donald H. Rumsfeld in 2003 stated that when the US signed the Geneva Convention against Torture, it was bound to follow the Convention only inasmuch as any part of it overlapped with legal protections within US Constitutional Amendments, and that domestic law was sufficient to prevent torture. Furthermore, the report declared that even those US criminal laws that did forbid torture[224] wouldn't

---

219. United Nations, "III: Geneva Convention Relative To The Treatment Of Prisoners Of War of 12 August 1949," 1949, *un.org/en/genocideprevention/documents/atrocity-crimes/Doc.32_GC-III-EN.pdf.*

220. United Nations, "IV: Geneva Convention Relative To The Protection Of Civilian Persons In Time Of War of 12 August 1949," 1949, *un.org/en/genocideprevention/documents/atrocity-crimes/Doc.33_GC-IV-EN.pdf.*

221. United Nations, "Convention Against Torture and Other Cruel, Inhuman or Degrading Treatment or Punishment," 1984, *ohchr.org/en/professionalinterest/pages/cat.aspx.*

222. One example of this is in the Taguba Report: "U.S. Abuse of Iraqi Detainees at Abu Ghraib Prison," *The American Journal of International Law* 98, no. 3 (July 2004): 595, *doi.org/10.2307/3181656.*

223. ""U.S. Abuse of Iraqi Detainees," 592-593.

224. For example, one domestic law included that "the Mississippi Supreme Court had outlawed waterboarding in the 1920's, describing it

apply to the interrogations at Guantánamo because the naval base was technically on non-US territory,[225] and neither would the laws apply to military operations involved in the War on Terror at large because they might prevent the president from using whatever means deemed necessary to interrogate prisoners of war and/or detainees. This last statement is perhaps the most troubling, because it opens the door to all kinds of inhumane behavior in the name of "getting information."

In 2001, the USA Patriot Act was passed, which basically states that anyone without US citizenship could be held without charge for up to one week (or longer, if that statute isn't properly enforced).[226] This suspension of due process is compounded by the fact that according to the United States Supreme Court in *Johnson v. Eisentrager*, "the US has no jurisdiction to entertain habeas [corpus] petitions brought by . . . espionage agents,"[227] (i.e. people suspected of terrorist sympathies or activities) and in *Al Odah v. United States*, a US Circuit Court upheld this reasoning and found that US law "preclude[s] the detainees from seeking *habeas* relief in the courts of the United States."[228] This has resulted

---

as torture." from James L. Dickerson's *Inside America's Concentration Camps: Two Centuries of Internment and Torture*, page 248, referencing *Fisher v. State*, 145 Miss. 116, 127, 110 So. 361 (1926); and *White v. State*, 129 Miss. 182, 187, 91 So. 903 (1922).

225. Kate Frisch, "During War, the Law is Silent," Or is it?: *Examining the Legal Status of Guantánamo Bay*, University of Richmond School of Law, 2016, scholarship.richmond.edu/cgi/viewcontent. cgi?article=1144&context=law-student-publications.

226. Sean D. Murphy, "U.S. Detention of Aliens in Aftermath of September 11 Attacks," *The American Journal of International Law* 96, no. 2 (2002): 470 – 75. doi.org/10.2307/2693944.

227. Sean D. Murphy, "Ability of Detainees in Cuba to Obtain Federal Habeas Corpus Review," *The American Journal of International Law* 98, no. 1 (2004): 188–90. doi.org/10.2307/3139278.

228. *Al Odah v. United States*, 321 F.3d 1141 (D.C. Circuit Court, 2003).

in hundreds of foreign detainees being arrested and held even for decades without any due process or possibility of trial. Of the 780 men who have been held at Guantánamo, 93 percent have been released without a formal charge.[229]

In addition to this, every person who has been kept in Guantánamo Bay is Muslim,[230] but needless to say, not all potential terrorists are Muslim. Much of the torture there has relied on religious harassment, including forced shaving of beards, force-feeding during Ramadan, and desecration of the Qur'an.[231] Guantánamo has been a sort of safe haven for Islamophobia, perpetuating a cycle of dehumanizing racism and religious discrimination.

Though President Obama penned an Executive Order of January 22, 2009 which was supposed to end the CIA's secret overseas prisons, ban coercive interrogation methods, and shut down the Guantánamo detention camp within a year,[232] as I write these pages in early 2022, the camp remains open. Though many leaders on the left are currently working to make it a higher political priority, it nonetheless remains low.[233]

229. "Guantánamo: Facts & Figures," Human Rights Watch, hrw.org/video-photos/interactive/2017/03/30/Guantánamo-facts-and-figures.

230. "Guantánamo By the Numbers," Center for Constitutional Rights, November 14, 2015, Updated May 2021, ccrjustice.org/home/get-involved/tools-resources/fact-sheets-and-faqs/guant-namo-numbers.

231. Maha Hilal, "Guantanamo: An enduring symbol of US Islamophobia," *Middle East Eye*, January 21, 2020, middleeasteye.net/opinion/guantanamo-persistent-symbol-us-islamophobia.

232. Executive Order 13492, January 22, 2009, Code of Federal Regulations, GovInfo, govinfo.gov/content/pkg/CFR-2010-title3-vol1/pdf/CFR-2010-title3-vol1-eo13492.pdf.

233. Rebecca Kheel, "House Democrats call on Biden to close Guantánamo 'once and for all,'" *The Hill*, August 5, 2021, thehill.com/policy/defense/566581-house-democrats-call-on-biden-to-close-guantanamo-once-and-for-all.

A Brief Nonviolent Policy Solution to Military Torture

Torture violates our shared inherent human dignity because it is an act of aggressive violence, so it should be eliminated from human experience. However, considering that torture is already banned under the Geneva Conventions, and that even several domestic statutes against torture have been passed, it would seem as though policy alone is not sufficient to end to torture in war. Therefore, people across the globe must demand an end to torture in any form, and as citizens, work to hold our respective nations accountable for war crimes that they have committed and continue to commit.

Part of holding our nations accountable is voting for officials who oppose torture, and then insisting they end this unjust practice wherever it is found.[234] This necessarily involves advocating for legal steps that could reduce the risk of torture ever happening: mandating regular and repeated Geneva Conventions trainings for all military personnel, discontinuing any military training or culture that precipitates abusive and torturous attitudes and behaviors, and dishonorable discharge and/or heavy sanctions for anyone in a government role (including military personnel) who implement torture at any level. And last but not least: all people detained by states and their militaries should have full access to pursue basic human rights (e.g. *habease corpus*), and all facilities in "exempt" jurisdictions that have been used to flout domestic and internatioal prohibitions on torture should be immediately shut down.

---

234. The second half of this, political accountability, is especially worth noting, because former President Barack Obama promised to shut down Guantánamo Bay Prison during his 2008 campaign, but failed to do so.

Additionally—and perhaps most importantly—civilians must demonstrate an unwillingness to tolerate torture any longer. This can only be achieved through widespread education on human rights.

Addressing Common Arguments in Support of Military Torture

Torture Saves Lives

"We need to use torture to get vital information that will prevent terrorism."

Contrary to popular belief, torture is profoundly ineffective at getting accurate intelligence from detainees. See "A Brief Ethical Analysis . . ." above, where I also discuss that we may not do evil that good may come of it; we may not use violence against humans who do not pose an imminent threat, even if it would be to save others.

"Torture is a deterrent to terrorism."

Contrary to this idea, multiple terrorists have actually cited the abuses of Muslims at CIA black sites, Abu Ghraib, and Guantánamo as their motive for getting involved with terrorist organizations.[235]

---

235. "Regional Ct Strategy For Iraq And Its Neighbors: Results And Recommendations from March 7-8 COM Meeting." March 18, 2006. *wikileaks.org/plusd/cables/06KUWAIT913_a.html.*

Terrorists Don't Deserve Due Process

"Suspending *habeas corpus* is necessary to achieve justice after 9/11."

This was the reasoning used in the Patriot Act, but in fact suspending *habeas corpus* for people accused of terrorism after 9/11 has prevented us from ever seeing the whole truth of that event. By depriving them of the right to a trial we have also deprived survivors and victims' families of authentic justice.

"They're not [US] citizens, so they don't get our constitutional rights."

When governments hold people indefinitely without charge or trial, in essence they are participating in a form of kidnapping. Non-citizens should have the civil right to freedom unless they are served with charges, in which case they should have a fair and speedy trial: to do otherwise amounts to a form of trafficking and is a violation of human dignity.

"Torture is only for the worst of the worst."

People who say this are implying that "bad people deserve it [torture] anyway." However, documentation shows that even children as young as thirteen or fourteen were arrested and transferred to Guantánamo,[236] not to mention that as of 2021, 93 percent of prisoners at Guantánamo have been released without formal

---

236. "Guantánamo's Children," UC Davis Center for the Study of Human Rights in the Americas.

charges.[237] It also shows a racist and Islamophobic double standard where, in certain nations, the US views child [adolescent] soldiers as victims to be treated with mercy and compassion and rehabilitation, but in the Muslim-majority nations where we've waged war, child soldiers have been treated as "enemy combatants." Some have been imprisoned without due process[238] and others have been killed.[239] But, regardless of who is being tortured, intentional harm such as torture is an affront to human dignity and should be ended.

"Support our Troops"

"The US has standards in place developed with medical experts to ensure that we torture 'humanely.'"

"Humane torture" is an oxymoron; it is not possible. Though the processes of modern torture have sometimes been "signed off" by physicians, this is an attempt to medicalize violence and assuage our consciences. Doctors are not a special class of human incapable of perpetrating harm: we must see past the MD and evaluate actions through a lens of human-centered ethics to determine whether they constitute violence.

---

237. "Guantánamo: Facts & Figures," Human Rights Watch.

238. ACLU publication of U.S. Violations of the Optional Protocol on the Involvement of Children in Armed Conflict, "Soldiers Of Misfortune: Abusive U.S. Military Recruitment and Failure to Protect Child Soldiers," ACLU, 2008, 33-36, *aclu.org/sites/default/files/pdfs/human-rights/crc_report_20080513.pdf*.

239. Jo Becker and Scott Shane, "Secret 'Kill List' Proves a Test of Obama's Principles and Will," *The New York Times*, May 29, 2012, *nytimes. com/2012/05/29/world/obamas-leadership-in-war-on-al-qaeda.html*.

"They do worse to us."

We should not be so ethically fragile as to allow our moral compasses to be dislodged by any terrorist organization or violent individual. Another person or group doing horrific violence (to us or those we care about) is not a reason to act unjustly or to violate human dignity. Even when responding to violence, we should respect the inherent, unchangeable dignity of those who have done us harm.

Fear of Recidivism

"These people are so abominable, we don't want them endangering society even if they were still held in detention."

Those who a government holds in detention deserve to face charges and receive a trial. Society can be kept safe from those suspected of criminal acts, including those accused of terrorism. To keep alleged terrorists detained is to keep them in a legal limbo without due process rights, essentially kidnapping them. We can either file charges in local jurisdictions, collaborate with the International Criminal Court in trying them, or send them back to the countries they came from.

Discussion Questions

1. When talking about torture, how would you respond to the question, "Wouldn't you do anything to save your family?"

2. The media often glorifies torture, as in the show 24. Before reading this chapter, how effective did you think

torture is? How has learning about its ineffectiveness impacted your perspective?

3. How can those who have been unjustly held prisoner and tortured be rehumanized? Think particularly of how you can fight Islamophobia and other forms of discrimination against people of color.

Further Reading Suggestions

1. Jérôme Tubiana and Alexandre Franc, *Guantánamo Kid: The True Story of Mohammed El-Gharani* (London: SelfMadeHero, 2019).

2. Mansoor Adayfi, *Don't Forget Us Here: Lost and Found at Guantánamo* (New York: Hachette Books, 2021).

3. James L. Dickerson, *Inside America's Concentration Camps: Two Centuries of Internment and Torture* (Brandon, MS: Sartoris Literary Group, 2019 edition).

4. Darius Rejali, *Torture and Democracy* (Princeton, NJ: Princeton University Press, 2007).

Ending Violence in Response to Crime

"Many that live deserve death.
And some that die deserve life.
Can you give it to them?
Then do not be too eager to
deal out death in judgement."

~ Gandalf, in J.R.R. Tolkien's
The Fellowship of the Ring

〽

Chapter 6

Police brutality

To enforce laws and sometimes stop crime, modern societies have instituted policing; but in recent years, countless instances of brutal, dehumanizing violence perpetrated by police and police-adjacent groups and individuals have come to light.

What is Police Brutality?

Police brutality is the use of undue or unnecessary force against civilians by law enforcement officers. It can include harassment, beatings, psychological coercion, torture, shootings, and other forms of violence. In some cases, it is fatal or has fatal consequences. In 2020, the [US] Police Violence Report issued by Mapping Police Violence stated that 1,126 people were killed by police violence, many by shootings, some by tasers, some by chokeholds, and some by vehicular force.[240] Additionally, police forces domestically and around the world frequently use tear gas, banned in wartime by both the Geneva Convention and US laws.[241]

---

240. Mapping Police Violence, "Police Violence Report 2020," *policeviolencereport.org/*.
241. Allison C. Meier, "Why Do Police Use Tear Gas When It Was Banned

In yet another instance of how the Consistent Life Ethic links many issues, this chemical irritant used to disperse crowds not only causes "burning sensations on the skin, choking, coughing, tearing, and sometimes nausea,"[242] but it can act as an abortifacient and is linked to miscarriage, too.[243,244,245] Though the particular methods of violence and dehumanization by police vary from case to case, between 2016 and 2019 Mapping Police Violence found 156,927 civilian complaints of police misconduct filed with 13,147 police departments around the United States.[246] Though not all complaints against police stem from brutality, the numbers closely track, and police brutality may often be under-reported, perhaps due to fear of backlash.[247]

in War?" *JSTOR Daily*, June 8, 2020, *daily.jstor.org/why-do-police-use-tear-gas-when-it-was-banned-in-war/*.

242. Meier, "Why Do Police Use Tear Gas?".
243. Associated Press, "U.N. says Israeli use of tear gas caused miscarriages, 11 deaths," *The Pittsburgh Press*, 1988, A5.
244. Mari Hayman, "Chile Suspends Use of Tear Gas Amid Concerns Over Miscarriages," *The Latin Dispatch*, May 19, 2011, *latindispatch.com/2011/05/19/chile-suspends-use-of-tear-gas-amid-concerns-over-miscarriages/*.
245. Richard Sollom and Holly G. Atkinson, Physicians for Human Rights, "Weaponizing Tear Gas: Bahrain's Unprecedented Use of Toxic Chemical Agents Against Civilians," *CUNY Academic Works* (August 2012): 28-29.
246. Mapping Police Violence, "Police Scorecard 2020," *policescorecard.org/*.
247. For this assertion, I can point to a complex thread of sources. First, from Matthew J. Hickman, "Citizen Complaints about Police Use of Force," U.S. Department of Justice, Bureau of Justice Statistics, June 2006, *bjs.ojp.gov/content/pub/pdf/ccpuf.pdf*: "Force complaints represent a subset of all force events. That is, not all force events result in citizens filing formal complaints. How often do citizens actually complain? Estimates from the 2002 Police-Public Contact Survey indicated that although 75% of citizens experiencing force thought the level of force used was excessive, about 10% filed a complaint with the agency employing the officer(s). About 1% filed a complaint with a CCRB." Then, a (lacking, but available) more recent source:

Police brutality, an all-too-common problem, is considered to be "one of the leading causes of death for young men" in the United States.[248] Police brutality exists across cultures and, while it cuts across lines of gender identity, race, class, and age, it disproportionately affects minorities and the most vulnerable members of a society. Transgender people, for example, experience police violence at a rate 3.7 times greater than do cisgender people,[249] and studies show that the rates of police killings "increase in tandem" with poverty rates.[250]

The tragic consequences of police violence are clear in its relationship to systemic racism. Black men are 2.5 times more likely than white men to have fatal encounters with the police, and studies show that Black people killed by the police are more than twice as likely as white people to be

---

Police-Public Contact Survey (PPCS) [1997-2018], Bureau of Justice Statistics, *bjs.ojp.gov/data-collection/police-public-contact-survey-ppcs#surveys-0*. Finally, the oldest of the sources states that, "In 1982, the federal government funded a "Police Services Study," in which 12,022 randomly selected citizens were interviewed in three metropolitan areas. The study found that 13.6 percent of those surveyed had cause to complain about police service in the previous year (this included verbal abuse and discourtesy, as well as physical force). Yet, only 30 percent of the people filed formal complaints. In other words, *most instances of police abuse go unreported.*" From ACLU's "Fighting Police Abuse: A Community Action Manual," August 1997, *aclu.org/other/fighting-police-abuse-community-action-manual.*

248. Frank Edwards, Hedwig Lee, and Michael Esposito, "Risk of Being Killed by Police Use of Force in the United States by Age, Race–Ethnicity, and Sex," *Proceedings of the National Academy of Sciences of the United States*, no. 34 (2019) 16793. *doi:10.1073/pnas.1821204116.*

249. "Trans Hate Violence Fact Sheet," NYC Anti-Violence Project, *avp.org/wp-content/uploads/2017/04/ncavp_transhvfactsheet.pdf.*

250. Justin Feldman, "Police Killings in the US: Inequalities by Race/Ethnicity and Socioeconomic Position," People's Policy Project, 2020, *peoplespolicyproject.org/wp-content/uploads/2020/06/PoliceKillings.pdf.*

unarmed.[251] People of color who die by police violence are "disproportionately likely to have their deaths classified as the result of accident, natural causes, or intoxication."[252] Racial disparities in deaths at the hands of police parallel poverty rates.[253]

Although police are given an average of 168 hours of training in use of arms, self defense, and use of force, they typically receive training for only a fraction of that time about domestic violence, mental illness, and sexual assault.[254] Qualified immunity, a judicial doctrine which prevents government officials from being prosecuted for offenses that do not violate "clearly established" law, often protects officers from consequences. Of the 1,126 US cases in which people were killed by the police in 2020, only 1 percent led to charges against officers.[255] Additionally, even when there are well-intentioned people working as police who claim that the problem stems from "a few bad apples," police unions (e.g. the Fraternal Order of Police [FOP]) and the "Blue Code [or Wall] of Silence" often prevent

---

251. Justin Nix, Bradley A. Campbell, Edward H. Byers, and Geoffrey P. Alpert, "A Bird's Eye View of Civilians Killed by Police in 2015," *Criminology and Public Policy* 16, no.1 (2017): 309–40. DOI:10.1111/1745-9133.12269.

252. Victor E. Kappeler, "Being Arrested can be Hazardous to your Health, Especially if you are a Person of Color," *EKU Online: Police Studies* (2014), *plsonline.eku.edu/insidelook/being-arrested-can-be-hazardous-your-health-especially-if-you-are-person-color*.

253. Justin M. Feldman, Sofia Gruskin, Brent A. Coull, and Nancy Krieger, "Police-Related Deaths and Neighborhood Economic and Racial/Ethnic Polarization, United States, 2015–2016," *American Journal of Public Health* 109, no.3 (2019): 458–64, DOI: 10.2105/AJPH.2018.304851.

254. Brian A. Reaves, "State and Local Law Enforcement Training Academies, 2013," Bureau of Justice Statistics Bulletin, 2016, *bjs.gov/content/pub/pdf/slleta13.pdf*.

255. "2017 Police Violence Report," Mapping Police Violence, 2017, *policeviolencereport.org/*.

cops who engage in violence from being let go,[256] thereby "spoiling the whole bunch." Troublingly, many cases of fatal police violence are not made public until a witness shares a recording because the police are invested in protecting "their own." This leads to some unsettling questions: How many deaths have gone unwitnessed? How much violence goes unrecorded?

A Brief Ethical Analysis of Police Brutality

Dr. Peter Kraska, a scholar of police and criminal justice, writes that in a militarized organization the "use of force and threat of violence" is seen "as the most appropriate and efficacious means to solve problems."[257] The Consistent Life Ethic tells us that aggressive violence is never the answer and shows the ineffectiveness of using force to solve problems, especially nonviolent crimes. In law enforcement, even in response to violent crime, principles of just defense such as last resort, just cause, and proportionality apply.[258] Though there may be select instances when an officer has used violent force in a truly limited, ethical self-defense, a great deal of police-perpetrated violence doesn't fit that description. Unfortunately, modern systems of policing tend to use violence as an automatic reaction; people who commit crimes are treated like subhuman combatants.

---

256. Noam Scheiber, Farah Stockman, and J. David Goodman, "How Police Unions Became Such Powerful Opponents to Reform Efforts," *New York Times*, June 6, 2020. Updated April 2, 2021, nytimes.com/2020/06/06/us/police-unions-minneapolis-kroll.html.

257. Kraska, "Militarization and Policing," 3.

258. See the subsection "How do Consistent Life Ethic adherents respond to aggressive violence?" in chapter 1, page 27.

Because police brutality is an act of intentional[259] and aggressive harm, it is always an act of dehumanization. We should always act to uphold all humans' dignity, and police brutality is an explicit rejection of the other, often in an attempt to assert superiority. It is especially egregious because the power police have is supposed to be used to protect the vulnerable; aggressive violence is a grave perversion of that role, as evidenced by police brutality's disproportionate effect on minorities.

Police brutality disguises attacks on life as law and order, and disguises increased militarization, targeting the vulnerable, as protective efforts. Because police are seen as necessary, authoritative, and essential, it follows that all of their actions would be seen similarly. Therefore, it's common for this internal logic to produce a prejudice against victims of police brutality, for people in the wider culture to assume that a victim "deserved it," and to turn a blind eye to police-perpetrated aggression. As long as people turn a blind eye to brutality in the justice system, real justice will never be served, and dehumanization by the police will run unchecked. Followers of the Consistent Life Ethic must work for real justice, and this begins by holding those in power accountable for the harm done to our communities.

---

259. There may be instances where police brutality was not completely intended, but rather was an act of reflex, without considering the humanity of the victim. This is likely often the case for military members in wartime combat, too. The individual culpability in immediate momentary intentionality (which can be questionable in the heat of the moment) versus the long-term, ingrained intentionality built into systemic training for violence combined with the difficulty of overcoming internal biases is complex and worth diving into for each of the issues in this book. In the system training and equipping individual police for violence discussed here, the system bears a substantial portion of the moral burden of "intention."

History of Policy and Culture around Police Brutality

Police brutality is not a new problem, nor is it solely an American problem. As early as 1848, an article titled "Police Brutality" appeared in the British magazine *Puppet-Show*, warning about the dangers of rampant police violence: "It is with shame and disgust that we have observed . . . how fast the Police Force is becoming an organized brutality. Scarcely a week passes without their committing some offence which disgusts everybody but the magistrates."[260] Instances of police brutality have been documented in nearly every nation, though Venezuela, Brazil, Syria, the Philippines, and India are among the nations with the most lethal policing.[261]

Particularly in the United States, South Africa, India, and many other former British colonies, the police have an especially fraught history in terms of racial or colorist violence. The institutionalization of white supremacy through the systematic enslavement of Black people and subjugation of people of color has echoed across the centuries. In South Africa, police brutality remains a problem despite efforts to diversify its ranks; many activists insist that the colorist legacy of apartheid (ended nearly thirty years ago) is still deeply ingrained in the post-colonial, democratic system.[262] In India, the history of oppression

---

260. "More Police Brutality," *The Puppet-Show*. 2, no. 27. 9 (1848): 14, *books.google.com/books?id=kbMOAAAAQAAJ&pg=RA2-PA14#v=onepage&q&f=false*.

261. Wikipedia, "List of killings by law enforcement officers by country," Last edited on July 20, 2021, *en.wikipedia.org/wiki/List_of_killings_by_law_enforcement_officers_by_country*.

262. For more on this history, See Eusebius McKaiser, "In South Africa, Police Violence Isn't Black and White," *Foreign Policy*, October 21, 2020, foreignpolicy.com/2020/10/21/in-south-africa-police-violence-isnt-black-and-white/; and also See Tanya Magaisa, "The

on the basis of social caste has been similarly repeated, despite the post-colonial police forces of the past seventy-five years being largely comprised of non-white Indians. People from lower classes have repeatedly been subject to beatings, torture, and even extrajudicial killings by police, with few legal consequences for the officers involved in such violent treatment.[263]

In the US, slave patrols dedicated to catching escaped enslaved people and quelling uprisings were one of the first instantiations of modern policing.[264] In the 1820s, the Texas Rangers were formed by Stephen F. Austin to protect the interests of white colonists in the region, particularly to eliminate the "threat" of Indigenous people and push out Mexicans and Mexican-American people who'd lived there for generations.[265] In the Northeast, however, racist policing intersected with nativism, where immigrant communities like the Irish, Italians, and Eastern Europeans were often the targets of police brutality.[266] Racism in policing continued after the Reconstruction era, too. Northern police forces began to target Black

Legacy of Racism in South Africa," Human Rights Watch, March 9, 2021, hrw.org/news/2021/03/09/legacy-racism-south-africa; and finally, See Isy India Thusi, "South Africa shows that diversity is not the answer to police violence," *The Hill*, September 10, 2011, thehill.com/opinion/civil-rights/515750-south-africa-shows-that-diversity-is-not-the-answer-to-police-violence/.

263. Mohit Rao, "Indian police use violence as a shortcut to justice. It's the poorest who bear the scars," CNN, December 2, 2020, cnn.com/2020/12/02/india/police-brutality-india-dst-intl-hnk/index.html.

264. Olivia B. Waxman, "How the US Got Its Police Force," *Time*, May 18, 2018, *time.com/4779112/police-history-origins/*.

265. Michael Sandlin, "A New History Tears Down the Myth of the Texas Rangers," *Texas Observer*. September 4, 2018, *texasobserver.org/a-new-history-tears-down-the-myth-of-the-texas-rangers/*.

266. Waxman,"How the U.S. Got Its Police Force."

communities, and Southern forces began enforcing new Jim Crow laws.[267] Police were often involved in or permissive of race riots and mass killings;[268] lynchings generally happened with the tacit approval, or at the very least tolerance, of the police force.[269]

From the 1992 police beating of Rodney King that launched the Los Angeles riots[270] to the killing of Daunte Wright in 2021,[271] in recent decades hundreds have been harmed by violent policing.[272] In 2020, a powerful wave of protest fought back against the trend of police brutality following the back-to-back-to-back killings of Elijah McClain, Rayshard Brooks, Breonna Taylor, Atatiana Jefferson, and George Floyd.[273] During the protests, even

267. Connie Hassett-Walker, "George Floyd's death reflects the racist roots of American policing," *The Conversation*, June 2, 2020, updated June 10, 2020, theconversation.com/george-floyds-death-reflects-the-racist-roots-of-american-policing-139805.

268. Derrick Bell, "Portent of Disaster and Discomforting Divergence," in *Police Brutality: An Anthology*, ed. Jill Nelson (New York: W. W. Norton & Company, 2000), 94-95.

269. Alex S. Vitale, *The End of Policing* (New York: Verso, 2018), 44.

270. Anjuli Sastry and Karen Grigsby Bates, "When LA Erupted In Anger: A Look Back At The Rodney King Riots," NPR, April 26, 2017, *npr.org/2017/04/26/524744989/when-la-erupted-in-anger-a-look-back-at-the-rodney-king-riots*.

271. Amanda Arnold, "Everything to Know about the Police Killing of Daunte Wright," *The Cut*, April 15, 2021, thecut.com/2021/04/minnesota-police-shooting-of-daunte-wright-what-to-know.html.

272. Many of these names and incidents can be found at: Alia Chughtai and Al Jazeera news, "Know Their Names: Black People Killed by Police in the U.S, interactive presentation," Al Jazeera News, 2020. interactive.aljazeera.com/aje/2020/know-their-names/index.html.

273. Many of these incidents can be found at: Alia Chughtai and Al Jazeera news, "Know Their Names: Black People Killed by Police in the U.S, interactive presentation," *Al Jazeera News*, 2020. *interactive.aljazeera.com/aje/2020/know-their-names/index.html*. Elijah McClain's story can be found at: Knez Walker, et al, "What happened to Elijah McClain? Protests help bring new attention to his death," ABC News, June 30, 2020, *abcnews.go.com/US/happened-elijah-mcclain-*

more people were brutalized and killed by militarized police forces.[274]

Rapid and widespread militarization of police has been precipitated by the 1033 program, a federal initiative that allows the military to give surplus equipment to police agencies (again demonstrating a link in CLE issues: much of this surplus comes from America's wars in Afghanistan and Iraq[275]). Agencies can order things like grenade launchers and tear gas and then form paramilitary police units (PPUs) modeled on special forces in the military. PPUs were originally designed for "reactive deployment of high-risk specialists for particularly dangerous events . . . such as hostage, sniper, or terrorist situations,"[276] but the vast majority of PPU deployments have been for drug raids, in particular "no-knock and quick-knock dynamic entries."[277] Use of PPUs in this way makes the "war on drugs" metaphor into a quite literal battle, and studies show that police paramilitary units are used disproportionately in neighborhoods with greater numbers of Black residents, even when studies control for local crime rates.[278] Militarization

protests-bring-attention-death/story?id=71523476.

274. Adam Gabbatt, "Protests about police brutality are met with wave of police brutality across US," *The Guardian*, June 6, 2020, *theguardian. com/us-news/2020/jun/06/police-violence-protests-us-george-floyd.*

275. Chris Joyner and Nick Thieme, "Police killings more likely in agencies that get military gear, data shows," AJC, October 8, 2020, *ajc.com/ news/police-killings-more-likely-in-agencies-that-get-military-gear-data-shows/MBPQ2ZE3XFHR5NIO37BKONOCGI/.*

276. Peter B. Kraska, "Militarization and Policing—Its Relevance to 21st Century Police," *Policing Advance Access,* December 13, 2007, *cjmasters.eku.edu/sites/cjmasters.eku.edu/files/21stmilitarization.pdf.*

277. Kraska, "Militarization and Policing," 7.

278. Jonathan Mummolo, "Militarization Fails to Enhance Police Safety or Reduce Crime but May Harm Police Reputation," *Proceedings of the National Academy of Sciences* 115, no.37 (Sep 2018): 9181-86; DOI: 10.1073/pnas.1805161115.

encourages a mentality that police officers are an occupying force rather than an agency to protect and serve, and it should come as no surprise that it does not foster good relationships within communities.

A Brief Potential Nonviolent Policy Solution to the Problem of Police Brutality

The three most common solutions suggested for police brutality are reform, defunding, and abolition. Among my teammates at Rehumanize International, we have proponents of each model. Again, whatever method of change you prefer, the most important aspect is that we together acknowledge the problems with the given system and make a substantial effort to shift law and culture with the central goal of upholding the life and dignity of each and every human involved. These solutions do intersect in some ways (for example, one might hold that significant defunding is necessary for reform), but each forms its own path forward for the future.

Those who advocate for reform see the justice system as seriously broken but still fixable. They believe that by requiring police departments to make certain reforms, such as limiting use of force, banning chokeholds, and making body cameras necessary, well-intentioned people with protective instincts and a sacrificial spirit can do police work safely and promote the safety of the community. Many also advocate for community policing, or recruiting candidates from the community being served to ensure police understand the culture of the place and feel like they are a part of it, rather than superior.[279] When com-

---

279. "US: 14 Recommendations for Fundamental Police Reform," Human

munity policing is not possible, cultural sensitivity training can lower the likelihood of police discriminating, consciously or unconsciously, against minorities. Advocates of reform argue that policing is not the problem; rather, the way policing is done is flawed and needs to be restructured so police are held accountable.

Others advocate for defunding the police. Proponents of defunding believe that too much money is spent on the police, resulting in bloated departments that sport military equipment and react excessively. They contend that violent crime is very little of what police deal with. If this is so, they argue, why spend so much money arming police to do what social workers or mental-health professionals could do better and nonviolently?[280] Cutting police budgets significantly would reduce the number of officers, and by extension the amount of police brutality. The money saved could be invested in community support systems. The police can continue to deal with violent crime, but traffic violations, low-level drug charges, and domestic disputes would be dealt with by an appropriate agency. Defunding, then, would be the first step toward large-scale societal changes.

Prison and police abolitionists believe that the police can never recover from their racist and violent roots, and so reform would simply be "[a] kinder, gentler, and more diverse war on the poor."[281] Defunding, abolitionists claim, would fail to address the root of the problem. They see the police system as too broken to be fixed and so should be completely abolished. Abolitionists, then, focus on reconstructing society in creative ways that do not rely on

---

Rights Watch, August 12, 2020, *hrw.org/news/2020/08/12/us-14-recommendations-fundamental-police-reform.*

280. Celeste Little, "What Does American Police Reform Actually Look Like?" *Clever,* August 19, 2020, *architecturaldigest.com/story/police-reform-community-services.*

281. Vitale, *The End of Policing,* 27.

force or police work. They seek to remedy the conditions that drive people to crime or make crime possible. Rather than focusing on punitive measures, abolitionists typically endorse alternative models such as restorative justice, which focus on helping offenders repair the harm they caused through their crime.[282]

Whether you support reform, defunding, or abolition, these core ideas lie at the heart of the problem: policing is not a war, and over-militarization of the police is inappropriate; people having mental health crises deserve appropriate, compassionate care; anyone working in potentially threatening environments should receive training in de-escalation and peaceful intervention; and legal loopholes like qualified immunity are immoral and obstruct authentic justice.

Addressing Common Arguments in Support of Police Brutality

Neighborhood Safety

"We need the police to deal with problems or crime associated with homelessness, mental illness, and drug abuse."

> The state has a responsibility to deal with problems such as homelessness, mental health, and drug abuse, but as they are now constituted, the police have been ineffective at addressing these issues. Instead, police often target vulnerable homeless, mentally ill, and

---

282. "Toolkit on Diversion and Alternatives to Detention," UNICEF, *unicef. org/tdad/index_56040.html*.

addicted people through raids and unnecessary arrests that often result in brutality and violations of human dignity. Currently, police are overworked and under-equipped to deal with these problems; the solution is to divert the responsibilities (and funding) for treatment of homelessness, addiction, and mental health to agencies and individuals who are better equipped to address these crucial issues nonviolently.

"It's smart to racially profile."

It's not smart to be racist, period. Crime statistics make it appear that people of color commit more crime because our local governments over-police communities of color. The Hamilton Project has shared data that "Black and white Americans sell and use drugs at similar rates, but Black Americans are 2.7 times as likely to be arrested for drug-related offenses."[283] It is likely, then, that other illegal activities would have similar statistical results that show a disparity in over-policing between races.

"Don't rob someone (or associate with people you know to be criminals) if you don't wanna be shot."

First, our rights (for those in the US) include a presumption of innocence, so shooting people without just cause is contrary not only to our dignity, but also to our rights. Next, the police are not omniscient and so should not

---

283. "Rates of Drug Use and Sales, by Race; Rates of Drug Related Criminal Justice Measures, by Race." The Hamilton Project, October 21, 2016, *hamiltonproject.org/charts/rates_of_drug_use_and_sales_by_race_rates_of_drug_related_criminal_justice.*

take up the role of judge, jury, and executioner; all those accused and charged with a crime should be allowed a fair trial. And last, it's worth mentioning that many of those who have been shot or brutalized by police have been unarmed or innocent of any crime.[284]

"Back the Blue"

"In light of how dangerous their jobs are, it's reasonable for cops to be on high-alert and follow the strategy that 'the best defense is a good offense.'"

Those who we trust with our lives should have the capacity and the training to handle the pressure and stress of situations involving weapons and people with mental illness or neurodivergence. Many police haven't been able to handle this pressure (as police violence against mentally ill and neurodivergent people has demonstrated time and again[285,286]), then the respon-

284. Though an incomplete assessment of all Americans, an NPR investigation has found that "Since 2015, police officers have fatally shot at least 135 unarmed Black men and women nationwide." See Cheryl W. Thompson, "Fatal Police Shootings Of Unarmed Black People Reveal Troubling Patterns," NPR, January 25, 2021, *npr. org/2021/01/25/956177021/fatal-police-shootings-of-unarmed-black-people-reveal-troubling-patterns*. One of those instances that particularly broke my heart was the story of Tamir Rice, who was just twelve years old when a police officer shot and killed him. See Vanessa Romo, "Justice Department Declines To Prosecute Cleveland Officers In Death Of Tamir Rice," NPR, December 29, 2020, *npr. org/2020/12/29/951277146/justice-department-declines-to-prosecute-cleveland-officers-who-killed-tamir-ric*

285. Jeffrey A. Fagan and Alexis D. Campbell, "Race and Reasonableness in Police Killings," *Columbia Law School Faculty Publications*, 2020, *scholarship.law.columbia.edu/faculty_scholarship/2656*.

286. Doris A. Fuller, H. Richard Lamb, Michael Biasotti, and John Snook, "Overlooked In The Undercounted: The Role of Mental Illness in Fatal Law Enforcement Encounters," Treatment Advocacy Center: Office of

sibility for responding to such incidents should fall to other agencies and individuals who can handle this pressure and who don't carry deadly weapons. Additionally, the doctrine of qualified immunity allows police to do things that otherwise they wouldn't (and shouldn't) be allowed to do, and allows "bad apples" to spoil the bunch. Well-intentioned people who want to serve their communities should stand up and declare that the government (and its agents) shouldn't get a free pass to engage in brutality.

"Police do some good things."

Similar to the answers in prior chapters on organizations that do some good things but also engage in violence (such as abortion, war, or torture), we should not absolve an organization of the harm and violence they do regularly because they do some good things. Instead, we must hold them accountable and try to figure out how to eliminate the violence from the organization or else shut it down completely. Even if there are people in police forces who are good, moral people, and have never participated in or covered up or minimized police brutality, they should be just as adamant in supporting efforts to prevent police brutality and stop systemic abuse of power that can run so rampant in departments all over the world.

Research & Public Affairs, December 2015, *treatmentadvocacycenter. org/storage/documents/overlooked-in-the-undercounted.pdf*

Discussion Questions

1. How much force do you think is necessary to keep the peace?

2. How can the victims of police brutality be remembered? How has your community honored past victims or helped their surviving family? How can we accompany and help the survivors of police brutality?

3. What nonviolent ways can you think of to bring down crime rates?

4. What do you see as the pros of defunding, abolition, or reform? What are the cons?

Further Reading Suggestions

1. Jill Nelson, editor, *Police Brutality: An Anthology* (New York: W. W. Norton & Company, 2001 reprint).

2. Mariame Kaba, *We Do This 'Til We Free Us: Abolitionist Organizing and Transforming Justice* (Chicago: Haymarket Books, 2021).

3. Patrisse Cullors and Asha Bandele, *When They Call You a Terrorist: A Black Lives Matter Memoir* (New York: St. Martin's Press, 2020).

4. Angela Davis, *Are Prisons Obsolete?* (New York: Seven Stories Press, 2003).

5. Howard Zehr, *Changing Lenses: Restorative Justice for Our Times* (Independence, MO: Herald Press, 2015 Twenty-fifth anniversary edition).

m

Torture in the justice system

Perhaps in an effort to deter crime, or maybe out of a retributive desire to inflict pain on those convicted of crime, in many nations (including the United States) prisons and "detention centers" become hotbeds of torture in our own backyards.

What is Torture in the Justice System?

As mentioned in chapter 5, torture is the use of violence for a tactical purpose, such as gaining strategic information, forcing a confession, or meting out punishment, typically empolyed by an authority, such as a public official (including prison personnel). The long, monotonous, and tragic theme of incarcerated people being tortured stretches back millennia. This chapter will focus on such torture not as a consequence of war, but in response to a violation of domestic law, although it will also include forced incarceration of innocents, as in enslavement.[287]

---

287. Though many incarcerated people were prisoners of war, we have separated torture in war into its own chapter (chapter 5), and will discuss torture of enslaved people (even those enslaved after war) here as under carceral torture. Additionally, many forms of capital

The many forms that carceral (or prison) torture has taken throughout history have this in common: those who hold the power of incarceration have inflicted dehumanizing pain and suffering on imprisoned people. This chapter will focus on enslavement, egregious neglect of basic human needs for those in custody, solitary confinement, and life without parole (LWOP) sentences.

Enslavement, also known as forced or coerced work of people under a carceral model, involves extracting labor (for no or little pay) often under the threat of further and more immediately-violent torture; this was the case in antiquity, in the chattel slavery of Black people in the Atlantic slave trade by Western European and American colonizer nations, and even today in the US and Chinese modern models of state-sponsored incarceration.

Unsanitary, unhealthy, neglectful, torturous living conditions are common in many prison or detention facilities around the world. For example, in US Immigration and Customs Enforcement (ICE) facilities, immigrants and refugees are often indefinitely detained, concentrated into tightly-packed camps, with sparse accommodations and neglectful treatment.[288] Not only is the separation of families for extended (if not indefinite) periods of time psychologically cruel in and of itself, but both adults and children are jammed into standing-room-only cages with no beds, chairs, or personal belongings other than their clothes and a metallic space blanket for when they may attempt to sleep.[289]

---

punishment were also meant to be extremely torturous, but the death penalty is substantial enough a topic to merit its own chapter (chapter 8).

288. "ICE Detention Facilities: Failing to Meet Basic Standards of Care," United States House Of Representatives Committee On Homeland Security: Majority Staff Report, September 21, 2020, *splcenter.org/ sites/default/files/ice_detetention_facilities_committee_report_ draft4_0.pdf.*

289. Suzanne Gamboa, "From bad to 'sheer inhumanity': Detention

Solitary confinement (sometimes referred to as "administrative segregation" or "isolation") is the intentional imprisonment of a sole individual within a cell (sometimes as small as a standard elevator). Solitary confinement is the norm in several maximum security prisons around the US, where as recently as 2017, some 61,000 incarcerated men, women, and children were being held in solitary confinement, some for years.[290] Men like Albert Woodfox and several of his Black comrades "on the inside" were tortured like this for decades: Woodfox spent over forty years in solitary confinement.[291] According to various accounts, including Woodfox's, this torture within incarceration often involves limited or no human contact, and confinement to a small space (which includes their toilet) for twenty-three hours a day. Under such conditions prisoners rarely see the sky, and even when they do it may be from solitary cages in an enclosed courtyard. Woodfox also recounts systematic beatings by guards,[292] dehumanizing and unnecessary strip-searches,[293] and liberal use of pepper spray and irritant gas to subdue the prisoners held in solitary.[294]

---

conditions for migrants worse under Trump, advocates say," NBC News, July 2, 2019, nbcnews.com/news/latino/bad-sheer-inhumanity-detention-conditions-migrants-worse-under-trump-advocates-n1025961.

290. Stephanie Wykstra, "The case against solitary confinement," Vox, April 17, 2019, vox.com/future-perfect/2019/4/17/18305109/solitary-confinement-prison-criminal-justice-reform.

291. Albert Woodfox, *Solitary: Unbroken by Four Decades in Solitary Confinement: My Story of Transformation and Hope* (New York: Grove Press, 2019).

292. Woodfox, *Solitary*, 103-105.

293. Woodfox, *Solitary*, 165-167.

294. Woodfox, *Solitary*, 116-119.

To compound this, some solitary confinement is worse than other kinds. In Albert Woodfox's experience, the worst was "the dungeon" or "the hole," designed to "mentally break" prisoners. The only contact with the outside was a food slot and guards would "[turn] off the water in the sink for days at a time, so [prisoners were] forced to drink water from the toilet."[295]

At Angola Prison (perhaps fittingly, or ironically, a former slave plantation in Louisiana), prisoners classified as Level 1 (the "worst of the worst") "had no yard time and fewer possessions. . . [they] had to wear paper gowns so they couldn't hang themselves. . . [some] guards enforced total silence."[296] And those who "acted out" while incarcerated at Level 1 or in the dungeon were "put in four-point restraints, handcuffed to a bed at the ankles and wrists, which forced a prisoner to lie in his own urine and feces."[297]

Solitary confinement seems to have the purpose of "breaking" prisoners via psychological torture. It causes extreme psychological distress in those incarcerated:

> Of 100 randomly selected people held at Pelican Bay, the supermax prison in California, . . . virtually all. . . reported heightened anxiety, irrational anger and irritability, confused thought processes, and being extremely sensitive to external stimuli. Some 70 percent felt themselves to be on the verge of a nervous breakdown, about 40 percent experienced hallucinations, and just under a third reported suicidal thoughts.[298]

---

295. Woodfox, *Solitary*, 168.
296. Woodfox, *Solitary*, 254.
297. Woodfox, *Solitary*, 254.
298. Craig Haney, "Mental Health Issues in Long-Term Solitary and 'Supermax' Confinement," *Crime & Delinquency* 49, no. 1 (January 2003): 124–156, https://doi.org/10.1177/0011128702239239.

Author Paul Singh documented his undercover investigation of medical prison torture in the United States in *Prison Torture in America: Shocking Tales from the Inside.* Singh's book recounts stories of individual prisoners throughout the nation whose medical conditions were overlooked, neglected, and downplayed by prison administrators. Several lived with cancer for years before diagnosis, many had to have limbs amputated due to medical neglect, and treatment of spinal injuries and severe lacerations was deferred.[299] Sometimes, lifesaving medications were intentionally withheld. Other times, mental health was entirely neglected and suicidal ideation allowed to fester. In numerous cases, including in ICE detention facilities, pregnant women have been forced to give birth in chains, or on the floor of their cell, without a physician or midwife; several times their infants were stillborn, miscarried, or perished shortly after birth.[300,301] In related cases, many prisoners have suffered medical torture through forced sterilization by physicians and state officials who embraced eugenic ideas.[302]

---

299. Paul Singh, *Prison Torture in America: Shocking Tales from the Inside* (San Francisco: Science Literacy Books, 2019).

300. Blake Ellis and Melanie Hicken, "Dangerous jail births, miscarriages, and stillborn babies blamed on the same billion dollar company," CNN, May 7, 2019, *cnn.com/2019/05/07/health/jail-births-well-path-ccs-invs/index.html.*

301. Opheli Garcia Lawler, "Nearly 30 Women Have Miscarried While Detained by ICE Since 2017," The Cut, March 4, 2019, *thecut.com/2019/03/nearly-30-women-miscarried-while-detained-by-ice-since-2017.html.*

302. This topic could be expanded upon, but there isn't enough space in this book to cover it all. For further reading, see my blog posts on the subject: "The History of Eugenics Behind U.S. Prison Walls," and "Contemporary Eugenics in U.S. Prisons," along with "Reproductive Injustice: Claims of Coerced Sterilization Under ICE Watch." All can be found on the Rehumanize Blog, from August 22-23, 2018, and September 17, 2020, at *rehumanizeintl.org/post/thehistoryofeugen-*

A more recent topic related to carceral torture is the sentence of "life without parole" (LWOP): under this sentence a convicted person has fewer opportunities for appeal, and will experience a different but longer death penalty—a drawn-out "death by incarceration."[303] Tragically, many people are serving LWOP sentences for crimes committed as juveniles. One of these men, Robert Saleem Holbrook, wrote the following appeal for clemency to the Pennsylvania Parole Board, outlining how a juvenile life without parole (JLWOP) sentence is mentally torturous:

> Just imagine what it is like to be a 35 year old man or woman condemned to die in prison for a terrible decision you made as a child. Imagine being denied the opportunity to demonstrate that the person you are at 35 is not the child you were at 16. . . . A cloud of hopelessness perpetually drifts over the head of a prisoner serving life without parole for a crime he committed or participated in as a child. He is forever condemned to his past despite the accomplishments and maturity he or she has developed as an adult. Only a justice system predicated on vengeance could justify such a sentence that holds children to the same accountability standards as adults.[304]

---

icsbehindusprisonwalls, *rehumanizeintl.org/post/contemporary-eugenics-in-us-prisons*, and *rehumanizeintl.org/post/ice-sterilization*.

303. "Factsheet: Life Without Parole in Pennsylvania," Decarcerate PA, *decarceratepa.info/content/factsheet-life-without-parole-pennsylvania*.

304. Robert Saleem Holbrook, "Statement for Decarcerate PA Action Day, April 5th," *Decarcerate PA Blog, decarceratepa.info/voices/robert-saleem-holbrook-statement-decarcerate-pa-action-day-april-5th-cjc*.

Just as having death by capital punishment hanging over one's head can constitute psychological torture,[305,306] prisoners (both current and former) like Holbrook attest that the constant barrage of thoughts such as "I will die here" and "There is no amount of personal betterment I can do to regain freedom" that LWOP sentences produce also constitute a form of psychological torture, again disproportionately impacting people of color. In 2014, even Pope Francis stated that maximum security prisons (like those described above) constitute torture, and that "life imprisonment is a hidden death penalty."[307]

These methods of psychological and physical violence within the carceral system constitute torture; regrettably, even though standards of law and culture have generally improved over the millennia, in the modern context torture of prisoners is still common.

A Brief Ethical Analysis of Torture in the Justice System

Whether perpetrated in a carceral setting through enslavement, solitary confinement, beatings, rape, medical neglect, LWOP, or any other method, torture disregards the dignity of those who are imprisoned; as such, it is contrary to the Consistent Life Ethic and must be ended. Torture

---

305. "The Death Penalty is a Human Rights Violation," The Center for Constitutional Rights, *ccrjustice.org/files/CCR%20Death%20Penalty%20Factsheet.pdf*.

306. The death penalty itself, I would argue, is also a form of carceral torture. However, it's a big enough topic to merit its own chapter.

307. Religion News Service, "Pope Francis: Life sentences are 'a hidden death penalty,'" *Crux*, October 13, 2014, *cruxnow.com/life/2014/10/pope-francis-blasts-supermax-prisons-as-torture/*.

does not keep society safe, and gravely harms the incarcerated. Behind prison bars, torture represents a desire for retribution or dehumanization. Like the death penalty, it reflects a society that, instead of offering those who have committed crimes some hope, rehabilitation, restoration, and a future, prefers to forget criminals completely, writing them off as "a lost cause."

History of Policy and Culture Around Torture in the Justice System

Some of the earliest documentation of torture includes artistic renderings in Assyrian, Mesopotamian, and Egyptian monuments,[308,309] while written laws such as the Code of Ur-Nammu (from c. 2100–2050 BCE) include references to a torturous "trial by ordeal."[310] And though documentation is sparser in other regions, there are ancient and medieval references to torture (sometimes as death penalty, sometimes in interrogation) from all corners of the world.

Until the early medieval era in Europe, crimes were often seen as interpersonal, so the state typically did not impose a formal trial by ordeal. During the medieval era, however, crimes began to be framed as contrary to "the King's peace" or the truth of the Church, so from the end of the twelfth century through the Inquisition the state or the Church ran judicial processes.[311] Torture, including

---

308. "Flaying of rebels," artist unknown, unknown date BCE, *commons.wikimedia.org/wiki/File:Flaying_of_rebels.jpg*.

309. "History of Torture," Museum of Torture, *tortureum.com/history-of-torture/*.

310. S. N. Kramer, "Ur-Nammu Law Code," *Orientalia* 23, no. 1 (1954): 48, *jstor.org/stable/43073169*.

311. It must be mentioned here that this conception of justice as "contrary to the King's peace" created a psychological distance between

use of "the rack" was meant to stamp out heresy or force confessions of wrongdoing.[312]

During the era of European colonialism in India, Asia, and the Americas torture was seen as standard and even necessary. The English Bill of Rights of 1689 laid out several rights of subjects of the Crown, including that "excessive bail ought not to be required, nor excessive fines imposed, nor cruel and unusual punishments inflicted,"[313] but not all colonized regions embraced these standards, and even among them, several groups were considered outside the purview of "the Crown" (e.g., enslaved people and Indigenous people), and were therefore excluded from consideration under such statutes. Enslaved people were regularly raped, whipped, beaten, trafficked away from their children or parents, starved, or treated as subhuman animals.[314]

Though the Thirteenth Amendment to the US Constitution technically freed enslaved people, that amendment still allowed slavery "as a punishment for crime whereof the party shall have been duly convicted."[315] This provision within the Thirteenth Amendment essentially created the backbone of the racist carceral leviathan that

---

the torturer (as a representative of the state) and the accused subject to torture. This emotional separation severely reduces any opportunity for interpersonal, community-based restorative justice and increases the likelihood of a vengeful, retributive justice in its place.

312. A. Lawrence Lowell, "The Judicial Use of Torture. Part I," *Harvard Law Review* 11, no. 4 (November 25, 1897): 223-224, *jstor.org/stable/pdf/1321315.pdf*.

313. "Bill of Rights 1688 [1689]," UK Parliament, 1688-1689, *legislation.gov.uk/aep/WillandMarSess2/1/2#commentary-c2144673*.

314. Dorothy Roberts, *Killing the Black Body: Race, Reproduction, and the Meaning of Liberty* (New York: Vintage Books, 1997, 2016 reprinting).

315. U.S. Constitution, Thirteenth Amendment. The whole text of the amendment states: "Neither slavery nor involuntary servitude, except as a punishment for crime whereof the party shall have been duly convicted, shall exist within the United States, or any place subject to their jurisdiction."

would dominate the US justice system from convict leasing during the 1870s all the way to prison slave labor today.[316]

Today, the United States has the highest per capita rate of incarceration in the world: 698 per 100,000, a total of 2.3 million people, imprisoned in the "Land of the Free,"[317] a number that does not include immigrants and refugees currently held in ICE detention facilities. The Clinton-era Illegal Immigration Reform and Immigrant Responsibility Act (IIRIRA),[318] followed by Bush's creation of the Department of Homeland Security and its Immigration and Customs Enforcement (ICE) division in 2003, created the legal backdrop for systematic dehumanizing incarceration of immigrants.

Incarceration is big business in the United States, both within private and public prisons and their probationary arms, whose combined total budgets come to over $80.7 billion annually.[319] Despite such huge sums alloted for prisons, prisoners are often made to work for little (if any) pay, basically functioning as slaves. According to the Prison Policy Initiative's most recent data, "The average of the minimum daily wages paid to incarcerated workers [in the US] for non-industry prison jobs is now 86 cents. . . [and the] average maximum daily wage for the same prison jobs [is]. . . $3.45 today."[320] Incarcerated people work for mere pennies an hour in prison facilities support roles like jani-

---

316. Ava Duvernay and Jason Moran, 13TH, USA, 2016.
317. Wendy Sawyer and Peter Wagner, "Mass Incarceration: The Whole Pie 2020," Prison Policy Initiative, March 24, 2020, *prisonpolicy.org/reports/pie2020.html*.
318. Dickerson, *Inside America's Concentration Camps*, 242.
319. Peter Wagner and Bernadette Rabuy, "Following the Money of Mass Incarceration," Prison Policy Initiative, January 25, 2017, *prisonpolicy.org/reports/money.html*.
320. Wendy Sawyer, "How much do incarcerated people earn in each state?," Prison Policy Initiative, April 10, 2017, *prisonpolicy.org/blog/2017/04/10/wages/*.

tors and cooks, in agricultural fields, or even in industrial factories for government facilities or the US military.[321,322] And up until passage of a new law in 2020,[323] prisoner-firefighters in California who were regularly risking their lives were paid less than $2 per day, and were often still restricted from becoming civilian firefighters upon their release.[324] However, there is currently a movement to abolish slavery in the Constitution by removing the "punishment clause" from the Thirteenth Amendment.[325]

Despite the fact that solitary confinement is prohibited by the Geneva Conventions, it is still ubiquitous in Supermax prisons worldwide, and is also used as punishment or "for safety" in penitentiaries and in facilities like ICE detention centers for immigrants and refugees. Despite the United Nations' statement in October of 2011 against solitary confinement, prisoners like Kalief Browder continue to be held in these torturous conditions.[326] The UN's declaration reads:

---

321. Whitney Benns, "American Slavery, Reinvented," *The Atlantic*, September 21, 2015, *theatlantic.com/business/archive/2015/09/prison-labor-in-america/406177/*.
322. "The Uncounted Workforce," NPR, June 29, 2020, *npr.org/transcripts/884989263*.
323. Vanessa Romo, "California Bill Clears Path For Ex-Inmates To Become Firefighters," NPR, September 11, 2020, *npr.org/2020/09/11/912193742/california-bill-clears-path-for-ex-inmates-to-become-firefighters*.
324. Eric Boehm, "As Prisoners, They Can Help Fight California's Huge Wildfires. As Free People, They're Banned From Being Firefighters," *Reason*, August 9, 2018, *reason.com/2018/08/09/inmates-are-helping-fight-californias-ma/*.
325. Brakkton Booker, "Democrats Push 'Abolition Amendment' To Fully Erase Slavery From U.S. Constitution," NPR, December 3, 2020, *npr.org/2020/12/03/942413221/democrats-push-abolition-amendment-to-fully-erase-slavery-from-u-s-constitution*.
326. Perhaps the most famous recent story of grievous psychological harm that resulted from a prisoner being held in solitary confinement is that of Kalief Browder. Browder was a sixteen-year-old ac-

A United Nations expert on torture today called on all countries to ban the solitary confinement of prisoners except in very exceptional circumstances and for as short a time as possible, with an absolute prohibition in the case of juveniles and people with mental disabilities.

"Segregation, isolation, separation, cellular, lockdown, Supermax, the hole, Secure Housing Unit (SHU)... whatever the name, solitary confinement should be banned by States as a punishment or extortion technique," UN Special Rapporteur on torture Juan E. Mendez told the General Assembly's third committee, which deals with social, humanitarian and cultural affairs, saying the practice could amount to torture.[327]

Though the statement doesn't prohibit solitary confinement outright, it places much stricter guidelines on when and how the practice should be used.

Nevertheless, the international community has not univocally condemned torturous life sentences: sixty-five nations impose LWOP.[328] In the US, the prevalence of LWOP sentences varies by state, and prior to 1972, only seven

---

cused of stealing a backpack who ended up being held pre-trial for three years at Rikers Island in New York City, two of which were spent in solitary. Both during his time in solitary and after his release he claimed to be suffering from intense paranoia and anxiety, and he attempted suicide several times, eventually dying by suicide at just twenty-two years old. See Jennifer Gonnerman, "Kalief Browder: 1993-2015," *The New Yorker*, June 7, 2015, newyorker.com/news/news-desk/kalief-browder-1993-2015.

327. "Solitary confinement should be banned in most cases, UN expert says," United Nations News, October 2011, *news.un.org/en/story/2011/10/392012-solitary-confinement-should-be-banned-most-cases-un-expert-says*.

328. "Life Imprisonment: Key Facts," Penal Reform International, penalreform.org/issues/life-imprisonment/key-facts/.

states had LWOP laws.[329] At and prior to that time, even prisoners with "life" sentences were often referred to their state parole board after ten to fifteen years, if they had a history of "good behavior." But in the "tough on crime" decades since, many states rushed to enact life without parole sentences. In the eighteen years after *Furman*, twenty-six states passed laws enforcing LWOP, and since 1991, seventeen more states added LWOP to their sentencing guidelines.[330] Today, approximately 160,000 people in the US are being held on LWOP,[331] of the roughly 479,000 people incarcerated on that sentence worldwide.[332]

Perhaps most disturbing about LWOP sentences is the number of people who committed crimes as children (under age eighteen) who were sentenced to life without parole (Juvenile LWOP, or JLWOP). In 2005, SCOTUS ruled that juveniles could not be sentenced to capital punishment,[333] but many were still held on LWOP sentences. In *Graham v. Florida*, heard in 2010, SCOTUS declared that non-homicide offenses do not warrant the most severe punishment available, so JLWOP was taken off the table for all juvenile crimes except for killing.[334] In the years since, twenty-five US states have enacted state-level legislation to prohibit the sentence of JLWOP for all crimes committed by juve-

---

329. The year 1972 is relevant because the Supreme Court ruling in *Furman v. Georgia* outlawed the death penalty nationwide, so many states looked for more "permanent" solutions to the "question" of murderers and others guilty of capital-level crimes. See Ashley Nellis, "Life Goes On: The Historic Rise In Life Sentences In America," The Sentencing Project, September 2013, *sentencingproject.org/wp-content/uploads/2015/12/Life-Goes-On.pdf*.
330. Nellis, "Life Goes On," 3.
331. Nellis, "Life Goes On," 1.
332. "Life Imprisonment: Key Facts," Penal Reform International.
333. *Roper v. Simmons*, 543 U.S. 551 (2005).
334. *Graham v. Florida*, 130 S.Ct. 2011 (2010).

niles, while the others still allow JLWOP.[335] Today, there are about 1,500 people around the country serving JLWOP sentences for crimes they committed as juveniles, constantly tortured by a lack of any discernible future or room to return to community.[336]

A Brief Potential Nonviolent Policy Solution to Carceral Torture

As I mentioned in chapter 5, "Military Torture," torture— an act of aggressive violence—is contrary to our shared inherent human dignity and should be abolished. In the US, torture is generally regulated by individual states in management of their prison systems, so the most of our focus in organizing to end carceral torture should be on a state level. This process will take a lot of education on torture and the rehumanization of prisoners by sharing their stories and fostering relationships that can build authentically restorative justice systems that respect and uphold their dignity.

One option is promoting legislation to limit or prohibit the use of solitary as stated in the UN standards promulgated in 2011, as well as laws and standards that would prohibit beatings and excessive strip-searches by prison guards. Other important legislation could outlaw JLWOP, and mandatory LWOP sentences. One other vital piece of law and advocacy is the protection of prisoners' rights to medical treatment, along with informed consent to all medical pro-

335. Josh Rovner, "Juvenile Life Without Parole: An Overview," The Sentencing Project, May 24, 2021, 3-4, *sentencingproject.org/publications/juvenile-life-without-parole/*.

336. Rovner, "Juvenile Life Without Parole," 1.

cedures and banning any coerced sterilization practices, particularly those used to reduce prison sentences.

And finally, it's worth mentioning that we can rehumanize those being held behind bars by "visiting the imprisoned": become pen pals with one (or more) incarcerated people, stop by in person, or do fundraisers for grassroots and legal organizations that help to restore dignity to prisoners.

Addressing Common Arguments in Support of Carceral Torture

Safety

"Corrections officers have been killed or harmed in the line of duty; they need the authority to prevent that kind of thing in the future (using whatever means are considered justified)."

It is true that many corrections officers—even well-intentioned ones—have been harmed in the course of their work. As it is, prisons function as a "crime university," removing many positive influences from the lives of those "on the inside" and promoting violent systems through prison politics. Therefore, corrections officers would be safer if we focused on rehabilitation and decarceration, and not on continuing the cycle of traumatization of prisoners. Regardless, we may not do evil that good may come of it, so torturing prisoners is not an acceptable course of action, even in the attempt to prevent future harm.

179

"Solitary confinement is necessary to keep the general prison population (or vulnerable individuals, like trans people) safe."

Solitary confinement is almost always used as a form of punishment, not as a form of isolation for prison safety. In the case of confining a "dangerous" prisoner away from the general population, this reason is often exaggerated and overused. Rarely are there people who are so dangerous that they cannot have a roommate, and even among those for whom it would be better if they remained alone, confinement need not be as dehumanizing and isolating as much of it is. In the rare cases of confining a vulnerable individual (like a trans person incarcerated with solely opposite-gender prisoners), there are better, more humane ways to protect that person. In general, solitary confinement should follow the principles handed down by the UN in 2011, which are listed above in the section on "History of Policy and Culture around Torture in the Justice System."

"Incarceration should be so terrible that people won't want to commit crimes."

People who use this argument want penalties to deter crime. However, materials from the US Department of Justice clarify that sending an individual to prison and increasing the severity of a punishment don't really deter crime.[337]

---

337. "Five Things About Deterrence," National Institute of Justice, May 2016, *ojp.gov/pdffiles1/nij/247350.pdf.*

(In relation to ICE detention): "It's necessary to separate children (for a long time) from the adult who brought them to the country because of the possibility of human trafficking."

Instead of building and policing a superfluous and rather ineffective border wall, our government could hire more people who are dedicated to background checks and helping refugee and immigrant families get settled in the United States. Additionally, extended family members such as aunts and uncles could be allowed to claim guardianship over minors traveling with them. This would help expedite the immigration process, reduce the amount of time that any individual was in any form of custody, and reduce the need for foster or group homes for these children, where they are at increased risk for domestic trafficking.[338]

(In relation to ICE detention): "Drugs, guns, and cartels are entering at the southern border."

First, the US government should stop violence-based foreign interventionism, which has often supplied military-grade weapons to other nations, amping up the drug war and regime change.[339] Ironically, dealing with

---

338. A study from New York state showed that at least 85 percent of children who had been trafficked for sex during a few months in 2006 had prior contact with the child welfare system; of those in upstate New York, 49 percent had been in a foster care placement; while of those from the New York City region, 75 percent had been in a foster home. See F. Gragg, et al, "New York prevalence study of commercially sexually exploited children," New York State Office of Children and Family Services, 2007, *blog.timesunion.com/capitol/ files/2007/04/Final%20Report%20NY%20CSEC%204-18-07.pdf*.

339. Kenneth N. Hansen and Robin L. Hoover, "Constructivism, Human Rights and the Mexican War on Drugs," under peer review at *Journal*

the consumption of illegal drugs might help, considering that the United States is historically the number one consumer of the drugs trafficked in by the violent cartels.[340] Second, customs enforcement ought to ensure that illegal and dangerous drugs are not entering the country. Additionally, the government can stop indefinite detention for immigrants by increasing staffing for background checks and expediting the legal immigration process. Such systems of background checks could prevent cartel members from entering the US.

Punishment And Moral Desert

"They're already in prison, so when there's bad behavior in prison, you need to 'up the ante' and increase the punishment."

Such thinking is used to justify any form of dehumanization and abuse against prisoners. The primary goal of prison should not be retribution and punishment, but rehabilitating and restoring to community those who have harmed that bond of community.

"Rapists deserve to be raped in prison."

Rape is bad and is violence, and it is terrible that it happens. We shouldn't wish harm or violence on anyone—even those who have done harm in the past. Also,

---

of *Borderland Studies*, img1.wsimg.com/blobby/go/e7d14fc5-46be-4910-a723-5e0e608c41a3/downloads/1cdv5bdrl_575708.doc; also Alfredo Carlos, "Mexico 'Under Siege': Drug Cartels or U.S. Imperialism?", *Latin American Perspectives* 41, no. 2 (2014): 43–59, jstor.org/stable/24575497.

340. Carlos, "Mexico 'Under Siege,'" 55.

the justice system sometimes imprisons the innocent, and wishing rape on someone wrongly convicted is a brutal iniquity. Again, the goal of prison should not be retribution and punishment, but restoration and healing of community. Rape does not serve the end of restoration or healing.

(In relation to children in ICE detention): "Their parents shouldn't have brought them here."

People leave their home nations for many reasons. The fact that they knew of the immigration detention situation in the United States and still came demonstrates how terrible their circumstances must have been. They deserve a safe place to live, and considering how many of the circumstances in their home nations are a product of US intervention, they deserve asylum status. Lastly, regardless of their guardians' motivations, the children kept in ICE detention cages likely had no choice in crossing the border. They shouldn't be punished for whatever crimes their parents may have committed. It's worth noting, however, that no one can ask for asylum status from the US without first being on US soil; many people attempting to cross the southern border are following the legal requirements for refugees and are not breaking the law.[341]

---

341. According to the American Immigration Council, "Asylum seekers who arrive at a U.S. port of entry or enter the United States without inspection generally must apply through the defensive asylum process. *Both application processes require the asylum seeker to be physically present in the United States.*" (emphasis added) See "Asylum in the United States Fact Sheet," American Immigration Council, June 2020, *americanimmigrationcouncil.org/sites/default/files/research/asylum_in_the_united_states.pdf*.

Economics

"It's a waste of taxpayer money to give people in prison 'good' things (e.g. TV, recreation, outside time, healthy food, books, restoration programs, etc.)."

> Several factors contribute to the high cost of prisons in the US, including mandatory minimums, LWOP sentences, death sentences (and the associated appeals process), and the inflated cost of basic necessities.[342] The high cost of US recidivism is largely due to the way prisons are structured as "crime universities," inculturating those behind bars into more and more contact with crime. Prisons with more humane apartment-style housing and rehabilitative-type programming (e.g. recreation, outside time, libraries, college or trade courses, restoration and counseling programs) are more likely to produce restorative outcomes with less recidivism and therefore less long-term cost to the taxpayer.[343]

"I'm paying for their housing; what do they need (living) wages for?"

> The cost of being in prison is extremely high. Within the prison economy, everything from sending an email to receiving a video call to getting tampons or extra food all have inflated prices. Not to mention that paying someone a living wage is basic economic justice: paying pennies an hour is akin to slavery, which is a form of violence and dehumanization.

---

342. "Economics of Incarceration," Prison Policy Initiative, *prisonpolicy. org/research/economics_of_incarceration/*.

343. "Introductory Handbook on The Prevention of Recidivism and the Social Reintegration of Offenders," United Nations Office on Drugs and Crime, 2018, *unodc.org/documents/justice-and-prison-reform/18-02303_ebook.pdf*.

Discussion Questions

1. Why do you think it's so easy for our society to forget about incarcerated people? How does the structure of our lives and our society contribute to neglecting those behind bars?

2. Which method of torture in the justice system mentioned in this chapter surprises you the most? Which are you most motivated to end?

3. Who do you know (or know of) who has been incarcerated? If you don't know someone personally, look up a story of someone who has been. How does hearing a first-hand account of incarceration (and the torture that person may have endured there) move you?

Further Reading Suggestions

1. Paul Singh, *Prison Torture in America: Shocking Tales from the Inside* (Menlo Park, CA: Science Literacy Books, 2019).

2. Ruth Delaney, Ram Subramanian, Alison Shames, and Nicholas Turner, "Reimagining Prison," Vera Institute of Justice, 2018, vera.org/reimagining-prison-web-report/american-history-race-and-prison.

3. Ashley Nellis, "Life Goes On: The Historic Rise in Life Sentences in America," The Sentencing Project, 2013, sentencingproject.org/wp-content/uploads/2015/12/Life-Goes-On.pdf

4. Joshua N. Aston, *Torture Behind Bars: Role of the Police Force in India* (Oxford, UK: Oxford University Press, 2020).

5. Albert Woodfox, *Solitary* (New York: Grove Press, 2019 reprint).

Chapter 8

The death penalty

The justice system's final and permanent response to crime is capital punishment: the death penalty. This form of violence persists because of a perception that it guarantees "justice" and "safety," but each and every human being, even those who are guilty of terrible crimes, has inherent dignity that must be upheld.

What is the Death Penalty?

A retributive justice system has many different "levels" of response to crime. Those convicted of misdemeanors might be given community service or probation, but those convicted of felonies are incarcerated. Only those convicted of the most heinous, or capital, crimes—which may include murder, aggravated rape, mass murder, terrorism, and sometimes treason[344]—are punished with the death penalty. Down through the ages, this irreversible form of state-sanctioned violence has been carried out via beheading,[345]stoning, poisoning, crucifixion, drowning,

---

344. Leonard D. Savitz, "Capital Crimes As Defined in American Statutory Law," *Journal of Criminal Law and Criminology* 46, no. 3 (1955).

345. The origin of the term "capital crime" is from the Latin word "capi-

drawing and quartering, burning at the stake, hanging, firing squad, gas chamber, electrocution, or lethal injection. Though more than 70 percent of nations have ended capital punishment in law or in practice,[346] in 2020 483 executions were recorded in eighteen countries.[347] According to Amnesty International, the most executions took place in "China, Iran, Egypt, Iraq and Saudi Arabia – in that order." Nearly all European nations have abolished the practice completely, and in the Americas only the United States executed any prisoners in 2020.

In 2021, thirty-one states in the US still authorized the most common form of capital punishment, lethal injection. It has been used to kill 1,354 death row inmates since 1976, when a Supreme Court decision allowed states to resume executions if proper legal procedures were followed.[348] Many states used a three-drug protocol involving an anesthetic such as sodium thiopental first, followed by Pavulon to cause muscle paralysis and respiratory arrest, combined with potassium chloride to stop the heart and ensure death.[349,350] Several states have adopted a one-drug

tal" meaning, "relating to the head (or top)," referring to the fact that these crimes were punishable by death (beheadings). See "Capital," *Lexico Oxford English Dictionary* online, lexico.com/en/definition/capital; and "Capital," Etymology Online Dictionary, etymonline.com/word/capital.

346. "International," Death Penalty Information Center, *deathpenaltyinfo.org/policy-issues/international*.

347. Amnesty International, "Death penalty in 2020: Facts and figures," *Amnesty International News*, April 21, 2021, amnesty.org/en/latest/news/2021/04/death-penalty-in-2020-facts-and-figures/.

348. "Methods of Execution," Death Penalty Information Center, *deathpenaltyinfo.org/executions/methods-of-execution*.

349. Amnesty International, "Lethal injections lead doctors to break medical oath," *Amnesty International News*, October 4, 2007, Accessed from archive, *web.archive.org/web/20140423183309/http://www.amnesty.org/en/news-and-updates/news/Lethal-injections-lead-doctors-to-break-medical-oath-041007*.

350. In another case of issues within the CLE being linked, potassium

protocol, a lethal dose of the anesthetic sodium thiopental, injected intramuscularly.[351] Even though the process is supposed to be painless and quick, the lungs of most people killed by lethal injection were heavier at the time of autopsy, with fluid in the lungs and foam in the airways, indicating that the inmates had died of "pulmonary edema, which can induce the feeling of suffocation or drowning."[352] Fearing moral backlash and so losing their execution drugs, many states have kept their lethal injection procedure secret, which may have ultimately precipitated the 2014 botched executions of Clatyon Lockett in Oklahoma and Joseph Wood in Arizona.[353]

---

chloride (KCl) has also been commonly used in second-and-third trimester abortions to induce heart attacks by lethal injection into the tiny fetuses while still in the womb. See N.B. Isada et al, "Fetal intracardiac potassium chloride injection to avoid the hopeless resuscitation of an abnormal abortus: I. Clinical issues," *Obstetrics and Gynecology* 80 no. 2 (1992): 296-99. See also Anna K. Sfakianaki et al, "Potassium Chloride–Induced Fetal Demise: A Retrospective Cohort Study of Efficacy and Safety," *Journal of Ultrasound in Medicine* 33, no. 2 (February 2014): 337-341.

351. Some criminal justice scholars propose that this shift toward the one-drug protocol came about because of the 2009 failed execution of Romell Broom in Ohio where a suitable vein for the three-drug intravenous (IV) protocol could not be located. See Megan McCracken and Jen Moreno, "Comments on the proposed 'Death Penalty Procedures,'" University of California, Berkeley: School of Law – Death Penalty Clinic, January 29, 2010, accessed via archive, *web.archive.org/web/20110814192348/http://www.law.berkeley.edu/files/Kentuckynews.pdf*.

352. Noah Caldwell, Ailsa Chang, and Jolie Myers, "Gasping For Air: Autopsies Reveal Troubling Effects Of Lethal Injection," NPR, September 21, 2020, npr.org/2020/09/21/793177589/gasping-for-air-autopsies-reveal-troubling-effects-of-lethal-injection.

353. Elliott Hannon, "Arizona Man Gasps and Snorts During Lethal Injection Execution That Took Nearly Two Hours," *Slate*, July 23, 2014, *slate.com/news-and-politics/2014/07/botched-lethal-injection-of-joseph-wood-takes-two-hours.html*.

Partly due to the reluctance of pharmaceutical companies to provide the aforementioned drugs, some states now use pentobarbital (a barbituate, like the drugs used in euthanasia) or fentanyl (a drug responsible for countless overdoses in the US) to execute people.[354] And because of pushback from the medical community, some states are reverting to archaic forms of judicial killing.[355]

Those older methods of execution insinuate retributive cruelty as part and parcel of justice. Electrocution, usually by electric chair, is the next most common form of execution; it is authorized in eight states and has been used to kill 163 people on death row since 1977. In an interview on her experiences as a death row chaplain, Sister Helen Prejean detailed the cruelty of the electric chair:

> They put a cloth soaked with saline solution on his shaved head and then the metal cap. A thick, curled wire runs from the cap to the generator. And then the straps go across his chest. . . . This huge, rushing, powerful, grinding sound of the fire being shot through his body. Three times. They run 1,900 volts, then let the body cool, and then 500 volts, and then 1,900 volts again. What's terrifying is that they've done autopsies of people who have been electrocuted, and the brain is mainly intact. We don't know what they feel. We really don't know, when we kill a human being, what's going on inside, the pain of it.[356]

---

354. "Overview of Lethal Injection Protocols," Death Penalty Information Center, *deathpenaltyinfo.org/executions/lethal-injection/overview-of-lethal-injection-protocols*.

355. Rose Rimler, "Will Pharmaceutical Companies Kill the Death Penalty?" *healthline*, October 16, 2019, *healthline.com/health-news/will-pharmaceutical-companies-kill-death-penalty*.

356. David Cook, "And Justice For All: Sister Helen Prejean On Why The Death Penalty Is Wrong," *The Sun*, Aug. 2010, *thesunmagazine.org/*

Other older methods of execution include lethal gas (such as cyanide or nitrogen), hanging, and firing squad.[357] Lethal gas is still legal in seven states and has been used to kill eleven people convicted of capital crimes. Hanging (legal in one state) and firing squad (authorized in four states) have been used to execute three people each since executions resumed in 1977.[358] Ultimately though, no matter the method all have a single purpose: to kill convicted persons as punishment for their crimes.

A Brief Ethical Analysis of the Death Penalty

Historically, the death penalty has been justified in terms of societal safety or retribution. In his discussion of capital punishment Thomas Aquinas, for example, described murderers as having entered the "state of the beasts," and so "fall[ing] away from the dignity of [humanity]." Therefore, in his analysis, killing by the state should be permitted.[359] Here I must push back against Aquinas, because even though I agree with him that "it be evil in itself to kill a man so long as he preserve his dignity," I definitely disagree that it is possible to lose our human dignity: I posit that our dignity flows from our human nature, our essence as rational beings, which we retain *even if* we make poor choices. We have our inherent human dignity simply because we

---

issues/416/and-justice-for-all.

357. For descriptions of these and other methods used in the death penalty, See "Description of Each Execution Method," Death Penalty Information Center, *deathpenaltyinfo.org/executions/methods-of-execution/description-of-each-method*.

358. "International and American Methods of Execution," Britannica Pro-Con.org, updated August 25, 2021, *deathpenalty.procon.org/international-and-american-methods-of-execution/*.

359. Thomas Aquinas, *Summa Theologica*, II-II, q. 64, a. 2, ad 3

are living human beings. Anyone who would dehumanize and treat humans as subhuman animals in the pursuit of justice is mistaken, because murderers, no matter what bad decisions they may have made or how grotesque their actions, are still human beings, creatures with a rational nature. This unchangeable humanity, not the actions of the human being, is what demands respect. Death row inmates are not monsters or beasts; they are still human.

Additionally, the ethical calculus should consider that the death penalty poses a threat to innocents, because humans are fallible and make mistakes. The state killing even one innocent person is too many. The state should not have such power. Fundamentally, however, the death penalty should be abolished because it violates the inherent dignity of human beings. The right to life is inalienable. All human beings deserve that right by virtue of their humanity, which is intrinsic and unchanging. No extrinsic quality, such as guilt, can revoke that right.

History of Policy and Culture around the Death Penalty

Judicial executions have existed from the dawn of human civilization, in every corner of the world. Ancient texts such as the Codes of Ur-Nammu and Hammurabi, and the Twelve Tables and the Justinian Code include references to the death penalty. Perhaps the most famous of these, the Code of Hammurabi, promulgated around 1750 BCE, prescribes execution for more than twenty-four criminal offenses.[360] This and similar ancient laws had

---

360. John D. Bessler, *The Death Penalty as Torture: From the Dark Ages to Abolition* (Durham NC: Carolina Academic Press, 2017), 3.

lex talionis—the law of retaliation—at the center of their understanding of justice: The offender should receive wrong had been done to the victim. This is where we get the common phrase, "an eye for an eye, a tooth for a tooth."

Since ancient times, many nations have held that those who committed crimes (especially violent crimes) deserved to "be punished in the most horrible of ways."[361] But not only was murder punished: crimes as widely varied as witchcraft, heresy, bigamy, sodomy, and theft have also historically been punished with execution. Peoples as diverse as the Chinese, the Inca, the Swedish, the Romans, the English, the Hawai'ians, East Africans, and many others all had some form of death penalty. The goal of the death penalty has historically been to deter potential criminals by making a show of the executions and making an example of the executed criminal.

In many nations the death penalty has been abolished, recognizing the inherent dignity of even the most hardened criminals. According to Amnesty International's most recent figures, there are:

- One hundred six countries where use of the death penalty is not allowed by law,

- Eight countries which permit the death penalty only for serious crimes in exceptional circumstances, such as those committed during times of war,

- Twenty-eight countries which have death penalty laws but haven't executed anyone for at least ten years, and have a policy or more formal commitment not to execute,

---

361. Timothy Brook, Jerome Bourgon, and Gregory Blue, *Death by a Thousand Cuts* (Cambridge, MA: Harvard University Press, 2008), 10.

- Fifty-six countries which retain death penalty laws and either carry out executions or have authorities who have not made an official declaration not to execute.[362]

In the United States, however, it has remained legal since colonial times until today, and over sixteen thousand people have been killed by the death penalty there.[363] Various colonial laws and then eventually state laws have dictated the legality of the practice on a state-by-state basis, with the adoption of the Constitution and the Bill of Rights only affirming the option for the practice. In what follows, I focus on my home nation because it is one of only two "developed" nations to still have and regularly use executions as a form of criminal justice.[364]

In June of 1972, in *Furman v. Georgia*, the United States Supreme Court overturned death sentences that were imposed under unacceptable procedures that rendered the penalty "cruel and unusual."[365] However, the five justices of the majority opinion could not agree on what made the death penalty cruel and unusual: Justices Brennan and Marshall considered capital punishment in and of itself to be cruel and unusual, and so unconstitutional; but the other three used other reasons including "racially discriminatory," "wanton and freakish," and "infrequently used, so, pointless."[366] The *Furman* decision led to death rows around the nation being emptied, as every state-level capital pun-

---

362. Reality Check team, "Death penalty: How many countries still have it?," BBC News, December 11, 2020, bbc.com/news/world-45835584.
363. Frank R. Baumgartner et al, *Deadly Justice: A Statistical Portrait of the Death Penalty* (New York: Oxford University Press, 2018), 1.
364. WION web team, "Japan hangs 3, defends 'capital punishment', calls it necessary for 'atrocious crimes'," WIO News, updated December 22, 2021, *wionews.com/world/japan-hangs-3-defends-capital-punishment-calls-it-necessary-for-atrocious-crimes-438987*
365. *Furman v. Georgia*, 408 US. 238. 1972.
366. *Furman v. Georgia*.

ishment law was deemed invalid and those under the death penalty were transitioned to life sentences, including some becoming eligibile for parole.[367]

The new standard was based on a "Four-Pronged Test" established by Justice Brennan:

> [A] punishment must not be so severe as to be degrading to the dignity of human beings. . . . [The state] must not arbitrarily inflict a severe punishment. . . . [The] severe punishment must not be unacceptable to contemporary society. . . . [And a] severe punishment must not be excessive. A punishment is excessive under the principle if it is unnecessary: the infliction of a severe punishment by the State cannot comport with human dignity when it is nothing more than the pointless infliction of suffering. If there is a significantly less severe punishment adequate to achieve the purposes for which the punishment is inflicted, the punishment inflicted is unnecessary, and therefore excessive.[368]

Following *Furman*, a 1973 bill that attempted to meet the Four-Pronged Test went to the Supreme Court in the case of *Gregg v. Georgia*. In the 1976 ruling, the majority opinion permitted the death penalty under Georgia's new standard and affirmed the condemnation of the convicted, Troy Gregg. The Court emphasized arguments that the death penalty deters crime. However, on the same day the justices handed down *Gregg*, they also handed down several "partner" rulings, two of which (*Woodson v. North Carolina* and *Roberts v. Louisiana*) included rejection of mandatory death sentences because mandatory sentences failed to consider the circumstances and selfhood of the convicted individual. Instead the Court held that the death penalty

---

367. Baumgartner et al, *Deadly Justice*, 1.
368. *Furman v. Georgia*.

should use a "narrow targeting" framework meant to use capital punishment only for "the worst of the worst."[369]

However, since the *Furman* decision in 1972, over 180 US death row inmates have been exonerated.[370] And, horrifically, an estimated 4 percent of all those on death row are innocent, but several may have been executed anyway.[371,372] It is possible that a substantial number of innocent people are still on death row, and that even today are facing execution.

Beyond questions of innocence, there is also troubling evidence that the death penalty is applied unfairly. Minorities are disproportionately sentenced to death; Black Americans make up just 13 percent of the US population[373] but comprise 42 percent of death row prisoners.[374] This data is even more distressing considering that *Gregg* rested heavily on arguments from deterrence, yet statistics point to the death penalty having no impact on deterrence from violent crime.[375] Even police chiefs don't view it as an effective deterrent.[376]

---

369. Baumgartner et al, *Deadly Justice*, 13.
370. "Description of Innocence Cases," Death Penalty Information Center, *deathpenaltyinfo.org/policy-issues/innocence/description-of-innocence-cases*.
371. Pema Levy, "One in 25 Sentenced to Death in the U.S. Is Innocent, Study Claims," *Newsweek*, April 28, 2014, *newsweek.com/one-25-executed-us-innocent-study-claims-248889*.
372. Hannah Knowles, "Four years after a man's execution, lawyers say DNA from the murder weapon points to someone else," *Washington Post*, May 4, 2021, *washingtonpost.com/crime-law/2021/05/04/ledell-lee-dna-execution/*.
373. "United States Quick Facts," United States Census Bureau, July 1, 2019, *census.gov/quickfacts/fact/table/US/PST045219*.
374. "Death Penalty Fact Sheet," Death Penalty Information Center.
375. Robert Brett Dunham, "Life After the Death Penalty: What Happens in States that Abolish the Death Penalty?," New York City Bar Association, August 14, 2017, *files.deathpenaltyinfo.org/legacy/files/pdf/DPIC_2017_Murder_Rate_Study.pdf*.
376. "Law Enforcement," Death Penalty Information Center, *deathpenaltyinfo.org/facts-and-research/new-voices/law-enforcement*.

Still today, there are substantial legal efforts and renewed interest on a state level in the US to abolish the death penalty. Some states have wavered back and forth in the effort: California has had proposition measures to abolish the death penalty on the statewide ballot several times but the measures have never passed the threshold necessary (instead a law was passed to speed up the legal process leading to execution).[377] Led by pro-life GOP legislators, Nebraska passed a law repealing the death penalty in 2015, but faced major backlash for doing so, such that just a year later the governor pushed a statewide referendum overturned the legislature's vote.[378] Recent polling indicates that around 60 percent of Americans support the death penalty; there's still a long way to go to change the culture.[379]

A Brief Potential Nonviolent Policy Solution to the Problem of the Death Penalty

Today, society has many nonviolent ways to be kept safe from people who have done grievous violence or threaten ongoing violence; these options render capital punishment unnecessary. At best, its continued use is useless vengeance; at worst, it opens the door for deadly dis-

---

377. Tess Owen, "Death penalty proponents win in California, Oklahoma, and Nebraska," *Vice News*, November 8, 2016, *vice.com/en/article/ gywxqm/death-penalty-proponents-win-in-california-oklahoma-and-nebraska*.

378. Taylor Dolven,"Nebraska's governor loves the death penalty so much it got him sued," *Vice News*, December 4, 2017, *vice.com/en/article/ qvzzj5/nebraskas-governor-loves-the-death-penalty-so-much-it-got-him-sued*.

379. Pew Research Center, "Most Americans Favor the Death Penalty Despite Concerns About Its Administration," June 2, 2021, *pewresearch. org/politics/2021/06/02/most-americans-favor-the-death-penalty-despite-concerns-about-its-administration/*.

crimination. At its core, the death penalty reveals a lack of creative thinking and tacit acceptance of a willingness to violate human dignity under an overly retributive and simplistic notion of "justice." At the least, in an effort to balance human dignity with societal safety, there is the nonviolent option of downgrading a death sentence to life in prison. And that is just the first of many possible options beyond society's self-imposed bounds of retribution and the cycles of trauma and harm.

Considering how to replace the death penalty, any system of justice ought be based in the inherent dignity of every human being, including the dignity of both the offender and the offended. Our model of justice should make amends and generate positive outcomes and healing, not a balance of harm. The death penalty is a final and fatal form of retributive justice. It does not seek to repair relationships between the offender and the offended; in fact, the needs of the offended party aren't really addressed. The focus is entirely on broken rules and punishment. If we aim to reduce recidivism and achieve true justice, we must build a system focused on restoring relationships between the offender, the offended, and the community as a whole.

Addressing Common Arguments in Support of the Death Penalty

Safety

"The death penalty protects the general population in prisons."

There are ways to keep people safe from those who pose a potential threat to themselves or others. The death penalty is not necessary to keep the general population safe.[380]

"The death penalty ensures that the criminal in question won't break out of prison or continue leading a life of crime even while incarcerated."

Prison breaks and continued involvement in criminal underground activities are extremely rare,[381] and do not justify killing individuals who otherwise pose no threat to the general population or those who work at the prison.

"The death penalty deters crime."

Generally, it does not.[382] The death penalty deters crime only by preventing the executed person from doing *anything* ever again.

"Some people (e.g. sociopaths) can't be rehabilitated."

Reliably identifying those who "are not treatable" according to their disposition would take just as long (if not longer) than the process of rehabilitation and restoration that could be done for most prisoners. Although, under a more restorative model of justice

---

380. "The Case Against the Death Penalty," ACLU, *aclu.org/other/case-against-death-penalty*.

381. "Handbook on the Management of High-Risk Prisoners," United Nations Office on Drugs and Crime, 2016, *unodc.org/documents/justice-and-prison-reform/HB_on_High_Risk_Prisoners_Ebook_appr.pdf*.

382. Daniel S. Nagin, "Deterrence in the Twenty-First Century," *Crime and Justice: A Review of Research*, vol. 42: *Crime and Justice in America: 1975-2025*, ed. Michael Tonry (Chicago: University of Chicago Press, 2013).

certain intransigent people might die while incarcerated because of their own stubbornness and attachment to violence, these rare cases do not justify violence against the many who, with ample care and resources, could change.

Justice

"Only the worst of the worst get the death penalty."

While death penalty proponents hope this is true, it is not. In recent memory, several people with severe intellectual and mental disabilities have been executed in the United States.[383] More than 185 people have been found innocent years after they were sentenced to death.[384] Ethically, any number of innocent people killed by capital punishment is too many.

"They deserve it."

Those who insist upon the death penalty believe that "an eye for an eye" is a just policy. The right to life is a human right based upon intrinsic dignity, not on something as changeable as guilt or innocence. Though there should be consequences for tearing a rift in community, these consequences should be oriented towards healing that rift, not heaping punishment on an offender.

---

383. "Alabama Seeks Execution of Another Person with Intellectual Disability," Equal Justice Initiative, October 19, 2021, *eji.org/news/alabama-seeks-execution-of-another-person-with-intellectual-disability/*.

384. "Innocence Database," Death Penalty Information Center, updated 2021, *deathpenaltyinfo.org/policy-issues/innocence-database*.

"The death penalty provides closure for families of victims."

Typically, imposing a death sentence in a murder case causes the victim's family to be dragged through a much longer and more emotionally taxing legal process because of the system of appeals.[385] Also, the death penalty cannot bring back the deceased or honor their memory. Instead, it continues the cycle of trauma, leaving yet another family to grieve a loved one (the executed offender). As has been shown in many instances, including the story of my CLE colleague Rachel Muha who lost her son Brian to senseless violence,[386] there are better, more compassionate and life-affirming ways to honor the life of the victim in these tragic cases.

"Life in prison is so cruel that it's kinder to kill someone if they'd just get life in prison anyway."

Death is an irrevocable punishment that cannot be undone. At least with life sentences, if a convicted person is found to be innocent less harm is done and that person can still live their life and receive restitution. Nonetheless, it must be restated that prison should not be so cruel and harsh that death would be preferable: the goal of incarceration should be rehabilitation and restoration.

---

385. Susan A. Bandes, "The Death Penalty and the Misleading Concept of 'Closure,'" *The Crime Report*, January 8, 2021; also "The Closure Myth," Equal Justice USA, *ejusa.org/resource/the-closure-myth/*.
386. Kate Morgan, "How A Mother Turned Her Grief Into Goodness," *Woman's Day*, December 8, 2019, womansday.com/life/inspirational-stories/a29833029/brian-muha-foundation-info-rachel-muha.

"We need it for crimes like treason, or racial terrorism, etc."

No crime is so bad that the offender should be considered "irrevocably lost." All human beings have a rational nature and the power to choose how to respond to our life situation. Even the person who has committed serial murder or treason or racial terrorism can change and become better. As long as society is kept safe, any offender should get the time and resources necessary for and restoration to community.

"The death penalty is licit according to my (interpretation of my) religion."

As stated in chapter 2, "Embryo Destruction," though we live in a religiously plural society and we honor freedom of religion, no religion can be allowed to violate the foundational human right to live free from violence. Without this right, no other rights exist, because all hinge on the first right—the right to life. If a religion holds a belief contrary to human dignity and our foundational right to live free from violence, people are free to hold that belief, but it should not dictate law.

Socioeconomic Factors

"The (racial) disparity in executions exists just because Black people commit more crimes."

See the answer to the similar question in chapter 6, "Police Brutality," which mentions the racial bias in policing. Additionally, it must be stated that racially biased jury selection and economic disparity in legal representation also contribute to the racial imbalance in executions in the United States.[387] There is also demonstrable bias when considering the race of the victim; those convicted of killing white people were more than four times as likely to receive a death sentence than those convicted of killing Black people.[388]

"We shouldn't be paying for someone to live on the taxpayers' dime."

Ironically, a life sentence in prison is economically cheaper than the death penalty, in large part due to the good and necessary appeals process involved in seeking a final and irrevocable sentence such as execution.[389] Additionally, the economic benefit of having one less mouth to feed and one less body to house does not outweigh the moral evil of an act of aggressive violence.

Discussion Questions

1. How does the media portray people convicted of capital crimes? Has it been dehumanizing or rehumanizing? How has it impacted your perspective?

387. "Reducing Racial Disparity in the Criminal Justice System: A Manual for Practitioners and Policymakers," The Sentencing Project, 2016, *sentencingproject.org/wp-content/uploads/2016/01/Reducing-Racial-Disparity-in-the-Criminal-Justice-System-A-Manual-for-Practitioners-and-Policymakers.pdf.*

388. Adam Liptak, "A Vast Racial Gap in Death Penalty Cases, New Study Finds," *New York Times*, August 3, 2020, *nytimes.com/2020/08/03/us/racial-gap-death-penalty.html.*

389. "Death Penalty Cost," Amnesty International USA, May 18, 2017, *amnestyusa.org/issues/death-penalty/death-penalty-facts/death-penalty-cost/.*

2. How can the families of victims who have been killed or severely harmed in capital crimes be accompanied? What do victims' families need? How do we balance respect for the dignity of the condemned people on death row with love and care for the victims?
3. What creative ideas do you have that might contribute to rehumanizing solutions in the justice system?

Further Reading Suggestions

1. John D. Bessler, *The Death Penalty as Torture: From the Dark Ages to Abolition* (Durham, NC: Carolina Academic Press, 2017).

2. Danel LaChance, *Executing Freedom: The Cultural Life of Capital Punishment in the United States* (Chicago: The University of Chicago Press, 2016).

3. Frank R. Baumgartner et al, *Deadly Justice: A Statistical Portrait of the Death Penalty* (Oxford, UK: Oxford University Press, 2017)..

4. Richard S. Jaffe, *Quest for Justice: Defending the Damned* (Liberty Corner, NJ: New Horizon Press, 2012).

5. Anthony Ray Hinton, *The Sun Does Shine: How I Found Life, Freedom, and Justice* (New York: St. Martin's Press, 2019).

6. Tim Junkin, *Bloodsworth: The True Story of the First Death Row Inmate Exonerated by DNA Evidence* (Chapel Hill, NC: Algonquin Books, 2005).

7. Bryan Stevenson, *Just Mercy: A Story of Justice and Redemption* (London: Oneworld Publications, 2015).

Ending Violence
in Response to Disability

Physician assisted suicide and euthanasia of people with disabilities is a deadly form of discrimination resulting from the fact that doctors and others do not see the lives of people with disabilities as valuable. This mirrors society's beliefs that our lives are not worth living and that it is better to be dead than disabled.

~Anita Cameron

Chapter 9

Euthanasia and filicide

I n the modern world, sometimes out of a desire to reduce human pain and suffering, and other times in an effort to cut costs in a dehumanizing medical system, euthanasia is seen as acceptable.

What are Euthanasia and Filicide?

The term "euthanasia" comes from the Greek root "eu-" meaning "easy" or "good," and the word "thanatos" meaning "death." Euthanasia is the direct killing of a patient by a physician or other individual; this may be voluntary (following the wishes of the patient), nonvoluntary (performed when explicit request of the patient is impossible), or involuntary (done against the wishes of the patient).[390] Assisted suicide refers to a situation in which a patient requests aid in dying and a physician prescribes lethal medication to be self-administered. Some proponents of euthanasia and assisted suicide may use "medical aid in dying" as a euphemism for either.[391] This chapter will focus

---

390. "Euthanasia," Missouri University School of Medicine, *medicine.missouri.edu/centers-institutes-labs/health-ethics/faq/euthanasia.*
391. B.L. Mishara and D.N. Weisstub, "Legalization of euthanasia in Que-

on euthanasia and its subtype, filicide, which is involuntary euthanasia against a member of one's family.

This book will not accept the sometimes-used distinction between "active" and "passive" euthanasia, which sometimes is called "euthanasia by omission." Such "passive" euthanasia is the intentional deprivation of nutrition and hydration (as occurred in the well-known cases of Terri Schiavo[392] and Michael Hickson[393]). Intentional starvation or dehydration is active killing, and from a CLE perspective is a form of violence. Additionally, the deprivation of any medication or treatment that would be considered "ordinary care" within the current medical context may also be considered active killing (e.g. insulin used to treat diabetes is "ordinary care"; intentionally depriving a diabetic patient of insulin so as to hasten death would be active killing).

According to common and recommended medical practices, euthanasia is often begun by giving patients heavy doses of an intravenous general anesthetic, numbing them and making them unaware of what is happening.[394] Then, killing is often accomplished using injected barbi-

---

bec, Canada as 'medical aid in dying': A case study in social marketing, changing mores and legal maneuvering," *Ethics, Medicine and Public Health* 1 no. 4 (November 2015): 450-55, DOI:10.1016/j.jemep.2015.10.021.

392. Mary Schindler, Robert Schindler, Bobby Schindler, and Suzanne Schindler Vitadamo, *A Life That Matters: the Legacy of Terri Schiavo*, 2nd edition (New York Grand Central Publishing, 2016).

393. Emily Czachor, "Black Disabled Man in Texas Dies After Being Denied COVID Treatment and Starved for Six Days, Wife Alleges," *Newsweek*, July 2, 2020, *newsweek.com/black-disabled-man-texas-dies-after-being-denied-covid-treatment-starved-six-days-wife-alleges-1515047*

394. Sigrid Dierickx et al, "Drugs Used for Euthanasia: A Repeated Population-Based Mortality Follow-Back Study in Flanders, Belgium, 1998-2013," *Journal of Pain and Symptom Management* 56, no. 4 (2018): 551-59.

turates, a class of drug used to induce a heart attack.[395] (Ironically, we see how violence is again linked: This type of drug is also still commonly used in the death penalty.[396]) Although rare, complications in these processes may cause patients pain and/or suffering. [397]

Filicide is distinct from the broader practice of medicalized euthanasia because it is more likely to occur in the context of the home, often using less medically sanitized means. According to the Autistic Self-Advocacy Network's Anti-Filicide Toolkit, "In the disability community, 'filicide' is used when talking about a parent or other relative murdering a child or adult relative with a disability."[398] Because it often happens at home, the number of disabled people killed by filicide is underreported; since the Disability Day of Mourning began in 2012 its memorial has included over seven hundred documented instances.[399] These statistics are compounded by the fact that the media often presents filicide as "understandable" or "justifiable, " reflecting the common perception that disabled people are burdensome and their systemic dehumanization based on ableist standards.[400]

395. Dierickx et al, "Drugs Used for Euthanasia."
396. David Kroll, "The Drugs Used In Execution By Lethal Injection," *Forbes*, May 1, 2014, *forbes.com/sites/davidkroll/2014/05/01/the-pharmacology-and-toxicology-of-execution-by-lethal-injection/?sh=46601d2a7103*.
397. J.H. Groenewoud et al, "Clinical problems with the performance of euthanasia and physician-assisted suicide in The Netherlands," *The New England Journal of Medicine* 342, no. 8 (2000): 551-56.
398. "Anti-Filicide Toolkit," Autistic Self-Advocacy Network, 2021, *autisticadvocacy.org/wp-content/uploads/2015/01/ASAN-Anti-Filicide-Toolkit-Complete.pdf*.
399. Disability Day of Mourning, *disability-memorial.org/*.
400. David Perry et al, "Media Coverage of the Murder of People with Disabilities by Their Caretakers," Ruderman Family Foundation, 2017, *rudermanfoundation.org/wp-content/uploads/2017/08/Murders-*

A Brief Ethical Analysis of Euthanasia

Because euthanasia and filicide intend the active and intentional killing of a human being, under the Consistent Life Ethic, they are prohibited. Even if the intention is to "stop the suffering," a human being may never be killed to prevent (further) suffering; the solution is to alleviate the suffering, not to eliminate the sufferer.

Generally, the argument for and ethical discourse around euthanasia stem from the concept of autonomy and the question of whether human beings have a "right to die" or "right to suicide." "Right to suicide" is relevant only for voluntary euthanasia, which is much more akin to physician-assisted suicide. Filicide, non-voluntary euthanasia, or involuntary euthanasia all unquestionably violate human autonomy. Still, even though individuals do have autonomy, no one has a right to exercise aggressive harm and violence, even towards oneself. Even in the case of voluntary euthanasia, consent may not always be possible or respected. Research shows that in the Netherlands there is a small percentage of assisted deaths—about one in two hundred—where the patient has not made an "explicit request."[401] Moreover, in the advanced illnesses often associated with euthanasia, it may be difficult or impossible to get such explicit requests. In the Netherlands, advanced dementia does not make a person ineligible to choose

---

by-Caregivers-WP_final_final.pdf.

401. van der Heide et al, "End-of-Life Practices in the Netherlands under the Euthanasia Act," *The New England Journal of Medicine* 356, no. 19 (2007): 1957–65, DOI:10.1056/NEJMsa071143.

euthanasia.[402] In 2019, euthanasia was performed for 162 patients with a dementia diagnosis.[403]

Additionally, Dutch legislation allows euthanasia for infants who are born with serious disorders,[404] children between the ages of twelve and sixteen (requiring both the child's and the parent's consent), and, as decided in the last two years, terminally ill children under twelve.[405] There are serious reasons to doubt a child's ability to give real consent, not the least of which is the risk that "the parents will become discouraged or exhausted by a child's illness and that the child will respond to a sense that the family would feel relieved if he or she were not there." In effect, such "euthanasia" would be an act of filicide.[406]

History of Policy and Culture around Euthanasia

The history of the modern movement for euthanasia is linked with the worldwide eugenic movement; although the stated reasoning might be to "reduce pain and suffering," the ableism within the medical field hints at the grotesque Nazi notion of "life unworthy of life."[407]

---

402. Alexander Marvar, "Euthanasia for Dementia Allowed by European Court," *Being Patient*, April 27, 2020, *beingpatient.com/euthanasia-for-dementia-netherlands/*.

403. J. Schuurmans, C. Crol, B. Chabot, et al, "Euthanasia in advanced dementia; the view of the general practitioners in the Netherlands on a vignette case along the juridical and ethical dispute," BMC *Family Practice* 22, no. 232 (2021), *doi.org/10.1186/s12875-021-01580-z*.

404. Leget et al, "Euthanasia and Physician-Assisted Suicide," 113.

405. "Netherlands backs euthanasia for terminally ill children under-12," BBC, October 14, 2020, *bbc.com/news/world-europe-54538288*.

406. Hendin, "The Dutch Experience," 241.

407. This phraseology *"lebensunwertes leben"* was commonly used by Nazi

In 1920s-era Germany, jurist Karl Binding and psychiatrist Alfred Hoche published a book, *Die Freigabe der Vernichtung Lebensunwertes Lebens* (*Permitting the Destruction of Life Unworthy of Living*). The text introduces the idea of legalizing the forced sterilization and "mercy killing" of people considered "unfit" for the growth and civic health of the nation, particularly disabled people. According to a 2018 paper on the subject, German physicians were easily drawn into this eugenic movement which "[drew] on ... Social Darwinism, [and] they argued that the burden on society by having to care for these individuals was too high and their human status too low, that the appropriate solution was the killing of these populations."[408] Even if the current acceptance of euthanasia is not so malicious and genocidal, the medical profession, sadly, still maintains a kind of ableism that suggests and accepts euthanasia for reasons of disability. Instead of offering non-lethal palliative care options, the killing of disabled and severely ill patients can be considered acceptable.

Euthanasia is often referred to as "mercy killing." For this reason euthanasia laws tend to apply to the terminally ill, *at least at first*. In both assisted suicide and euthanasia, the implication is that death is preferable to the pain and suffering caused by the patient's illness or disability. Such ableism operates at all levels of society, including the medical field.[409]

---

physicians and in Nazi propaganda, referencing the disabled as subjects for euthanasia and other eugenic practices. For more information see US Holocaust Memorial Museum, "Search Results for 'Life unworthy of life:'" *ushmm.org/search/results/?q=life+unworthy+of+life*.

408. Michael A Grodin et al, "The Nazi Physicians as Leaders in Eugenics and 'Euthanasia': Lessons for Today," *American Journal of Public Health* 108, no. 1 (2018): 53-57.

409. Heidi L. Janz, "Ableism: the undiagnosed malady afflicting medicine," *CMAJ: Canadian Medical Association Journal* 191, no. 17 (2019): E478-E479.

To facilitate the recent movement for legal euthanasia, Dr. Herbert Hendin, executive director of the American Suicide Foundation, travelled to the Netherlands in the 1990s to study its policies and practices regarding euthanasia and assisted suicide. He found that, although safeguards were in place, doctors who ignored the rules or endangered patients faced few penalties. In many cases, instead of waiting for patients to request euthanasia physicians suggested it, and performed it even when patients' illnesses did not fit the criterion of "suffering that cannot be relieved"or on people for whom there were still alternate forms of pain treatment.[410]

Some of the most distressing parts of Hendin's investigation are case stories of individual patients. In one, a doctor ended the life of a Dutch nun who was in excruciating pain. Her religious beliefs did not permit euthanasia, but the doctor felt that it was the compassionate thing to do, so without permission he euthanized her.[411] Another physician ended the life of a cancer patient who said she did not want euthanasia. "It could have taken another week before she died," the doctor said; "I just needed this bed."[412] In another case, a wife gave her "sick, elderly husband" the choice of euthanasia or going to a care home. Although the doctor was aware that the man was being coerced, euthanasia was still allowed to go forward.[413]

These cases highlight how the idea of being "free from disability" has led physicians and family members to kill disabled patients rather than continue to give them care.

---

410. Herbert Hendin, "The Dutch Experience," *Issues in Law & Medicine* 17, no. 3 (2001): 229.
411. Hendin, "The Dutch Experience," 232.
412. Hendin, "The Dutch Experience," 232.
413. Hendin, "The Dutch Experience," 235.

In the effort to create a world "free from disability," medical professionals often seek to do so by eliminating those with disability, as demonstrated by the often coerced and widely socially accepted abortions of prenatal children with Down syndrome in nations such as Iceland.[414]

Though legal euthanasia may at first include only "fatal diagnoses," over time many such laws have come to include those experiencing intractable pain and suffering, and even varying levels of disability. A 2022 report from Belgium states that the second leading cause of euthanasia (at 17.7 percent of all performed) was "'polypathologies,' ranging from dementia and heart disease to incontinence and hearing loss."[415] Such reasoning troubles those who promote disability rights, because these justifications for euthanasia reflect the symptoms common in various disabilities.[416]

In nations with more lenient euthanasia laws, such as the Netherlands or Belgium, even the euthanasia of minors has been legalized, including for those with a common diagnosis like severe clinical depression.[417] (In the United States, however, euthanasia for mental illness has not yet

414. Julian Quinones and Arijeta Lajka, "'What kind of society do you want to live in?': Inside the country where Down syndrome is disappearing," CBS News, August 14, 2017, *cbsnews.com/news/down-syndrome-iceland/*.

415. Federal Commission for the Control and Evaluation of Euthanasia, "Euthenasie – Chiffres de l'année 2021" ("Euthanasia figures for 2021"), March 31, 2022, *organesdeconcertation.sante.belgique.be/sites/default/files/documents/cfcee_chiffres-2021_communique-presse-total.pdf*.

416. "Disability Groups Opposed to Assisted Suicide Laws," Not Dead Yet, *notdeadyet.org/disability-groups-opposed-to-assisted-suicide-laws*.

417. Scott Kim, "How Dutch Law Got a Little Too Comfortable with Euthanasia," *The Atlantic*, June 8, 2019, *theatlantic.com/ideas/archive/2019/06/noa-pothoven-and-dutch-euthanasia-system/591262/*.

been approved.) Laws legalizing euthanasia or physician-assisted suicide can come to overlook the comorbidity of depressive symptoms that accompany many painful or fatal diagnoses. This creates a medical caste system in which physio-typical people receive a standard of care that treats mental illness in order to prevent death, but disabled and severely ill patients are given the option to have themselves killed through voluntary euthanasia or to participate in their own death through physician-assisted suicide.[418]

Euthanasia laws vary from nation to nation, and within nations that have multiple jurisdictions may vary by locality. Such laws may change and some may be rejected. Still, most of these pushes for euthanasia and the acceptance of filicide stem from the same violent, systemic ableism.

A Brief Potential Nonviolent Policy Solution to the Problem of Euthanasia

The law should prohibit euthanasia and filicide, and physicians who perform euthanasia and the caregivers who kill vulnerable disabled people should be prosecuted. In addition, of course, there are many other cultural initiatives and policies whereby the dignity of those who are disabled or severely ill can be upheld. These include policies that offer access to robust palliative care, compassionate chronic pain treatment (including access to opiates for those not prone to addiction), and above all anti-ableist educational programs that highlight and center the voices of disabled people. Regarding filicide, the dignity of disabled people must never be up for debate;

---

418. Hee-Ju Kang et al, "Comorbidity of depression with physical disorders: research and clinical implications," *Chonnam Medical Journal* 51, no. 1 (2015): 8-18, DOI: 10.4068/cmj.2015.51.1.8.

additionally, disabled people should receive ample support to live as independently as possible, and caregivers should also receive broad and far-reaching resources to deal with and prevent burnout and exhaustion. For example, government fiscal support or tax relief could allow a primary caregiver to have some time off for necessary rest. Above all, though, the inherent human dignity of people with disabilities and severe illnesses must be taken as a given, and violence never seen as a solution.

Addressing Common Arguments in Support of Euthanasia

Disability

"They're (mostly) not conscious of what's happening to them."

> First, many people who are euthanized are aware of what's happening to them, and euthanasia laws are being expanded to include more categories of people.[419] Second, killing individuals merely because they may not be conscious of what is happening to them at that time is never justified. It is an injustice to kill those who are asleep, or blackout drunk, or even in a coma. Human beings have an inherent, foundational right to live free from violence. That right is not diminished by a person's level of consciousness at any point in time.

---

419. Ronald W. Pies and Annette Hanson, "Twelve Myths About Physician Assisted Suicide and Medical Aid In Dying," HCP*live*, July 7, 2018, hcplive.com/view/twelve-myths-concerning-medical-aid-in-dying-or-physicianassisted-suicide.

"They may never 'wake up.'"

While this may be possible, they *definitely* won't wake up if they are euthanized! Again, individuals have a right to the necessities of life (food, water, shelter), and to the opportunity and time to recover from their traumatic injury or illness. It may be debated whether disabled people have a right to extraordinary medical care (although I think they do), but killing them is never morally acceptable.

"They shouldn't have to suffer throughout their life. It's better to end it before it's really had a chance to start" (for the young). Or (for the elderly) "they've already had a long full life. They wouldn't want to live like this."

Although this reasoning can stem from a basically good desire to end suffering and pain for those we love, it results in violence and ableism. In the case of pain, the nonviolent alternative of comprehensive palliative care should be used to ease suffering as much as possible. And in the case of disability, no one has the responsibility or the right (especially those who are nondisabled) to decide what determines another person's quality of life, especially whether another person should be subjected to violence. Abled people regularly underestimate disabled peoples' level of happiness and fulfillment,[420] and therefore tend to push death onto those who are only seeking accommodations and resources. It's also important to note that treat-

---

420. P. M. Rothwell et al, "Doctors and Patients Don't Agree: Cross Sectional Study of Patients' and Doctors' Perceptions and Assessments of Disability in Multiple Sclerosis," *BMJ* [*British Medical Journal*], *clinical edition* 314, no. 7094 (May 1997): 1580-83, DOI:10.1136/bmj.314.7094.1580.

ments, accommodations, and even cures that improve the lives of disabled people are being researched and developed every day. Just fifty years ago, a child with spina bifida would have a radically different life than a similar child diagnosed in utero today.

"People's stated wishes (to not live like this) should be respected."

Those who are suicidal (or who seek someone to kill them), should receive preventive interventions, and as much as possible, their material conditions should be helped. Additionally, society needs to be made aware that disability is not taboo or horrific, but a part of the natural life cycle of human beings, who *always* have inherent, unchangeable dignity.[421]

"Burdensome"

"The [disabled person] is a physical/financial burden on the family/system."

People are not burdens; treating them as such dehumanizes them and contradicts human dignity. Additionally, humans don't exist for the good of the family or system; families and systems exist for the good of each human being and each one's dignity. People must not be killed just because they have costly needs or rare conditions; doing so for merely utilitar-

---

421. Here I say "a part of the natural life cycle of human beings" because as we age, we can develop disability conditions that require mobility aids, hearing aids, visual aids (like glasses), or more direct care. The change in our levels of ability is natural and normal, and we should expect that each of us will, someday in our future, become disabled.

ian purposes reduces human beings merely to a means to economic ends.

"The caregiver didn't ask for this."

Typically, news stories repeat this message, with appeals from murderous caregivers who tell the press (or a judge), "You would never understand. You have no idea how hard it is to take care of a disabled/autistic/ neurodivergent child." Of course, the disabled wards didn't ask for the situation either: neither for their disability, nor for a cold and ableist guardian. We don't get to pick and choose what our children will be like— doing so reduces children to commodities and dehumanizes them as objects. Instead, we must welcome the children we do have and work to accommodate their abilities and meet their needs. In the US, if parents or guardians are unable or unwilling to do so, or if they think they may hurt their disabled ward, they can seek Safe Haven or child relinquishment as a last resort option to spare the life of the child.[422]

Denial of Treatment

"Starvation/dehydration isn't active killing; it's just 'letting die.'"

Basic food and nutrition or sustenance is a human right. To deprive someone—particularly the vulnerable

---

422. Safe Haven laws exist in all fifty states; they allow parents to safely and anonymously relinquish an infant at specified facilities. In the case of older children, though full immediate relinquishment may not be possible, local agencies for child welfare exist to help create plans for child safety (up to and including foster placement, adoption, or reunification, if so desired by the adults). For more information on Safe Haven laws, See childwelfare.gov/pubpdfs/safehaven.pdf.

such as children and disabled people—of those things when they are easily available is an act of aggressive violence. It is not merely "letting die." In Terri Schiavo's court case, starvation and dehydration were mandated despite the fact that she had loved ones who offered to take responsibility for her and provide her food and water. Nevertheless, the court mandated a decisive choice to kill her.

"Other humans don't have a right to my help."

This argument is often heard in libertarian circles, whose proponents might say that "duties or responsibilities to others don't exist." However, even from this perspective, we have the basic responsibility to not kill fellow humans, and not killing means that we don't intentionally starve or dehydrate someone to death. For extraordinary healthcare beyond food and water and readily available medication, moral philosophers in the CLE realm do have various opinions on how much a person is owed. But those in medical fields understand well that the basic principle of medical care is healing, not harm, and that their role is to help people, no matter their background or level of ability.

Discussion Questions

1. What is the difference between euthanasia and assisted suicide? How is the distinction relevant?

2. When have you seen the media enforce assumptions about the quality of life of people with disabilities, the elderly, or people with mental illness? What movies, books, or shows have you seen that use stereotypes about these groups?

3. What stories of filicide have you seen in the news media? How did they portray the killing of the disabled person? How do you think that impacts society's acceptance of such killings by caregivers?

Further Reading Suggestions

1. Harriet McBryde Johnson, *Too Late to Die Young: Nearly True Tales from a Life* (London: Picador Books, 2006)

2. "Anti-Filicide Toolkit," Autistic Self-Advocacy Network, bit.ly/3dTYD2v.

3. Gregor Wolbring, "Why Disability Rights Movements Do Not Support Euthanasia: Safeguards Broken Beyond Repair," Independent Living Institute, 1998, independentliving.org/docs5/Wolbringeuthanasia.html.

4. Smitha Nizar, *The Contradiction in Disability Law: Selective Abortions and Rights* (Oxford, UK: Oxford University Press, 2016).

5. Mary and Robert Schindler, Bobby Schindler, and Suzanne Schindler Vitadamo, *A Life That Matters: The Legacy of Terri Schiavo* (New York: Grand Central Publishing, 2006).

Chapter 10

Assisted suicide

Though like euthanasia in its proximity to disability and the problem of pain and suffering, assisted suicide presents unique ethical and policy questions for the CLE thinker.

What is Physician-Assisted Suicide?

Physician-assisted suicide [PAS] often functions similarly to euthanasia, as explored in the prior chapter. The legal process varies from place to place, but in Oregon, the first in the United States to legalize PAS, it looks like this:

To request a prescription for lethal medications, a patient must be:

- An adult (18 years of age or older),
- A resident of Oregon,
- Capable (defined as able to make and communicate health care decisions), and
- Diagnosed with a terminal illness that will lead to death within six months.

Patients meeting these requirements are eligible to request a prescription for lethal medication from a licensed Oregon physician.

To receive a prescription for lethal medication, the following steps must be fulfilled:

- The patient must make two oral requests to his or her physician, separated by at least 15 days.

- The patient must provide a written request to his or her physician, signed in the presence of two witnesses.

- The prescribing physician and a consulting physician must confirm the diagnosis and prognosis.

- The prescribing physician and a consulting physician must determine whether the patient is capable.

- If either physician believes the patient's judgment is impaired by a psychiatric or psychological disorder, the patient must be referred for a psychological examination.

- The prescribing physician must inform the patient of feasible alternatives to [assisted suicide], including comfort care, hospice care, and pain control.

- The prescribing physician must request, but may not require, the patient to notify his or her next-of-kin of the prescription request.

To comply with the law, physicians must report to the Oregon Health Authority (OHA) all prescriptions for lethal medications. Reporting is not required if patients begin the request process but never receive a prescription.[423]

The drug protocol for PAS has shifted in recent years away from single barbiturates, to one with two drug cocktails: "DDMA, consisting of diazepam, digoxin, morphine sulfate, and amitriptyline (57% of ingestions); or DDMA-Ph, consisting of DDMA with the addition of phenobarbital (39% of ingestions)."[424,425] In physician-assisted suicide (unlike in euthanasia, which is expressly prohibited by Oregon law), the dosage must be self-administered, whether through ingestion (orally or through feeding tube) or injection. Some argue that assisted suicide gives patients autonomy, allowing them to control their own death. But a brief look at assisted-suicide legislation clearly shows that, rather than granting autonomy, it actually can put people in a highly vulnerable position.

Although legislation in states where assisted suicide is legal requires that prescriptions be "voluntarily requested," these laws do not provide safeguards to ensure this. For example, as elder-law attorney Margaret Dore notes, the Washington Death with Dignity Act allows "someone

423. "Death with Dignity Act Requirements document," Oregon State Legislature, *oregon.gov/oha/PH/PROVIDERPARTNERRESOURCES/ EVALUATIONRESEARCH/DEATHWITHDIGNITYACT/Documents/ requirements.pdf*.

424. "Oregon Death with Dignity Act 2021 Data Summary," Oregon Health Authority, Public Health Division, Center for Health Statistics, February 28, 2022, oregon.gov/oha/PH/PROVIDERPARTNERRE-SOURCES/EVALUATIONRESEARCH/DEATHWITHDIGNITYACT/ Documents/year24.pdf.

425. Yet again, we see a connection between CLE issues of violence. You might recall from the chapter 3 section on "What is Abortion?" that some abortions (particularly on fetuses in the second and third trimester) are performed using digoxin, which is used to cause a heart attack, killing the prenatal child. The drug is used here for the same reason, to cause a heart attack in PAS patients, killing them.

else to talk for the patient during the lethal-dose request process."[426] In the State of Washington, it is legal for one of the witnesses for the initial assisted-suicide request to be the patient's heir, even though an heir would "benefit from the patient's death"—a deeply concerning conflict of interest.[427] In addition, there is no oversight to make sure the prescription is voluntarily *taken*. Whether the actual act of dying is autonomous is arguable: Washington requires that the dosage be "self administered," but the Act defines self-administering as "ingesting medication to end his or her life"[428]—so, as Dore points out, "Someone else putting the lethal dose in a feeding tube or IV nutrition bag also would qualify."[429]

Once the prescription has been filled, doctors have no way of knowing if the patient was pressured or forced into administering it, which could lead to surreptitious usage and hidden euthanasia. Whatever happens, once the patient has passed away, the death certificate lists "the underlying terminal disease as the cause of death"[430] rather than the administered dosage, making it difficult to investigate a death and to collect data on assisted-suicide rates.

Even if PAS were perfectly administered in all cases and there were no risk of euthanasia, suicide—the taking of

---

426. Margaret Dore, "'Death with Dignity': What Do We Advise Our Clients?," *Bar Bulletin*, 2009, *kcba.org/kcba/newsevents/barbulletin/BView.aspx?Month=05&Year=2009&AID=article5.htm*.

427. Dore, "'Death with Dignity.'"

428. "Instructions for Medical Examiners, Coroners, and Prosecuting Attorneys: Compliance with the Death with Dignity Act," Washington State Department of Health, 2009, *doh.wa.gov/Portals/1/Documents/Pubs/422-148-DWDAInstructionsForMedicalExaminers.pdf*.

429. Dore, "'Death with Dignity.'"

430. "Instructions for Medical Examiners," Washington State Department of Health.

one's own life—is already the tenth leading cause of death in the United States and the second leading cause of death for people between the ages of ten and thirty-four.[431] PAS only adds to that deadly toll. Every suicide is a great loss. Hope and healing need to be offered to all because every person, without exception, is worthy of life. Although much stigma has been associated with suicidal ideation, those who ponder taking their own life need compassionate treatment and support systems, rather than negative correction or legal avenues to end their lives. .

A Brief Ethical Analysis of Physician-Assisted Suicide

Some argue that everyone has a right to "die with dignity," and that euthanasia and assisted suicide dignify an otherwise degrading death. As Janet Good, an assisted-suicide advocate, put it, "Pain is not the main reason we want to die. It's the indignity. Every client I've talked to . . . they've had enough when they can't go to the bathroom by themselves. Most of them say, 'I can't stand my mother, my husband . . . wiping my butt.'"[432] Gilles Genicot, co-chairman of the Euthanasia Control and Evaluation Commission in Belgium, said in an interview that the Belgian euthanasia law "humanizes the deaths of terminally ill patients."[433]

431. CDC, "Web-based Injury Statistics Query and Reporting System (WISQARS)," National Center for Injury Prevention and Control, 2020, *cdc.gov/injury/wisqars/index.html*.

432. Richard Lei, "Whose Death Is It, Anyway?," *The Washington Post*, 1996, *washingtonpost.com/archive/lifestyle/1996/08/11/whose-death-is-it-anyway/54f4daef-9a40-4fd5-bac4-628fbef78f01/*.

433. Gilles Genicot, "The Right to Die in Belgium: An Inside Look at the World's Most Liberal Euthanasia Law," Interview by Megan Thompson, PBS *NewsHour*, January 15, 2015, *pbs.org/newshour/show/*

In the view of Good and Genicot, disability and illness dehumanize by causing suffering and making the person dependent on others. In their view, choosing death brings a person dignity; it "humanizes," because it restores the autonomy that is an assumed part of being human.

But what is this conception of dignity? The Consistent Life Ethic holds that dignity, like value, is intrinsic to being a human being; it cannot be taken away by disability or dependence. Conceptions of dignity predicated on health, ability, and independence are ableist and ageist. As the disability rights group Not Dead Yet writes, "In a society that prizes physical ability and stigmatizes impairments, it's no surprise that previously able-bodied people may tend to equate disability with loss of dignity. This reflects the prevalent but insulting societal judgment that people who deal with incontinence and other losses in bodily function are lacking dignity."[434]

We should never accept direct killing, including killing via PAS, as a solution to suicidal ideation or advanced illness. Mercy that sees dependence as undignified is not mercy. Mercy that seeks to kill is not mercy. Those who are suffering need radical compassion and hospitality.

History of Policy and Culture around Physician-Assisted Suicide

Assisted suicide, under certain provisions, is currently legal in many countries, including Belgium, Canada, Luxembourg,

---

right-die-belgium-inside-worlds-liberal-euthanasia-laws.

434. "Disability Rights Toolkit for Advocacy Against Legalization of Assisted Suicide," Not Dead Yet, *notdeadyet.org/disability-rights-toolkit-for-advocacy-against-legalization-of-assisted-suicide*.

the Netherlands, Spain, Switzerland, New Zealand, Portugal, and parts of Australia. Some US states have legalized PAS, including California, Colorado, Hawaii, Maine, Montana, Ne w Jersey, New Mexico, Oregon, Vermont, Washington, and the District of Columbia.

Switzerland was the first of these nations to adopt a lenient policy on assisted suicide, early in the twentieth century. Its lax policy concerning assisted suicide has led to a sort of "death tourism" where people from other nations travel there to end their lives. It is troubling that, "according to a recent study, around 25% of people who die by assisted suicide in Switzerland do not have any serious or terminal illness, but are just old, or are simply 'tired of life.'"[435,436] Following Switzerland's legalization in 1918, it took seventy to eighty years for other nations even to consider legalizing assisted suicide.

A prime proponent of voluntary euthanasia and assisted suicide in the United States was a man the media nicknamed "Dr. Death"—Jack Kevorkian. In the late 1980s, in Detroit newspapers Kevorkian started advertising his services in "death counseling."[437] Then he started covertly practicing voluntary medical euthanasia and assisted suicide until the State of Michigan revoked his medical license in 1991.[438] After losing his license he resorted to

---

435. Roberto Adorno, "Nonphysician-assisted suicide in Switzerland," *Cambridge Quarterly of Healthcare Ethics* 22 no. 3 (April 2013): 246-53, DOI:10.1017/S0963180113000054.

436. This may represent most strikingly a disenfranchisement of the elderly as a class; but certainly those "tired of life" should first be treated with robust mental healthcare and opportunities to find joy in life once again.

437. Paul Finkelman, ed., *Encyclopedia of American Civil Liberties* (Oxfordshire, England: Routledge, 2013), 888.

438. Associated Press, "Kevorkian medical license revoked," *Lodi News-Sentinel*, November 21, 1991, 8.

more gruesome methods, eventually resulting in his arrest and several high-profile court cases which, unfortunately, gave him positive notoriety and allowed his assisted suicide movement to gain more traction.[439]

Kevorkian picked up momentum because proponents of legal assisted suicide and euthanasia typically come from a place of compassion; they say that they don't want people to suffer unbearable pain, and that is understandable. No one wants that. However, statistics show that patients who request assisted suicide are concerned not primarily about pain, but about disability. A study of the results of Oregon's Death with Dignity Act found that 92% of patients who chose assisted suicide in 2021 cited being "less able to engage in activities" as one of the concerns that led to them requesting assisted suicide.[440] Ninety-three percent cited "loss of autonomy," 68 percent cited "loss of dignity," 54 percent cited becoming a "burden on family," and 47 percent cited "losing control of bodily functions."[441]

In healthy, young, physio-typical people many of these reasons would be flagged as evidence of suicidal depression.[442] It appears that fear of disability is driving people to suicide. Rather than offering compassionate, psychologically informed care, assisted suicide advocates are essentially

439. Keith Schneider, "Dr. Jack Kevorkian Dies at 83; A Doctor Who Helped End Lives," *The New York Times*, June 3, 2011.

440. "Oregon Death with Dignity Act: 2021 Data Summary," Oregon Health Authority, Public Health Division, Center for Health Statistics, February 28, 2022, 13,.oregon.gov/oha/PH/PROVIDERPARTNERRE-SOURCES/EVALUATIONRESEARCH/DEATHWITHDIGNITYACT/Documents/year24.pdf

441. "Oregon Death with Dignity Act: 2019 Data Summary," 12.

442. Kathleen M. Foley and Herbert Hendin, *The Case against Assisted Suicide. [Electronic Resource]* : *For the Right to End-of-Life Care* (Baltimore, MD: Johns Hopkins University Press, 2002), *catalog.library.vanderbilt.edu/permalink/01VAN_INST/13em2a7/alma991043275545303276.*

saying that disabled people should not receive the same treatment offered to others. In effect, proponents of PAS confirm that among the disabled, suicidal ideation is "correct," while in others it is a symptom of mental illness. We should not simply accept that fears of disability are allowed to drive people to suicide. Everyone deserves suicide prevention care—including those who are ill or disabled.

We often assume that a doctor is the best person to assess a patient's quality of life, but a growing body of evidence shows that people who have never experienced disability consistently misjudge the quality of life of people with disabilities, whose self-assessments are substantially higher.[443] Many bioethicists refer to this phenomenon as the "disability paradox."[444] Some studies show that nondisabled people who are *not* healthcare workers are better at assessing the quality of life of disabled people than nondisabled healthcare workers themselves.[445] Doctors are not the best experts to assess quality of life in such grave cases as euthanasia and assisted suicide.

A Brief Potential Nonviolent Policy Solution to the Problem of Physician-Assisted Suicide

Because physician-assisted suicide is an act of violence and contrary to the Consistent Life Ethic, it should never be legalized or socially encouraged. That isn't to say that

---

443. Rothwell, "Doctors and Patients Don't Agree," 1580–83.
444. Gary L. Albrecht and Patrick J. Devlieger, "The Disability Paradox: High Quality of Life against All Odds," *Social Science & Medicine* 48, no. 8 (1999): 977–88, DOI: 10.1016/S0277-9536(98)00411-0.
445. Ron Amundson, "Quality of Life, Disability, and Hedonic Psychology," *Journal for the Theory of Social Behaviour* 40 no. 4: 374–92, doi. org/10.1111/j.1468-5914.2010.00437.x.

there should be criminal penalties for those who attempt suicide, but rather, the goal should be to prevent the prescription of lethal drug cocktails by physicians with the intent to aid in suicide. Instead, we should direct people experiencing suicidal ideation to robust mental healthcare and, if necessary, pain relief.

As a community, we must develop better safety nets for ill and disabled people, and doctors must communicate that disability and illness do not affect an individual's worth or dignity. With current medical technology, pain can be managed. Suffering can be lessened. Steps can be taken to address a patient's concerns, such as home care services to relieve feelings of burdening family.

We have a responsibility to protect people from harm, including self-harm. Communities should work together to bring down suicide rates by working on compassionate prevention and support. One of the simplest ways to do this is limiting the means of committing suicide: for example, heavy alcohol use and gun ownership are strong risk factors for turning suicidal ideation into a completed suicide.[446] Strategies could be developed that equitably assess suicide risk and safety protocols for gun owners and their families, or maybe promote alcohol recovery programs more aggressively among psychiatric patients with a history of suicidal ideation and alcohol abuse. At the very least, individuals with knowledge of a loved one's depression or ideation should do their best to remove alcohol and firearms from the situation, thereby reducing risk of death. Additionally, reporting on, writing about, or otherwise discussing suicide must never romanticize

---

446. Glenn Sullivan, "How to Lower the Suicide Rate," *Psychology Today*, March 30, 2020, psychologytoday.com/us/blog/acquainted-the-night/202003/how-lower-the-suicide-rate.

or sensationalize it, and it is especially important not to include explicit details about suicide attempts. One of the most effective things we can do is to reduce the stigma attached to mental illness and to asking for help. Each life is precious, and it is important that society be structured to protect every life.

Another way to help people who would otherwise consider or be offered euthanasia or assisted suicide is investing in palliative care. If fear of disability and illness are driving people to make these choices, the medical establishment must re-examine how it communicates diagnoses and how it treats those who have terminal illnesses. Palliative care "affirms life and regards dying as a normal process."[447] It does not strive to hasten death, nor does it deny death's ultimate inevitability. Instead, it strives to improve quality of life as much as possible at each stage of a patient's illness by keeping the person comfortable, in control, and cared for. Doctors must be trained to make available these options that holistically honor the dignity of the patient.

Palliative care also offers help for people who are in extreme pain. As noted earlier in this chapter, pain is not one of the principal reasons for choosing assisted suicide and euthanasia; but where pain is a significant concern for a patient, palliative sedation is an option that does not involve the direct taking of life, and it is available across the United States and most of the world. Used only when no other kind of treatment has been found effective, palliative sedation involves medicating a patient to the point where they no longer experience pain, sometimes to the point

---

447. Cecilia Sepúlveda, Amanda Marlin, Tokuo Yoshida, and Andreas Ull-rich, "Palliative Care: The World Health Organization's Global Perspective," *Journal of Pain and Symptom Management* 24, no.2 (2002): 91–96, DOI:10.1016/S0885-3924(02)00440-2.

of being unconscious.[448] Having it as an option can give patients security about the possibility of future pain without feeling that they have no choice but to end their life.

Addressing Common Arguments in Support of Physician-Assisted Suicide

Right to Die

"People have a right to die." Or, "You can't tell me what to do with my body."

> Ultimately, I probably couldn't stop those who wish to kill themselves if they were intent enough on doing so. I would certainly refer them to mental healthcare resources and try to help as much as possible to ease that person's suffering, though. In most places you cannot be prosecuted for attempting suicide, although there are some legal structures which allow a person to be involuntarily admitted to a (mental) hospital for expressing the intent to do so. However, the concept that "people have a right to die" can lead to creating a legal right and then a medical industry around doing so. Systems like this attack human dignity and normalize self-inflicted harm. Additionally, these systems put immense pressure on disabled people to die because of the dehumanizing way our culture views them as "burdensome." The solution to suicidality or a desire to

---

448. Molly L. Olsen, Keith M. Swetz, and Paul S. Mueller, "Ethical Decision Making with End-of-Life Care: Palliative Sedation and Withholding or Withdrawing Life-Sustaining Treatments," *Mayo Clinic Proceedings* 85, no. 10 (2010): 949–54, DOI:10.4065/mcp.2010.0201.

die is holistic mental healthcare and community care, not violence and death.

"I don't wanna suffer." Or, "Making someone live in pain is cruel."

Extensive palliative care options exist and should be much more accessible to all who need them. Furthermore, pain is not one of the main reasons why people seek assisted suicide; rather, people seek PAS because they fear disability. This points to a devaluation of disabled lives, a deep-seated ableism that despises disabled people because they are vulnerable and require help with intimate care.

"Let them die on their terms; it's easier for the family to deal with grief this way."

I know from my own experience that disability and terminal illness can be hard to deal with or to see a loved one go through. Helping someone to participate in their own death, however, spreads the trauma of violence, perpetuating a cycle of trauma and a violent ableism that ripples from that one individual into the community. Instead, we should seek rehumanizing palliative care and encourage families to talk about death and disability in an anti-ableist way that sees them as natural aspects of the human experience.

Disability

"I would never want to live with that condition/disability."

> Disabled people can hear it when such cruel things are said. Sure, logically, it makes sense that we wouldn't want a debilitating condition or disability; but saying that we wouldn't want to *live* if we had that condition is ableist and dehumanizing. As mentioned in chapter 9, "Euthanasia and Filicide," abled people regularly underestimate the level of happiness and fulfillment of disabled people[449] and therefore tend to push death onto those who want and need accommodations and resources.

"If you are disabled, you are a 'burden' on your family, taxpayers, society, etc."

> People are not burdens; treating them as such is contrary to human dignity. Additionally, humans don't exist for the good of the family or system; families and systems exist for the good of each human and each person's dignity. We must not kill people because they have costly needs or rare conditions; to do so reduces human beings in a utilitarian fashion, as a means to economic ends. Even if disability accommodations are pricey, they should be considered expected necessary expenses of living in a human-centered society.

"The healthcare system (including our hospice system) is so bad and having a long-term disability/chronic illness within

---

449. Rothwell et al, "Doctors and Patients Don't Agree."

this system is so awful that it would be cruel not to 'give people a way out.'"

It is absolutely true that someone with a disability/ chronic illness will have an extremely difficult challenge navigating the US healthcare model (including the hospice system). I can attest to this fact. However, the response to such a dehumanizing system is to fix the system—upend it if necessary!—so as to build it on a foundation of human rights and dignity instead of financial profit, bureaucracy, and scientific advancement. The solution should be to create a rehumanizing healthcare system, not to kill vulnerable disabled people.

Medicalization of Suicide

"If someone wants to die, it's better that a doctor be involved."

This stance may stem from the concept of "safety": A person doesn't want to end up badly disfigured or further disabled from an attempted suicide. But it implies that assisted suicide is substantially or ethically different from "normal" suicide. This implication is yet another instance of the medicalization of violence, in which violence is seen as acceptable because it is performed in a clinical setting. However, we should not make violence easier. There *should* be a stigma against it, and we should not enable physician participation, because violence is contrary to human dignity.

"There are safeguards in place to make sure that people who are just depressed won't be given assisted suicide."

Again, this reveals the ableist double-standard wherein a nondisabled person who experiences the desire to die is considered "not of sound mind"; but if disabled persons request medical aid in dying, they are offered suicide-on-demand. This stems from the idea that "disabled lives aren't worth living," and perpetuates violent ableism. Additionally, it's worth noting that in certain nations, such as the Netherlands and Belgium, otherwise nondisabled depressed people like Aurelia Brouwers, a twenty-nine-year-old who suffered from several mental illnesses,[450] have requested PAS and received it.[451] My nation's northern neighbor, Canada, is moving to legalize Medical Aid in Dying (MAiD)—or voluntary euthanasia—for non-terminal psychiatric patients and people with disabilities.[452] It seems that the longer medical aid in dying is around, the more the restrictions are loosened and expanded.

Discussion Questions

1. Why do you think it is considered an act of mercy to assist disabled or dependent persons in ending their life, while we simultaneously build safety nets to stop nondisabled people from ending theirs?

2. What kinds of pain are considered to "destroy" dignity?

---

450. Linda Pressley, "The troubled 29-year-old helped to die by Dutch doctors," BBC News, August 9, 2018, bbc.com/news/stories-45117163
451. Lars Mehlum, et al, "Euthanasia and assisted suicide in patients with personality disorders: a review of current practice and challenges," *Borderline Personality Disorder and Emotion Dysregulation* 7, no. 15 (July 30, 2020), bpded.biomedcentral.com/articles/10.1186/s40479-020-00131-9#Tab1.
452. Mark S. Komrad, "First, Do No Harm: New Canadian Law Allows for Assisted Suicide for Patients with Psychiatric Disorders," *Psychiatric Times* 38, no. 6 (June 7, 2021): 10-11.

Why do you think that is so?

3. Perhaps this chapter made you aware of the strong disability rights movement that opposes PAS. How might you follow the work of disability activists, such as those with organizations like Not Dead Yet, who campaign against physician-assisted suicide because of its ableist foundations? If you don't know of or follow any, why not?

Further Reading Suggestions

1. "Disability Rights Toolkit for Advocacy Against Legalization of Assisted Suicide," Not Dead Yet, notdeadyet. org/disability-rights-toolkit-for-advocacy-against-legalization-of-assisted-suicide.

2. ""Suicide Prevention and Assisted Suicide," Center for Disability Rights, cdrnys.org/wp-content/uploads/2015/12/Assisted-Suicide-Position-Paper.pdf.

3. Kathleen Foley and Herbert Hendin, editors, *The Case Against Assisted Suicide: For the Right to End-of-Life Care* (Baltimore: Johns Hopkins University Press, 2002).

Ending Dehumanization, Rehumanizing the World

Unless one lives and loves in the trenches, it is difficult to remember that the war against dehumanization is ceaseless.

~ Audre Lorde

⑪

Chapter 11

Resisting the inculturation of violence

Violence and degradation of humans are often brushed off and ignored, or supported and promoted. Our world is so steeped in prejudice and dehumanization that it can be hard to pinpoint where such evils are happening and to call them out. Such violence and degradation can be found in music, in the videos we watch, in the news, even in casual mealtime conversation with family or friends. But we can do something. We must register our noncompliance with these systems of human degradation and speak clearly for human dignity.

Dehumanization, Language, and Culture

Dehumanizing language negatively shapes perception: groups of people come to be seen as "less-than" or "sub-human." A subconscious process of moral disengagement allows others to be viewed as less than us, which enables a distinct psychological separation, which in turn makes it easier to allow or commit violence against them.[453]

---

453. Albert Bandura, "Moral disengagement in the perpetration of inhu-

How do our words dehumanize?

	Non-person	Animal	Inanimate Object	Deficient Human	Parasite	Disease	Waste Product
Indigenous Americans	"An Indian is not a person within the meaning of the Constitution." George Canfield, American Law Review, 1881	"The Indian... is an untamable, carnivorous animal." Dr. Josiah Nott, 1847	"[Indians are] anthropological specimens." American press coverage, 1904	"Indians [are]... inferior to the [Indians]." Henry Clay, Secretary of State, 1825	"Clear the country of that vermin [Indians]." Colonel Henry Bouquet, 1763	"The Iroquois had proved more deadly... than the pestilence." Historian Francis Parkman, 1902	"[Indians are] the very dregs, garbage...of Earth." Poet Christopher Brooke, 1622
Black Americans	"In the eyes of the law... the slave is not a person." Virginia Supreme Court decision, 1858	"The negro is... one of the lower animals." Prof. Charles Carroll, 1900	"A negro of the African race was regarded... as an article of property." US Supreme Court decision, 1857	"A subordinate and inferior class of beings." US Supreme Court on the status of Black people, 1857	"They [Negroes] are parasites." Dr. E. T. Brady, 1909	"Free blacks in our country are... a heritage of contagion." American Colonization Society, 1815-30	"The negro race is... organic and psychic debris." Dr. William English, 1903
Jewish Europeans	"The Reichsgericht itself refused to recognize Jews... as 'persons' in the legal sense." 1936 German Supreme Court Decision	"The [Jewish] prisoners here are animals." Nazi anatomy prof. Dr. August Hirt, 1942	"Transit material." Portrayal of Jews dispatched to Nazi Death Camps, 1942-44	"The inferior Jewish race." Dr. Rudolph Ramm, Nazi medical educator, 1943	"The Jew is a parasite." Nazi propaganda booklet, 1944	"Some day Europe will perish of the Jewish disease." Joseph Goebbels, Nazi Propaganda Minister, 1939	"What shall we do with this garbage?" Christian Wirth, extermination expert, 1942
Elders & Disabled People	"True guilt arises only from an offense against a person, and a Down's is not a person." The Atlantic Monthly, 1968	"Until a living being can take conscious management of life... it remains an animal." Prof. George Ball, 1981	"I came to see those patients as work objects." Nursing home staff member, 1977	"A life... devoid of those qualities which give it human dignity." Assessment of a child with disability, Dr. Harry Hartzell, 1978	"That's a real parasite." Medical staff characterization of a debilitated patient, 1989	"[Registering the feeble-minded] would be the first step in the regulation and elimination of defective strains from the community." W.E. Fernald, 1913	"There's a lot of rubbish [patients] this morning." ER doctor, 1979

Preborn Humans	"The word 'person,' as used in the 14th amendment, does not include the unborn." US Supreme Court decision, 1973	"Like... a primitive animal that's poked with a stick." Dr. Hart Peterson on fetal movement, 1985	"People's body parts [embryos] are their personal property." Attorney Lori Andrews, 1986	"The fetus, at most, represents only the potentiality of life." US Supreme Court decision, 1973	"The fetus is a parasite." Prof. Rosalind Pollack Petchesky, 1984	"Pregnancy when not wanted is a disease... in fact, a venereal disease." Prof. Joseph Fletcher, 1979	"An aborted baby is just garbage... just refuse." Dr. Martti Kekomaki, 1980
Refugees & Immigrants	"These are illegal people. Thus, they are not people at all." Opinion article, 2006	"You have got a swarm of people... wanting to come to Britain..." British Prime Minister David Cameron, 2015	"The people who are here illegally would therefore be owned by the state and become an asset." Iowa radio host Ian Mickelson, 2015	"Remember it is not racist to prevent undesirables from entering our country." Diane Francis, 1999	"Letting in parasites, [but] turning away entrepreneurs," The Daily Telegraph, 2013	"[Asylum seekers are] a dreadful human epidemic..." Sunday Times, 2002	"[Other nations] send to our shores the dregs of [their] population..." Leland Stanford, 1862
Enemy Combatants	"We believe that RFRA's use of 'person' should... exclude nonresident aliens." US Court of Appeals, 2008 On prisoners in Guantanamo Bay	"You could pass some people and they shout at you saying, 'Look at that cockroach,' 'Look at that snake.'" Esperance Nyiranugira, on what Hutu thought of Tutsi, 2009	"By calling them names,' he said, 'they're not people anymore. They're just objects.'" The Guardian, 2007	"A lot of guys really supported the whole concept that if they don't have darker skin, they're not as human as us, so we can do what we want." Josh Middleton, US Army 82nd Airborne Division 48, 2007	"Yellow vermin." American press during WWII about the Japanese	"Al Qaeda Mutating Like a Virus" Newspaper headline, 2003	"They [Iranians] are... human debris." Rush Limbaugh, radio broadcaster, 2004
Incarcerated Inmates	"Prisoners are not people,' testimony of former North Korean prison camp guard. "The Guard: The story of a North Korean defector." DW.com, 2014	"He's an animal. A terrible animal." said Carl Elliott, 81, whose daughter was David Alan Gore's sixth known and final victim. (Gore was executed for the murders of six women), 2012	"In prison, you look at people as objects," Mark Delaplane, dying prisoner, 1996	"When you kill criminals, it is not a crime against humanity. The criminals have no humanity," Rodrigo Duterte, president of the Philippines, 2017	"Prisoners are parasites we cannot afford." Letter to the editor, The New York Times, 1992	"We think it... necessary for a state to provide precautionary measures against the moral pestilence of... convicts." US Supreme Court decision, 1837	"Society has used the juvenile courts to create a caste system where there are throw-away people." James Bell, 2009

Note: Many of the quotes on this table were the fruit of research by William Brennan in his book Dehumanizing the Vulnerable.
Additional categories were added and research was done by team members of Rehumanize International.

Sometimes, the motivation for dehumanization stems from potentially good intentions: the desire for national security, for safe communities, for stable families, for individual survival.

Humans should not be dehumanized, even in order to achieve good ends. This book has documented many examples of dehumanization, and this chapter will explore common examples of culture and language that dehumanize, along with suggested alternatives. So as the dehumanization that has seeped into our culture is presented here, the voice of William Wilberforce, English slavery abolitionist, should be ringing in your mind: "You may choose to look the other way but you can never say again that you did not know."

Facing the grotesque history of dehumanization challenges me to work day in and day out to build a culture of peace and life. I aim to live the principle that Maya Angelou states so well, and I hope you will, too: "Do the best you can until you know better. Then when you know better, do better." Instead of settling into comfort with the prevailing culture of violence, our language and actions should reflect the fact that every human being has inherent dignity by the virtue of our unique selfhood and our shared humanity.

Ableism

I have come to understand ableism—the all-too-common bias against disabled people—largely because I myself have newly become disabled with fibromyalgia and a handful of other chronic conditions that cause a laundry list of

---

manities," *Personality and Social Psychology Review*, Special Issue on Evil and Violence (1999): 193-209.

painful and lifestyle-limiting symptoms. I was somewhat familiar with the term "ableism" several years ago because of disabled friends and self-advocates who had brought it to my attention, and the more I learned about my own diagnoses and how they limit my life, the more familiar I became. Ashley Eisenmenger's piece "Ableism 101" from *Access Living* explores this neologism from a disability justice perspective:

> Ableism is the discrimination of and social prejudice against people with disabilities based on the belief that typical abilities are superior. At its heart, ableism is rooted in the assumption that disabled people require "fixing" and defines people by their disability.[454]

Ableism is the idea that nondisabled people are inherently "more worthy" of rights and protections than disabled people. Ableism sees disability as bad, sometimes to the point of wanting to eradicate disability and those with disability conditions. In the most extreme terms, ableism can lead to disability-selective abortions, forced sterilizations of people with disabilities, and hardline eugenics that demands everyone with a disability be executed because they are seen as "useless eaters" who take up excessive resources without contributing much.[455]

Ableism is often deeply linked with utilitarian ideas of human worth and dignity. The philosopher Peter Singer, for example, deems people with lower levels of ability to have less worth.[456] This philosophy implies not only that

---

454. Ashley Eisenmenger, "Ableism 101: What it is, what it looks like, and what we can do to fix it," *Access Living News Blog*, December 12, 2019, *accessliving.org/newsroom/blog/ableism-101/*.

455. "People with Disabilities," United States Holocaust Memorial Museum, *ushmm.org/collections/bibliography/people-with-disabilities*.

456. Grace Lapointe, "When Ableism Intersects with Utilitarianism," *Me-*

disabled people are less worthy of rights, but also that human beings get human rights and dignity only at around two years of age! In its "purest" form, such utilitarian ableism denies human rights to preborn children and even infants and toddlers, and so allows violence against them because they are less "able" (and therefore "less worthy") than adults.

To root out ableism from your sphere of influence, remove these common phrases from your vocabulary: "You are so retarded." "That guy is crazy." "That's so lame." "You're acting so bi-polar today." "He's such a spaz." "My ideas fell on deaf ears." "She's a psycho." If you or someone you know says something casually ableist like this, please stop the conversation, call attention to the phrase and its ableism, perhaps explaining how such language stigmatizes those with disabilities and offer a replacement phrase. Replacement suggestions include: "You're being silly." "That's not cool." "You're acting very hot and cold today." "He's so clumsy." "My idea fell on closed minds." "She's acting really rude/insensitive/mean."

A common form of ableism in the culture results in not thinking of or intentionally excluding disabled people in event planning. Facilities and events not being accessible highlights a world that rejects people with disabilities and continues the cycle of disabled people not being considered or welcome. Event planners should make sure that the space has accessible entrances, that accommodations are made for food allergies, and that options like captions, sign language interpretation, and audio descriptions are offered. If you attend an event that does not offer such accommodations, contact the organizers and lodge a complaint.

---

dium, January 21, 2020, *gracelapointe.medium.com/when-ableism-intersects-with-utilitarianism-9d0473a60882.*

Ableism is reflected in the pervasive pressure that friends, family, and physicians place on parents to consider abortion if their preborn child has a disability. So if you or a friend are pregnant with a baby with some sort of disability, it's vital that you rehumanize that child. Begin by not using the pronoun "it"; instead, use "he/him," "she/her," or "they/them" for the baby. Next, perhaps most vitally, never, ever insinuate that it would be better for them, the baby, their family, or the world if that child were dead. Instead, affirm that each and every human being has the same inherent dignity and remain joyful about this child, just as you would for a nondisabled child. You can also (help) do research on their child's condition, and help them create a life-affirming plan that will educate the whole family and community of support on the condition and demonstrate how they can assist.

Granted, most of these ableist actions don't have intentionally violent aims, but they all contribute to a culture that dehumanizes disabled people. It is vital for us to rehumanize: to see disabled people with their whole selves, to engage disabled people as peers, and to challenge the culture to see disability not as bad, but simply a part of life.

Ageism

Ageism is prejudice and discrimination because of a person's age. Though ageism might be considered to be principally a bias against elders, it also exists against children, too, including the tiniest of children: embryonic and fetal humans. This prejudice deems certain humans as unworthy of dignity or community or human rights based on their age. Ageism denies that each and every human being has inherent dignity; instead, it maintains that a person's worth depends on age.

In the case of abortion and embryo destruction, because the preborn child is still very young (and as a consequence small, ugly, dependent, and not-yet-able to do certain things),that child is said to not have rights or dignity, that killing such a child is acceptable. In the case of euthanasia or assisted suicide, some proponents might say that an elderly person "has had a long, full life," and in an overlap with ableism, that the disabilities (like loss of continence or full mental capacity) that often come with age are ample reason to deprive that person of the right to live free from violence.

To root out ageism from your sphere of influence, remove common phrases from your vocabulary: (for elderly people) "old fart," "geezer," "gramps," "old bag," "biddy," "old fogey"; (for preborn children) "clump of cells/tissue," "it," "the pregnancy," "parasite," "spawn," etc. If something casually ageist surfaces, stop the conversation, call attention to the ageism involved, and offer a replacement term. For example: older adult, elder, mature adult, senior citizen; and preborn child, baby, prenatal human, "inside baby," child, etc.

Another form of ableism in the culture involves considering only "younger applicants" for a job position, or signaling in the job listing that younger applicants are preferred. If you are involved in the hiring process at your workplace, ensure that age-identifying questions or criteria are not part of the discernment process. Instead, promote the idea that an inclusive and diverse workplace should include age diversity.

A particularly violent form of ableism surfaces when someone (particularly a physician) suggests euthanasia or something similar to an elder in your family. If a doctor or family member or friend suggests that you (or your family members) should create or enact a plan for euthanasia or assisted suicide, push back by calling attention to older adults' inherent dignity as members of the human family. Point out that every person's existence is a moral good, no matter how "useless" they might seem, and that killing is not the answer to any suffering that might be a consequence of age or disability. Offer to be part of a caretaker team for your elder family member(s), and promote the values of generational memory, mentorship, and presence that older community members bring to the table.

Classism

Classism is a bias against people based on socioeconomic class. The most obvious historical examples include European feudal systems and Indian caste systems that were defined by endogamy—the requirement to marry within one's social, economic, or religious group.[457] Classism is less overt in the United States than in those cultures, especially because it is said that "anyone can achieve the American dream." However, today's global society is still structured around capital and big business, so classism is part and parcel of our existence. There are often subtle ways that people of all classes put down those with lesser financial means, which generally also tracks with the issue of racism (and colorism).

Classism intersects with systemic issues of violence inasmuch as the poor are more likely to be coerced into participating in violence because of their financial situation. Youth from poor families are intensively targeted by military recruitment officers in high schools around the

---

457. "Caste Systems," LibreTexts, February 20, 2021, socialsci.libretexts. org/@go/page/8157.

US.[458] Likewise according to research in the *British Medical Journal* (BMJ), "75% of women requesting abortion in the US are in poverty or in the low-income bracket. The poorest 12% of women account for almost 50% of abortions and the poorest 30% for 75% of abortions."[459] Similarly, in relation to retributive justice systems worldwide, the United Nations warns that

> If you are poor, the chances of being sentenced to death are immensely higher than if you are rich. There could be no greater indictment of the death penalty than the fact that in practice it is really a penalty reserved for people from lower socio-economic groups. This turns it into a class-based form of discrimination in most countries, thus making it the equivalent of an arbitrary killing.[460]

To uproot classism in your sphere of influence, begin by eliminating some common phrases from your lexicon: "That was so ghetto!", "bougie," "low life," "trash(y)," "they have no class," "low class," "parasite(s)," "welfare queen(s)," "moocher," "freeloader," etc. If you or someone you know says something casually classist, please make an effort to stop the conversation, call attention to the classism, perhaps including how such language stigmatizes and

---

458. Michael Springer-Gould, "The Weaponization of Poverty: An Investigation into United States Military Recruitment Practices In High Schools Of Low-Income Communities In The Inland Empire," *Pitzer Senior Theses*, Claremont College, 2020, *scholarship.claremont.edu/ cgi/viewcontent.cgi?article=1117&context=pitzer_theses*.

459. L. Eaton, "A woman's right to choose: five minutes with . . . Stella Creasy," BMJ 367, no.8222 (November 7, 2019): 259, *doi*:10.1136/bmj. l6424.

460. U.N. Office of the High Commissioner, "Death penalty disproportionately affects the poor, UN rights experts warn," United Nations News Release, October 10, 2017, *ohchr.org/en/NewsEvents/Pages/ DisplayNews.aspx?NewsID=22208&LangID=E*.

degrades those who are poor, and offer a replacement phrase. Some replacement suggestions include: "That was so rude/in need of repair" (depending on context), "extravagant/snobbish," poor person/people, low-income people, working class, families/people in need, etc.

Another prevalent form of classism involves maintaining institutional standards that disadvantage people who rent or whose housing is transient. If you are in a leadership role that looks at housing status, including rental versus ownership, or considers those who live in brick-and-mortar homes as better than those who live in mobile homes, try to eliminate the bias from within that system. Scholarships, classes, work-from-home policies, hiring, and even paychecks can be biased towards brick-and-mortar homeowners because they are seen as "more stable." This standard discriminates against lower-income families who still deserve safe housing and an equal right to access education and work opportunities.

A subtly dehumanizing form of classism involves demeaning people who use welfare programs such as WIC, free school meals, SSI/SSDI, food stamps, Section 8 housing, and more. If you've ever said anything to this effect around your peers or in a social media argument, consider that people would likely not subject themselves to the invasive process of accessing these welfare programs if they were not truly in need of assistance, and it is likely that compounding historical and current factors have contributed to their need for government assistance. Also, consider that there are ample restrictions on how working-class people use such resources, and that direct cash payments have been shown to be an effective way of helping low-income families escape the cycle of poverty.[461]

461. Nurith Aizenman, "Researchers Find A Remarkable Ripple Effect When

Homophobia/Transphobia

Like disability, homophobia is something I have learned more about because of my own experience as bisexual and my connection to the global LGBTQIA+ community. Even though strides are being made in LGBTQIA+ acceptance and inclusion, homophobia—which can range from bias to hatred against gay (or transgender/transsexual) people—is all too common in societies around the world. Homophobia and transphobia stem from underlying ideas that being gay and/or transgender is bad, immoral, "aberrant," or even sinful, and so rendering people who are gay or transgender inherently less worthy of rights and protections. This can result in job and housing discrimination, families disowning their gay or trans members, and at its worst, violence against LGBTQIA+ people. Every member of our human family has inherent dignity, and this should be emphasized especially with those who often face discrimination and hate.

Homophobia and transphobia intersect with issues of violence and dehumanization in the legal sphere and beyond. Disturbingly, the "Gay/Trans Panic Defense" is still used in the courtroom. The LGBT Bar defines this defense as "a legal strategy which asks a jury to find that a victim's sexual orientation or gender identity is to blame for the defendant's violent reaction, including murder."[462] Though since 2014 sixteen US states have banned this strategy and ban laws have been introduced to legislatures in ten more, in many places it remains an option for those accused of violence against gay and trans people.

You Give Cash To Poor Families," NPR, December 2, 2019, *npr.org/ sections/goatsandsoda/2019/12/02/781152563/researchers-find-a- remarkable-ripple-effect-when-you-give-cash-to-poor-families*.

462. "Gay and Trans 'Panic' Defense," The National LGBT Bar Association, 2019, updated 2021, *lgbtqbar.org/programs/advocacy/gay-trans- panic-defense/*..

Perhaps more disturbing than this, however, is the reality that sixty-seven UN member nations still criminalize same-sex sexual activity de facto or through law,[463] six of which prescribe the death penalty for those convicted. According to ILGA World—the International Lesbian, Gay, Bisexual, Trans and Intersex Association—"the death penalty is the legally prescribed punishment. . . [in] Brunei, Iran, Mauritania, Nigeria (12 Northern states only), Saudi Arabia and Yemen."[464] ILGA also reports that Afghanistan, Pakistan, Qatar, Somalia (including Somaliland) and the United Arab Emirates may also leave the door open for using the death penalty against people convicted of same-sex acts.[465] Extrajudicial killing and violent oppression of LGBTQIA+ people have been documented in many regions with Islamic Sharia law, including Chechnya, in Russia.[466] Regardless of what one believes about the nature of sexuality, religion should not be used to "justify" violence or oppression. Adults consenting to sex acts or wearing drag or presenting in a gender non-conforming way do violence to no one. They should not be treated as criminals: to do so is an act of homophobic discrimination.

Gay and trans people currently face a world with less discrimination than decades (and centuries) past, but if a "gay gene" or "trans gene" were discovered, genetic

---

463. Lucas Ramon Mendos et al, State-Sponsored Homophobia 2020: Global Legislation Overview Update, (Geneva: ILGA World, December 2020): 113, ilga.org/downloads/ILGA_World_State_Sponsored_Homophobia_report_global_legislation_overview_update_December_2020.pdf.

464. Lucas Ramon Mendos et al, State-Sponsored Homophobia 2020, 31

465. Lucas Ramon Mendos et al, State-Sponsored Homophobia 2020, 31

466. Mehdi Hassan, "Chechnya Is Trying to Exterminate Gay People. Our Silence Only Emboldens Vladimir Putin and Ramzan Kadyrov," *The Intercept*, June 28, 2020, theintercept.com/2020/06/28/welcome-to-chechnya-gay-men/.

testing could lead to sexuality- or gender-identity selective abortions, similar to what is already done in parts of the world where male babies are more prized and so females are aborted. Selective abortions are also done currently through genetic and phenotypic testing on preborn children to kill intersex fetuses.[467] Those intersex babies who are born are often subject to surgical mutilation, but they cannot consent to these "non-lifesaving procedures to change natural variations in genital appearance or reproductive anatomy."[468]

To root out the homophobia and transphobia in your sphere of influence, here are some expressions to delete from your vocabulary: "That's so gay!", "No homo!", "fag(got)," "dyke," "queer," "tranny," etc. If you or someone you know says something casually homophobic or transphobic, please stop the conversation to call attention to the homophobia/transphobia in the phrase, including how such language stigmatizes and degrades those who are gay or trans, and offer a replacement phrase. Some things you could say instead include: "That's so uncool/pointless" (depending on the context), "as a platonic friend" or "platonically," a gay person, a trans person, etc. Also consider how you talk about LGBTQIA+ people in general conversation, keeping in mind that careless language can lead to dehumanizing tropes and caricatures of what gayness or transness means or is like in lived experience.

One form of homophobia that's made frequent headlines over the past couple of decades is an institution firing or not hiring someone who reveals they live with a same-sex partner/spouse. If you are involved in human

---

467. Katie M. Saulnier, Hortense Gallois, Yann Joly, "Prenatal Genetic Testing for Intersex Conditions in Canada," *Journal of Obstetrics and Gynecology Canada* 43, no. 3 (March 1, 2021): 369-371.

468. "FAQ: What is intersex?," InterACT Advocates, updated January 26, 2021, *interactadvocates.org/faq/*

resources at your workplace, please be sure to apply the standards of basic dignity and respect in your decisions, and uphold the rights of all to be free from workplace discrimination. Even in religious contexts that have "theological morality standards," consider how those standards are applied (or not applied) between straight and LGBTQIA+ employees. Be equitable. Do not favor straight employees who may not be living up to your institution's standards of morality, yet single out for exclusion the LGBTQIA+ members of your community and workplace.

There is a deep-seated phobia of "non-normative" bodies and of intersex people that perhaps stems from the way that their existence challenges social perceptions of gender and sex. This fear often leads to support for and use of "intersex normalization surgery" on babies and children. If you or someone close to you is carrying or has given birth to a child known to have intersex traits, do not speak in a way that would normalize such an unnecessary and invasive surgery. These procedures can result in a child's long-term loss of fertility, sexual function, and emotional well-being, all out of a parent's desire to raise a "normal" child. In fact, around 1.6 percent of the global population (around the same rate as redheads), has some form of intersex condition. Most intersex conditions are not life-threatening and do not require immediate surgery.[469] Please remind the family that every child is precious and worthy of dignity; when the child comes of age, the family should let that child determine what (if any) non-necessary surgical interventions are used on their one precious body.

---

469. "FAQ: What is intersex?," InterACT Advocates.

Racism

Racism has two dimensions: an internal bias against certain people based on a combination of socially-constructed standards (like skin color) that make up the concept of "race," and the systemic support for practices that uphold these standards in order to favor one race (usually white) over another. In the United States, racist language is woven into the fabric of the nation and its founding, as white supremacy is reflected in colonial law, the Declaration of Independence, the Constitution, and many of the policies that came thereafter.[470] Policies that contributed to the genocide of Indigenous peoples and prolonged and permitted the institution of slavery that dehumanized Black Americans were written into these founding documents. Though at first white landowners promoted a sort of "nativism" that excluded new immigrants from white communities, in time the concept of whiteness in American society came to include Italian, Irish, Polish, Russian, and other immigrants whose ancestors came from Europe and who "passed" enough as white. To this day, most Black, Indigenous (including Latinos with Indigenous roots, who because of modern ethnic categorization confusingly enough are often considered a separate category), Arab, and Asian people

---

470. Annette Gordon-Reed, "America's Original Sin: Slavery and the Legacy of White Supremacy," *Foreign Affairs*, January/February 2018, *foreignaffairs.com/articles/united-states/2017-12-12/americas-original-sin*.

(including those from the South Asian subcontinent) are all considered "people of color."[471,472]

Today, at least when it comes to US policy, racism is an intersecting factor in almost every major issue of violence. The violence that disproportionately impacts

471. Mistinguette Smith, "After Asian American hate, I'm reclaiming racial solidarity and the term 'people of color,'" USA Today, May 11, 2021, usatoday.com/story/opinion/voices/2021/05/11/people-of-color-better-than-bipoc-shows-racial-solidarity-column/4938922001/. A similar perspective on who "people of color" includes is also represented in the "Person of color" Wikipedia page: wikipedia.org/wiki/Person_of_color.

472. Colorism is worth mentioning here because it is often the outward gauge of racism in society. Those who are "more white" are often favored over those with darker complexions. This is especially relevant in my life, because despite having substantial Indigenous (Mexican) ancestry, I pass as white to the point that most people expect me to be Scotch-Irish. I even received a scholarship that was largely given to white-passing Latino students who were able to check the box "Hispanic/Latino" but who didn't face the cultural costs of having a dark complexion and therefore of facing most forms of racism (colorism) in US society. For a larger discussion of colorism in the US, see Kimberly Jade Norwood, "'If You Is White, You's Alright. . . .' Stories About Colorism in America," Washington University Global Studies Law Review 15, no. 4 (2005): 585, openscholarship.wustl.edu/law_globalstudies/vol14/iss4/8.

various communities of color includes abortion,[473] war,[474] military torture,[475] police brutality,[476] torture in the justice

---

473. The following comparison of study and census results indicates that people of color are disproportionately likely to have abortions compared to their white counterparts. In the most recent study available, white women had 33.4 percent of all abortions, Black women had 38.4 percent of abortions, and Hispanic women had 21.0 percent of abortions, despite making up 61.6 percent, 12.4 percent, and 18.7 percent of the U.S. population, respectively. See Katherine Kortsmit et al, "Abortion Surveillance—United States, 2019," Table 6, Centers for Disease Control and Prevention, November 26, 2021, cdc.gov/mmwr/volumes/70/ss/ss7009a1.htm#T6_down; also see Nicholas Jones, Rachel Marks, Roberto Ramirez, and Merarys Ríos-Vargas, "2020 Census Illuminates Racial and Ethnic Composition of the Country," United States Census Bureau, August 12, 2021 *census.gov/library/stories/2021/08/improved-race-ethnicity-measures-reveal-united-states-population-much-more-multiracial.html*.

474. Recent ongoing wars have targeted Somalia, Libya, Uganda, Iraq, Iran, Afghanistan, and Syria, all of which are comprised of racial and ethnic groups that are consistently "other"ed in the predominantly white US culture. See "List of wars involving the United States," Wikipedia, last updated October 17, 2021, *en.wikipedia.org/wiki/List_of_wars_involving_the_United_States*; and See Horace G. Campbell, "The Quagmire of US Militarism in Africa," *Africa Development / Afrique et Développement* 45, no. 1 (2020): 73–116, jstor.org/stable/26936565.

475. Torture of Arab and African (particularly Muslim) people at Guantánamo Bay Prison, Abu Ghraib Prison, and CIA black sites was common throughout the War on Terror. See Kristen T. Valentine, "Punishing the 'other': race, ethnicity, and the American justice system," University of Louisville, *Electronic Theses and Dissertations*, Paper 1479, *doi.org/10.18297/etd/1479*.

476. A recent (2021) study shows that Black Americans are killed by police shootings at a rate of thirty-seven per million, Hispanics at a rate of twenty-eight per million, but white Americans at a rate of fifteen per million. See "Police Shootings Database," *The Washington Post*, updated September 30, 2021, *washingtonpost.com/graphics/investigations/police-shootings-database/*.

system,[477] and capital punishment.[478] Additionally, people of color from Haiti, Mexico, Guatemala, and other Latin

---

477. The 2010 national census (2020 census data is still being tabulated on this subject), reveals that Black people were incarcerated at a rate of 2,306 per 100,000 people, while American Indians or Alaska Natives were imprisoned at a rate of 1,291 per 100,000, Latino people were incarcerated at a rate of 831 per 100,000, and white people were imprisoned at a rate of 450 per 100,000 people. See "U.S. incarceration rates by race & ethnicity, 2010," Prison Policy Initiative, prisonpolicy.org/graphs/raceinc.html?gclid=CjwKCAjw2bmLBhBREiw AZ6ugo7EmoDYqKeeFW4pnvUh6I5oW2nHyWoub2erW_JCiY1MXXzC5PD8NhoCyF8QAvD_BwE; People of color made up a disproportionate amount of the prison population in solitary confinement. A 2015 study published at Yale by Judith Resnik reports, "Black male prisoners made up 40 percent of the total prison population in those 43 jurisdictions, but constituted 45 percent of the 'restricted housing population,' another way to describe those in solitary confinement. In 31 of the 43, the percentage of black men who spent time in solitary wasn't proportional to their slice of the general population— it was greater. Latinos were also disproportionately represented in solitary: on the whole, 21 percent of inmates in confinement were Latino, even though this group constituted only 20 percent of the total population. Overall, in 22 of the 43 jurisdictions, Latinos were overrepresented in relation to their general-population numbers." Study referenced in article: Juleyka Lantigua-Williams, "The Link Between Race and Solitary Confinement," *The Atlantic*, December 5, 2016, theatlantic.com/politics/archive/2016/12/race-solitary-confinement/509456/; original study found through web archive: Association of State Correctional Administrators at the Arthur Liman Public Interest Program, "Aiming to Reduce Time-In-Cell: Reports from Correctional Systems on the Numbers of Prisoners in Restricted Housing and on the Potential of Policy Changes to Bring About Reforms," Yale Law School, November 2016, accessed via archive, *web.archive.org/web/20161222084512/https://law.yale.edu/system/ files/area/center/liman/document/aimingtoreducetic.pdf*.

478. According to the most recently available information from the Death Penalty Information Center, the percentage of people on death row in the US breaks down along the following lines: 41.29 percent are Black despite making up 12.4 percent of the population, and 42.37 percent are white, despite making up 61.6 percent of the population. See "Death Row U.S.A. Spring 2021," NAACP Legal Defense Fund quarterly report, Spring 2021, *naacpldf.org/wp-content/uploads/ DRUSASpring2021.pdf*.

American nations made up the majority of the immigrant population held in indefinite detention camps by ICE during the Trump administration.[479] Racism plays a part in all of these systems of violence waged in and by the United States, because racism is perhaps our first and foundational national sin.

However, the United States isn't the only region of the world infected by racism and its cousin, nationalism. One of the factors that has precipitated and amplified the war that began on February 24 of this year (2022) with a Russian invasion against Ukraine is a storied history of nationalist prejudice between the neighboring countries.[480]

---

479. Emily Ryo and Ian Peacock, "The Landscape of Immigration Detention in the United States," American Immigration Council Special Report, December 2018, *americanimmigrationcouncil.org/sites/ default/files/research/the_landscape_of_immigration_detention_ in_the_united_states.pdf*.

480. This topic is undoubtedly charged at the moment, as Russia unjustly fired the first weapons in this war, making a violent and wrongful invasion, and Ukraine has just cause to defend their national community. However, I think that most peace activists would agree that seeking peace requires an effort to put down arms and see the root issues at play, including prejudice like nationalism. For more, See "Ukrainian Pacifist's Message to the World: U.S., NATO & Russia Share Responsibility to Avoid War," Democracy Now!, February 16, 2022, democracynow.org/2022/2/16/yurii_sheliazhenko_russian_invasion_ukraine; and also see Samuel B. Parker, "The Russo-Ukrainian War and the Nuclear Threat: How Did We Get Here, and What Do We Do Now?" Rehumanize blog, March 1, 2022, rehumanizeintl.org/ post/the-russo-ukrainian-war-and-the-nuclear-threat-how-did-we-get-here-and-what-do-we-do-now, and John Whitehead, "Staving Off War: The Russia, Ukraine, and NATO Stand-Off," Rehumanize blog, January 1, 2022, rehumanizeintl.org/post/staving-off-war-the-russia-ukraine-and-nato-stand-off. The additional dimension of racism against refugees from other nations when contrasted with white Ukrainians has also been something to ponder, not to mention the preferential treatment of white Ukrainian refugees when compared to the prejudicial treatment against Ukrainian refugees of color. See Sophie Trist, "Two Wrongs Don't Make a Right: Constructively Discussing Race in the Russo-Ukrainian War," Rehumanize blog, March

To uproot racism in your sphere of influence, here are some common sayings to erase from your phraseology: "I've been gypped!", "She sold me down the river!", "Barbarian," "long time, no see!", "Indian giver," "nigger," "kike," "polack," "slant," "chink," "gook," "redskin(s)," "thug," "gypsy," "ape," "beaner," "wetback," "coon," "flip," "jap," "paki," "cabbage eater," "raghead," "sambo," "shylock," "spic," "spook," "squaw," "eskimo," "yellow," "wop," etc. If you or someone you know says something casually racist like one of these words or phrases, please make an effort to stop the conversation, call attention to the wording and its racism, perhaps including how such language stigmatizes and degrades those who are of the targeted race and suggest a replacement term that fits the circumstance without being racist. Some replacements for the phrases above include: "I've been cheated," "I've been betrayed," "foreigner," "it's been a while," "[someone] gave me a gift and later took it back" (describe the action). For the rest, just *don't use racial slurs!* It's easy to eliminate racial slurs from your lexicon simply by using the correct racial/national name of the person in question, like: Black, Jewish, Polish, Japanese, Chinese, etc. Slurs are intended to dehumanize and distance the user from the humanity of the target; push back against them by rehumanizing the people in question.

One other frequent and insidious form of racism is at play when managers choose not to offer a job to someone who has a Black or "ethnic" name. This internal (and often unconscious) bias has been demonstrated many times in national studies and class-action lawsuits. Managers tend to pursue applicants with "whiter-sounding" names.[481] So,

---

21, 2022, rehumanizeintl.org/post/two-wrongs-don-t-make-a-right-constructively-discussing-race-in-the-russo-ukrainian-war
481. Payne Lubbers, "Job Applicants With 'Black Names' Still Less Likely

if you are involved in the hiring process at your workplace, ensure that race-identifying questions or criteria are not part of the discernment process. Consider even removing names from the applications and resumes so that sort of subconscious bias can't influence your decision. Instead, promote racial diversity as part of an inclusive and diverse workplace.

Another form of racism that I've witnessed time and time again: people overlooking or excusing police brutality because the victim in question was a "thug." If you (or someone you know) are tempted to call victims of police brutality "thugs" because they had what you'd consider "a mean look," stop and rehumanize. In an act of brutality in policing, George Zimmerman, a neighborhood watch member, killed Trayvon Martin, a teenaged boy.[482] Afterwards, I saw Martin dehumanized in mainstream and social media as a "thug" because he was wearing a hoodie and liked to take over-serious selfies flipping the bird or wearing a "grill." None of these actions are worthy of his being killed. The common practice of dehumanizing Black and Brown people (particularly men and boys) as "violent thugs" began centuries ago in an effort to justify violence against Black and Brown men and boys by keeping white society hyper-vigilant.[483] Reject the cycle of dehumanization by refusing to participate in any racism—subtle or otherwise.

---

to Get Interviews," *Bloomberg News*, July 29, 2021, bloomberg.com/news/articles/2021-07-29/job-applicants-with-black-names-still-less-likely-to-get-the-interview.

482. A. Munro, "Shooting of Trayvon Martin," *Encyclopedia Britannica*, February 19, 2021, *britannica.com/event/shooting-of-Trayvon-Martin*.

483. Calvin John Smiley and David Fakunle, "From 'brute' to 'thug:' the demonization and criminalization of unarmed Black male victims in America," *Journal Of Human Behavior In The Social Environment* 26, no. 3-4 (2016): 350-66, DOI:10.1080/10911359.2015.1129256.

Sexism

As a woman, I've certainly been on the receiving end of "prejudice, stereotyping, or discrimination, typically against women, on the basis of sex."[484] From casually sexist remarks thrown our way as we walk down the street, to systemic barriers that constrain women's careers, long-term earning power, and families, sexism has been baked into many cultures for millennia. Aristotle, one of Western culture's philosophical fathers, stated, "females are weaker and colder in nature, and we must look upon the female character as being a sort of natural deficiency."[485] In the medieval Christian Church that followed, Gregory of Tours reported that at a council in Macon, "One of the bishops arose and said that a woman is not able to be called 'a human.'"[486] Even Thomas Aquinas called women's individual nature "defective and misbegotten," insisting that women needed to exist essentially only to help in the work of reproduction.[487] A history of patriarchal structures prevented women's full inclusion in all aspects of society (such as voting, property ownership, the ability to work outside the home, and to attend university) until fairly recently, but much progress has been made in many Western nations, including my own nation, the US.

In the East, the misogyny in Confucianism deeply impacted Chinese culture. The *Analects* say, "Women and

484. "Sexism" in Lexico, online *Oxford English Dictionary*, lexico.com/en/definition/sexism.
485. Aristotle, *On the Generation of Animals*, Book IV, accessed from The Electronic Scholarly Publishing Project, *esp.org/books/aristotle/generation-of-animals/html/contents/aristotle-generation-book4.html*.
486. Gregory of Tours, *The History of the Franks*, Book Eight, Section 20.
487. Thomas Aquinas, *Summa Theologiae*, Question 92, Article 1, English Second and Revised Edition, trans. Fathers of the English Dominican Province, (print 1920, online 2017), *newadvent.org/summa/1092.htm*.

servants are hard to deal with" (17.25). The fact that women were compared (and bunched with) servants from lower social strata "implies that women are of equal status with the lower social class."[488] Practices like sex-selective abortions and infanticide, foot-binding, subjugation to male family members, concubinage, and widow suicide flow from the central idea in Chinese tradition and culture "that male children are more desirable because they possess the capability to care for the elderly, work toilsome jobs, and perform critical ancestral practices."[489] Similar practices and ideas exist in the South Asian subcontinent, too. In India, patriarchal traditions about dowry and the general social disenfranchisement of women mean that daughters are often unwanted and so in poorer families face inequitable food allocation and in wealthier families, sex-selective abortions.[490]

In Africa, patriarchal cultures create systems of inequality wherein women and girls face high rates of domestic violence, female genital mutilation, and dowries.[491] In Indigenous cultures on Turtle Island (also known as North America), there is a stronger history of matriarchal family structures,[492] but in the modern era a devas-

---

488. Juliana Batista, "The Confucianism-Feminism Conflict: Why a New Understanding is Necessary," *Xinmin Pinglun*, August 29, 2017, schwarzmanscholars.org/events-and-news/confucianism-feminism-conflict-new-understanding-necessary.

489. Juliana Batista, "The Confucianism-Feminism Conflict."

490. Sugandha Nagpal, "Sex-selective Abortion in India: Exploring Institutional Dynamics and Responses," *McGill Sociological Review* 3, no. 2 (February 2013): 18-35.

491. Cyril-Mary P. Olatunji, "An Argument for Gender Equality in Africa," CLCWeb: *Comparative Literature and Culture* 15, no. 1 (2013): doi.org/10.7771/1481-4374.2176

492. For just one example of this, See Holly Kear, "Elusive Matriarchy: The Impact of the Native American and Feminist Movements on Navajo Gender Dynamics," *Historical Perspectives: Santa Clara University Undergraduate Journal of History*, Series II 11 no. 11 (2006), scholar-

tating trend of missing and murdered Indigenous women and girls (MMIWG),[493] high rates of domestic and sexual violence,[494] and (overlapping with racism) a dark history of eugenic sterilizations and medical malpractice has arisen.[495] Despite (or perhaps because of) the deep-seated sexism in so many cultures, the internet has led to a beautiful connection of feminist movements all over the planet.

Certainly we must work to end gender-based violence at home (in the form of domestic violence) and in the larger world (both domestic and state-sponsored). However, as mentioned earlier, this book's main focus isn't to educate on violence that is already culturally frowned upon or illegal. Therefore, although we must work to end the violence of sexism that can harm women physically and psychologically, a deeper and more pressing issue at this time in most contexts worldwide is undoing the patriarchal structures that favor men, see women as non-normative, and contribute to the violence of abortion.

To eliminate the sexism in your sphere of influence, cut this common lingo out of your vocabulary: "Don't be a sissy/pussy!", "Are you gonna cry like a girl?", "Grow a pair!", "Man up!", "You're great, for a woman...", "She's bossy!", "bitch," "cunt," "nag," "catty," "drama queen," "banshee," "feminazi," "slut," "tease," "man-eater," "hysterical," etc. If you or someone you know says something casually sexist, please try to

commons.scu.edu/historical-perspectives/vol11/iss1/11

493. "Murdered & Missing Indigenous Women," Native Women's Wilderness, nativewomenswilderness.org/mmiw

494. Victoria C. Olive, "Sexual Violence in a Native American Community: Native American Women Speak Out," University of Washington Masters thesis, 2015, digital.lib.washington.edu/researchworks/bitstream/handle/1773/35108/Olive_washington_0250O_15288.pdf

495. Brianna Theobald, "A 1970 Law Led to the Mass Sterilization of Native American Women. That History Still Matters," *Time*, updated November 28, 2019, time.com/5737080/native-american-sterilization-history/

stop the conversation, call attention to the sexist phrase, including how such language stigmatizes and degrades women, and offer a non-sexist replacement that fits the circumstance. Some suggestions include: "don't quit on me!" (don't make fun of people for crying or having emotions, support them instead!), "be/get strong," "be brave," "you're great," "she's driven and delegates well," and finally, call women "women," maybe sometimes "ladies"; and never use slurs meant to demean women or their body parts, ever.

Sexism can also rear its ugly head when companies decide not to hire or promote a woman because she expresses interest in having (more) children. If you are involved with the hiring processes at your workplace, make sure that you and the hiring team aren't passing over a candidate for hiring or promotion simply because she might want to have kids sometime soon. This demonstrates how the wombless cisgender male body is seen as normative, because it's practically unheard of for men to get passed over for jobs or promotions because they want to have kids. In fact, one study shows that having a child helps a man's earning potential, acting like a sort of "bonus," but for women, having a child acts as a "penalty," depressing wages fairly quickly, and potentially long-term.[496] So if this sort of thing happens at your workplace, make your

---

496. Recent studies show that having a child causes a substantial drop in earnings for many new mothers for the first years after the birth of a child, and can prevent that woman from ever "getting back on track" to her pre-baby earnings trajectory. See Danielle H. Sandler and Nichole Szembrot, "Cost of Motherhood on Women's Employment and Earnings: New Mothers Experience Temporary Drop in Earnings," United States Census Bureau, June 16, 2020, census.gov/library/stories/2020/06/cost-of-motherhood-on-womens-employment-and-earnings.html; also See Claire Cain Miller, "The Motherhood Penalty versus the Fatherhood Bonus," *The New York Times*, September 7, 2014, *nytimes.com/2014/09/07/upshot/a-child-helps-your-career-if-youre-a-man.html*.

protest heard, because such situations are unjust, and can lead women and families to feel pressure to have abortions.

A particularly subtle but harmful form of sexism involves perpetuating pregnancy and maternity stigma in communities, churches, and schools. As I've often discussed with young people who worry over how their parents or church will react to their unplanned pregnancy, though extramarital sex may be a sin, pregnancy and motherhood certainly are not. We must encourage and enable young people (particularly young women) in these circumstances to hold their heads up high. In our very anti-life culture, choosing life can be hard when some among your peers and your church may shame you instead of support you. So be a witness to the value and dignity of her life and the life of her child: To every person facing a difficult pregnancy show compassion, love, and support. Reject the shaming, gossip, and taboo culture around young and unwed pregnancy.

Resist is a Verb

Dear reader, I am so, so glad that you have made it this far. Thank you for sticking it out and learning all you can about all these important topics. I am encouraged that you have invested the time and the energy to read: It shows me that you care, and care passionately about human rights for *all* human beings! **Now, I encourage you to get out there and make big waves.**

This book isn't meant to be one where you put it down and move on with your life as it was before. When you have finally turned the last page here, I hope that you are spurred to action. Indeed, to resist the inculturation of violence, we must **do something**. "Resist" is a verb, it is an action word. "Rehumanize" is too. So now I earnestly challenge you to read on in chapter 12, "Put These Ideas into Action," and then together let's build a world beyond violence and dehumanization.

Discussion Questions

1. Examine your life and your actions honestly. Where have you participated in ideologies of dehumanization over the years? Which was the hardest to uproot? Which do you still struggle to uproot? Why?

2. Which ideologies of dehumanization have you suffered under? Or perhaps a friend or family member? You don't have to name it out loud, but think back to when it happened. What do you wish you or someone else present had done differently?

3. How do you think we can have better conversations about these ideologies of dehumanization, considering how embedded many of them are in the cultures we live in today?

Further Reading Suggestions

1. Marina Carlos, illustrated by Freaks, *I'll figure it out: How ableism impacts disabled people's lives* (Self-published, 2020).

2. Alice Wong, editor, *Disability Visibility: First Person Stories from the Twenty-First Century* (New York: Vintage Books, 2020).

3. Ashton Applewhite, *This Chair Rocks: A Manifesto Against Ageism* (New York: Celadon Books, 2020).

4. Barbara Jensen, *Reading Classes: On Culture and Classism in America* (Ithaca, NY: ILR Press, 2012).

5. Bill Henson and Meg Baatz, *Guiding Families of LGBT+ Loved Ones* (Houston: Posture Shift Ministries, 2018).

6. Jason Reynolds and Ibram X. Kendi, *Stamped: Racism, Antiracism, and You* (New York: Little, Brown Books, 2020).

7. Erika Bachiochi, *The Rights of Women: Reclaiming a Lost Vision* (South Bend, IN: University of Notre Dame Press, 2021).

8. William Brennan, *Dehumanizing the Vulnerable: When Word Games Take Lives* (Chicago: Loyola Press, 1995).

Chapter 12

Put these ideas into action

There are plenty of ways to live out the principles described in this book, all involving different levels of commitment. At minimum, you could simply avoid committing acts of aggressive violence against human beings in your own life. In the event of an unplanned pregnancy choose life; do not become an executioner; do not commit war crimes, etc.

Looking at the Consistent Life Ethic simply as a list of actions that are wrong and not taking part in them would be sufficient and perfectly tolerable. However, we know that this philosophy is more than that. Because the modern world is plagued both by violence and by a sense of apathy about or acceptance of that violence, it is critical that we unsettle this status quo. Even if you talk the talk, you've still got to walk the walk. And that action can begin wherever you are. All politics is local, and violence is taking place in your community.

Live Peace & Justice daily

Ultimately, the things we do daily, weekly, monthly in our own communities are more important than a single vote in nearly any election. Enact justice. Live peace. Daily. Right where you are. Voting every four years cannot be our sole action towards supporting human rights. The work begins again each day; it doesn't end because the election's over.

How we choose to live, daily, for and in solidarity with the marginalized and oppressed will always have more of an impact than your one vote for president, or senate, or any other major political office. Statistically, your vote will have an infinitesimally small impact on the outcome of a race,[497] but 100 percent of the time, it will impact your own conscience. Your vote indicates which groups of humans you are willing to sacrifice "for the greater good." Rather than justifying compromise, make a commitment to yourself and to your community to live justice daily. Don't expect politicians to do it for you.

Use your Freedom for Community

Though "freedom" has been touted as my nation's ultimate value, I challenge our hyper-individualistic inter-pretation. I recently learned that the word "free" comes from the Indo-European word "friya," meaning "beloved."[498] (Fun fact, my name, Aimee, also means "beloved.") Oh, and the word "friend" also comes from that same root word. Historically, "a free person" was someone who was "joined to a tribe of free people by ties of kinship and rights of

---

497. The following study is representative of the impact of an individual vote only on a national election, but the same principle tracks down even to state-level races as well. See Andrew Gelman, Nate Silver, and Aaron Edlin's "What Is The Probability Your Vote Will Make A Difference?" in *Economic Inquiry* 50, no. 2 (April 2012): 321–26, *stat. columbia.edu/~gelman/research/published/probdecisive2.pdf.*

498. David Hackett Fischer, *Liberty and Freedom: A Visual History of America's Founding Ideas* (New York: Oxford University Press, 2005), 5.

belonging."[499] Freedom was "the idea that—together—we can ensure that we all have the things we need: love, food, shelter, safety."[500] It was a model of interdependence; we need to recover this idea that no human is an island: our freedom is for community, is for solidarity, is for mutual aid.

A holistically pro-life culture will be marked by mutual aid, solidarity, and community; living those principles starts wherever you live. It takes effort to connect with your community. Building actual relationships with those in need is hard. It can be physically exhausting to help a mom care for a colicky baby when she needs emergency babysitting. It can be emotionally challenging to uproot structural racism in your hearts and your communities by pursuing reconciliation and reparations. And it can be hard on your self-control to part with the ten dollars you were going to spend on a fancy drink at Starbucks in order to buy a pack of diapers or wipes for a family in need in your neighborhood. But we can't create a pro-life culture if we continue to stay up in our ivory towers and just talk about abortion or euthanasia or police brutality or war as if they're merely academic topics to be debated. These issues of violence really impact individual humans, and it's our responsibility to really get our hands dirty and meet people where they are.

I challenge you to do the hard work of building community, of living solidarity, and constantly giving your life in mutual aid to others in that community. I challenge you to build integrated lives, where your convictions and your actions align. This philosophy, the Consistent Life Ethic, is

499. Hackett Fischer, *Liberty and Freedom*, 5.
500. Mia Birdsong, *How We Show Up: Reclaiming Family, Friendship, and Community* (New York: Hachette Go, 2020), 18.

much more than passively saying no to violence; rather, we must actively affirm the value of each individual human life.

We must agitate against the systems and institutions of injustice and confront those who uphold and defend them. Fundamentally, this is the work of "changing hearts and minds." The most effective way to do this is regular, in-person contact with those who agree as well as those who disagree on these vital issues. In other words, if the problem is violence and dehumanization, the answer is connection, community, and *rehumanization*.

Build a Culture of Encounter

We promote connection, community, and encounter best when we engage in a culture of encounter. John Koenig, author of the *Dictionary of Obscure Sorrows* (a project he originated on the social media site Tumblr), created a neologism to name an idea that can revolutionize the way we see our fellow human beings and change the world.

> **sonder – n.** The realization that each random pass-erby is living a life as vivid and complex as your own—populated with their own ambitions, friends, routines, worries and inherited craziness—an epic story that continues invisibly around you like an ant-hill sprawling deep underground, with elaborate pas-sageways to thousands of other lives that you'll never know existed, in which you might appear only once, as an extra sipping coffee in the background, as a blur of traffic passing on the highway, as a lighted window at dusk.[501]

---

501. This definition was originally found via the Tumblr project page, here: "Sonder," *Dictionary of Obscure Sorrows, dictionaryofobscuresorrows*.

This concept of having quiet but practical moments of empathy for others didn't originate on social media, though. Almost every culture and religion contains a version of the Golden Rule, as well as the familiar axiom, "You must walk a mile in another's shoes."

Before Koenig's *Dictionary of Obscure Sorrows*, one of the early modern Personalist philosophers, John Henry Newman, beautifully expressed the idea of selfhood and practical empathy in his "The Individuality of the Soul":

> Nothing is more difficult than to realize that. . . every one of all the millions who live or have lived, is as whole and independent a being in himself, as if there were no one else in the whole world but he. . . [Each human] has his own hopes and fears, desires, judgments, and aims; he is everything to himself, and no one else is really any thing. . . He has a depth within him unfathomable, an infinite abyss of existence.[502]

Recognizing that we all carry within us "an unfathomable, infinite abyss of existence" fills me with awe. Sometimes, it makes me feel overwhelmed, frozen in the magnitude of it.

Recently, though, despite how stunned I'd been, I emboldened myself to continue this necessary work of building a culture of encounter. I began reading Pope Francis's most recent encyclical letter, *Fratelli Tutti* ("On Fraternity and Friendship"), in which he expresses his concern that people will be less and less often be "called by name, less and less will this unique being be treated as a

---

com/post/23536922667/sonder. In years since, the project has been turned into a book: John Koenig, *The Dictionary of Obscure Sorrows* (New York: Simon & Schuster, 2021), x.

502. John Henry Cardinal Newman, "The Individuality of the Soul," found in *Parochial and Plain Sermons* (San Francisco: Ignatius Press) 1997: 784-792.

person with his or her own feelings, sufferings, problems, joys and family." He goes on to explore what it means to create an authentic culture of encounter, meeting people where they are and building community:

> To speak of a "culture of encounter" means that we, as a people, should be passionate about meeting others, seeking points of contact, building bridges, planning a project that includes everyone... that can accept differences.... All this calls for the ability to recognize other people's right to be themselves and to be different. Without [this recognition], subtle ways can be found to make others insignificant, irrelevant, of no value to society. While rejecting certain visible forms of violence, another more insidious kind of violence can take root: the violence of those who despise people who are different.... The path to peace does not mean making society blandly uniform, but getting people to work together, side-by-side, in pursuing goals that benefit everyone. A wide variety of practical proposals and diverse experiences can help achieve shared objectives and serve the common good. The problems that a society is experiencing need to be clearly identified, so that the existence of different ways of understanding and resolving them can be appreciated. The path to social unity always entails acknowledging the possibility that others have, at least in part, a legitimate point of view, something worthwhile to contribute, even if they [have ever] acted badly.[503]

It brings me great joy to see a religious leader responding to the beautiful diversity of humanity with such an affirmative and hospitable approach. Not only does Pope

---

503. Pope Francis, *Fratelli Tutti*, (Vatican City: The Holy See) October 2020: §193, 216-218, 228, *vatican.va/content/francesco/en/encyclicals/documents/papa-francesco_20201003_enciclica-fratelli-tutti.html*

Francis seem to be a fan of radical inclusivity, but he, too, sees that by knowing and understanding the depths of people's lives and experiences, we will be better positioned to build a culture of peace.

This call to encounter others in their individuality brings to mind a couple lines from one of my personal heroes, Catherine of Siena, who once said that "Love follows knowledge,"[504] and "One who knows more, loves more."[505] I agree wholeheartedly. Spending more time with someone and learning who they are with their joys and fears, with their hopes and regrets, with their stories and their selfhood, cannot help but bring us to love them—even if we feel little affection towards them, or we're annoyed by them or frustrated by them, the intimate knowledge of who they are brings an immense love, an immense desire for their well-being and for their good.

If we have *sonder* for our fellow human beings—the riders we sit next to on the bus, the carpoolers we pass on the highway, the elderly couples drinking coffee at diner tables, the homeless LGBTQIA+ teens slouching on park benches, the classmates we argue with in recitations, our parents when they get on our nerves—the world will change. Sonder brings the "Golden Rule" to a much more intense, personal level. It conveys the magnitude of our own life to the passing lives of others.

To have sonder is to rehumanize: to transfer to every single human being our own understanding of how difficult and beautiful and awful and awesome it is to be human. If we really had this sonder for others, if we learned their stories, if we loved the humans behind the human rights, then consistency would be a given instead of an outlier, and nonviolence would be the rule

---

504. Catherine, of Siena, *The Dialogue* (New York: Paulist Press) 1980, §1.
505. Catherine of Siena, *The Dialogue*, §66.

instead of the exception. If we had this powerful, practical empathy for each and every human being, there's no way that we could wish violence on anyone. We could no more ask that a bomb be dropped on them and their family, we could no more be comfortable with their killing by scalpel, vacuum, and forceps. We would have to actively oppose and work to end all acts of violence. We would have to stand for a Consistent Life Ethic.

It's hard to understand who someone else is, through and through. Knowledge indeed is power; and knowledge of the other inevitably leads to an empowering love to choose the good of the other. Whenever the temptation arises to yell or to scream or to engage in a violence towards another person, remember "sonder." For just a moment, imagine the complexity of their beautiful and awful and awesome life. And allow yourself to love your enemies. Think about it this way: We can't degrade those who disagree with us in order to "win" the argument or solve the problem, because ultimately, such degradation or dehumanization contradicts our end goal. It blocks building an integrated, inclusive, and rehumanizing community where *every* human stands for every human.

Transform our Communities

To truly transform our world, we must first transform our communities. And the degree to which our communities are human-centered depends on us.

So where should you start? First, figure out who you know in your area with whom you can work to end violence against all human beings. Seek out the local Rehumanize Chapter.[506] Contact them and join their efforts! If there isn't

---

506. You can find this info at *rehumanizeintl.org/community*.

one, seek out the clubs, community groups, religious congregations, social organizations, or fraternal societies that share similar or overlapping goals to the ones laid out in this book. If you find one, consider having them sign on to be a Rehumanize Ally group. Rehumanize Allies are existing organizations that choose to sign onto our pledge to assert the principles of the Consistent Life Ethic. An allied group can be any group—multi-issue or single-issue-focused—that affirms the dignity of every human being. They are not required to work directly on every issue within the Consistent Life Ethic framework; however, their activism cannot contradict Rehumanize International's position on any life issues.

Becoming a Rehumanize Ally is a great choice for anyone ready to get started with Consistent Life Ethic organizing alongside like-minded people. Groups receive instant access to the Rehumanize International team's guidance, web-based lectures and training, event and campaign assistance and promotion, and the opportunity to work with us hosting in-person events in your area such as speaking engagements or even the Rehumanize Conference.

If you don't already belong to a preexisting group, perhaps you could start one yourself! Local Rehumanize Chapters are fully dedicated to the mission and vision of Rehumanize International. Like Rehumanize Allies, they can access support and opportunities to train with and learn from our core team, as well as receive materials. Rehumanize Chapters offer practical support to educate, connect, and restore those elements in their communities that a culture of violence deforms: the sense of the deep value and dignity of each individual person. For more information on Rehumanize Chapters and Allies visit: *rehumanizeintl.org/community.*

If you don't have access to a group or you aren't yet ready to dive in that deep, that's perfectly all right too. There are plenty of things you can do by yourself or with just one or two friends! Below are a few suggestions, but we encourage you to brainstorm other ideas that may best suit your skills and interests. You can find more ideas like this in my day-by-day weekly action planner book, *A Consistent Life: The Young Advocate's Guide to Living Peace & Justice Daily*, which can be found at *rehumanizeintl.org/shop* and Amazon.

Other ways to get active now

Education:

- Start conversations with your friends and family about the Consistent Life Ethic and advocate for your positions.

- Set up a table in a public square with literature on an issue that is important to you.

- Attend online and in-person events with Rehumanize International and other like-minded organizations and encourage people to come.

- Share posts on social media.

- Wear t-shirts, buttons, patches, and other merch with Consistent Life Ethic messaging—visit *rehumanizeintl.org/shop* if you need some!

- Write blog posts, articles, and op-eds.

Service:

- Sidewalk advocacy outside an abortion clinic—if you've never done this before, visit *rehumanizeintl.org/sidewalk-outreach* for tips on effective outreach.

- Host a fundraiser or items drive for a local service non-profit (think: pregnancy center, domestic violence shelter, immigrant and refugee resource center).

- Write letters to incarcerated people, including those on death row.

- Volunteer at a soup kitchen or food bank or set up a donation box in the public square.

- Visit with residents at a nursing home or maternity home.

- Help elderly or disabled community members with yard work or chores.

- Create and distribute portable first-aid and toiletry kits for people experiencing homelessness.

Activism:

- Attend the National March for Life or your local/state march.

- Organize an anti-war rally in your city.

- Campaign for local institutions (think: banks, universities) to divest from the military industrial complex, the abortion industry, or private prisons and detention centers.

- Speak to your elected officials about life issues.

- Host speakers and teach-ins on life issues.

- Hang up flyers or wheat-paste.[507]

---

507. "Wheat[-pasting] is a way to get art and messaging into public spaces," said Mark Strandquist, an artist from Philadelphia, in the following piece by Molia Wollan, "How to Wheat-Paste Posters," *The New*

Art:

- Host a poster-making night or art build for an upcoming rally.

- Get together to create submissions for Create | Encounter, Rehumanize International's arts contest.

- Use sidewalk chalk to take your art to the streets.

- Hold a knitting/crafting night to create hats and blankets to donate to people in need.

Again, these are just some suggestions for ways to get activated in the movement for every human life. I'm so excited to have you on board, and I look forward to seeing all the good that you will do to create a world beyond violence—a world with human rights for all human beings!

Discussion Questions

1. Recall that "freedom" is derived from the Indo-European root "friya," which means "beloved." How does your perspective of the word and the concept change, knowing the root of "freedom" is so deeply rooted in our belovedness in the context of community?

2. What have you recently done to build a culture of peace and life in your community? What creative ideas do you have that you would like to get started on?

3. What has helped motivate you to get involved with human rights activism? What could help you stay

---

York Times, June 10, 2020, *nytimes.com/2020/06/09/magazine/how-to-wheat-paste-posters.html.*

involved and connected with this activism? How can you implement those things in your own work in your community?

Further Reading Suggestions

1. Mary Grace Coltharp and Aimee Murphy, *A Consistent Life: The Young Advocate's Guide to Living Peace & Justice Daily* (Pittsburgh, PA: Life Matters Journal, 2018).

2. Mia Birdsong, *How We Show Up: Reclaiming Family, Friendship, and Community* (New York: Hachette Go, 2020).

3. Marshall Ganz, *Organizing: People, Power, Change* (Washington, DC: Leading Change Network, 2014), commonslibrary.org/wp-content/uploads/Organizers_Handbook.pdf.

N◖P

New City Press

New City Press is one of more than twenty publishing houses sponsored by the Focolare, a movement founded by Chiara Lubich to help bring about the realization of Jesus' prayer: "That all may be one" (John 17:21). In view of that goal, New City Press publishes books and resources that enrich the lives of people and help all to strive toward the unity of the entire human family. We are a member of the Association of Catholic Publishers.

www.newcitypress.com
202 Comforter Blvd.
Hyde Park, New York

Periodicals
Living City Magazine
www.livingcitymagazine.com

Scan to join our mailing list
for discounts and promotions
or go to www.newcitypress.com
and click on "join our email list."